To my dear friend Fred,
    This all began at your
feet back in '68.

        Hans S Pawlisch

        2 April 1986

Cambridge Studies in the History and Theory of Politics

EDITORS

Maurice Cowling   G. R. Elton
J. R. Pole

SIR JOHN DAVIES AND THE CONQUEST OF IRELAND

This book is dedicated to my grandparents

DR OTTO AND MRS ANNA PAWLISCH

of Reedsburg, Wisconsin

SIR JOHN DAVIES AND THE CONQUEST OF IRELAND

A study in legal imperialism

HANS S. PAWLISCH

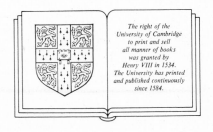

The right of the
University of Cambridge
to print and sell
all manner of books
was granted by
Henry VIII in 1534.
The University has printed
and published continuously
since 1584.

CAMBRIDGE UNIVERSITY PRESS

Cambridge

London   New York   New Rochelle

Melbourne   Sydney

Published by the Press Syndicate of the University of Cambridge
The Pitt Building, Trumpington Street, Cambridge CB2 1RP
32 East 57th Street, New York, NY 10022, USA
296 Beaconsfield Parade, Middle Park, Melbourne 3206, Australia

First published 1985

Printed in Great Britain at the University Press, Cambridge

Library of Congress catalogue card number: 84–9407

British Library cataloguing in publication data
Pawlisch, Hans S.
Sir John Davies and the conquest of Ireland
– (Cambridge studies in the history and theory of politics)
1. Law – Ireland – History and criticism
2. Law and politics
340'.115'09415   KDK156

ISBN 0 521 25328 4

Contents

Preface

This book had its genesis ten years ago at the University of Wisconsin–Milwaukee where Professors John McGovern and James Brundage encouraged an interest in legal history and economic development that was subsequently extended to early modern Irish history. For their encouragement and advice I can only begin to make grateful acknowledgement.

It remains to enumerate my many other debts. This study owes much to friendly criticism volunteered by the seventeenth-century seminar at the Institute of Historical Research in London and by Professor G. R. Elton's Tudor seminar at Cambridge. For fair-mindedness, wise counsel and warm encouragement it is necessary to make special thanks to Professor Elton whose uncommonly effective scholarly assistance is an experience shared by those who know both the man and the mind. Dr Paul Brand of University College, Dublin, and Mr Kenneth Nicholls, of University College, Cork, generously read and commented on an earlier draft of this work. I am also grateful for helpful criticism obtained from my former colleague Dr Mary O'Dowd of the Queen's University of Belfast and from Professor Nial Osborough of the Law Department at Trinity College, Dublin. Many others offered help, advice and encouragement, and I can only name a few. Much support was tendered by Dr Ian Roy of King's College, London, and by Professor David Harkness of the Queen's University of Belfast. I also benefited from numerous discussions with Mr Bob Hunter of the New University of Ulster, Mr Fred O'Brien of University College, Cork, Professor R. Dudley Edwards of University College, Dublin, Dr Richard Fraher of Harvard University, Professor Brian Levack of Texas University, Dr Michael Weinzierl of the University of Vienna and Mr Migwe Thuo of Volunteer Service Overseas – all of whom convinced me of the existence of a truly international community of scholars. Warm acknowledgement is also made to Mrs Nancy Carpenter, whose criticisms of early drafts of this work were fundamental in shaping its final form.

The librarians and staffs of various archives in which I conducted my research were always helpful and co-operative. I wish to thank the following institutions for granting permission to cite materials stored in their archives: the Public Record Office, London, the British Museum, London, Lambeth Palace Library, London, the Bodleian Library, Oxford, the National Library of Ireland, Dublin, the Library of Trinity College, Dublin, the Public Record office, Dublin, Marsh's Library, Dublin, the King's Inns Library, Dublin, and the Library of the Queen's University of Belfast. Special gratitude must be expressed to the American Bar Foundation, which awarded me a fellowship in legal history during the year 1976/7, and to the Institute for Irish Studies at the Queen's University of Belfast, which awarded me a senior fellowship during the year 1981/2.

Reedsburg, Wisconsin
24 August 1983

Abbreviations

AHR	*American Historical Review*
AJLH	*American Journal of Legal History*
An. Hib.	*Analecta Hibernicum*
Arch. Hib.	*Archivium Hibernicum*
BIHR	*Bulletin of the Institute of Historical Research*
BL	British Library
BNJ	*British Numismatic Journal*
Bodl.	Bodleian Library, Oxford
C	*Code* of the *Corpus Iuris Civilis*
Cal. Car.	*Calendar of the Carew Manuscripts Preserved in the Archepiscopal Library at Lambeth*, London, 1867–73
CLJ	*Cambridge Law Journal*
CSPD	*Calendar of State Papers Domestic Series*, London, 1860–1911
CSPI	*Calendar of State Papers, Ireland*, London 1860–1912
CSP – Rome	*Calendar of State Papers Relating to English Affairs, Preserved Principally at Rome, in the Vatican Archives and Library*, ed. J. M. Rigg, 2 vols., London, 1916
CSP – Spain	*Calendar of Letters and State Papers Relating to English Affairs, Preserved Principally in the Archives of Simancas, 1558–1603*, ed. Martin Hume, 4 vols., London, 1894
CUL	Cambridge University Library
D	*Digest* of the *Corpus Iuris Civilis*
DNB	*Dictionary of National Biography*, 23 vols., London, 1909
EHR	*English Historical Review*

Erck	J. C. Erck (ed.), *A Repertory of the Inrolments on the Patent Rolls of Chancery in Ireland Commencing with the Reign of James I*, Dublin, 1846.
Griffith	M. C. Griffith (ed.), *Irish Patent Rolls of James I: Facsimile of the Irish Record Commissioners' Calendar prepared prior to 1830*, Dublin, 1966
HJ	*Historical Journal*
HLQ	*Huntington Library Quarterly*
HMC	Historical Manuscripts Commission
IER	*Irish Ecclesiastical Record*
IHS	*Irish Historical Studies*
IMC	Irish Manuscripts Commission
Inst	*Institutes* of the *Corpus Iuris Civilis*
Irish Fiants	Calendar of Fiants, Henry to Elizabeth, *Reports of the Deputy Keeper of the Public Records in Ireland*, nos. 7–22 (Dublin, 1875–90)
Lam. Pal.	Lambeth Palace Library
L & P Hen. VIII	*Calendar of Letters and Papers, Foreign and Domestic, Henry VIII*, ed. J. S. Brewer, 21 vols. London, 1862–1932
LQR	*Law Quarterly Review*
Morley	Henry Morley (ed.), *Ireland under Elizabeth and James I, Described by Edmund Spenser, by Sir John Davies and by Fynes Moryson*, London, 1890
MTR	C. H. Hopwood (ed.), *Middle Temple Records*, 4 vols., London, 1904
NILQ	*Northern Ireland Legal Quarterly*
NLI	National Library of Ireland
NYULR	*New York University Law Review*
P & P	*Past and Present*
PRO	Public Record Office, London
PROI	Public Record Office of Ireland, Dublin
PRONI	Public Record Office of Northern Ireland, Belfast
RIA Proc.	*Proceedings of the Royal Irish Academy*
RSAI	*Journal of the Royal Society of Antiquaries of Ireland*
SHR	*Scottish Historical Review*
SP	State Papers Ireland, Elizabeth – George III
TCD	Trinity College, Dublin
TRHS	*Transactions of the Royal Historical Society*
UJA	*Ulster Journal of Archaeology*

Part I

INTRODUCTION

I

Law as an instrument of colonization

The sixteenth and early seventeenth centuries in Ireland constitute one of the great watersheds in Irish history, a decisive period that witnessed the reduction of the whole island to effective English sovereignty. This conquest was not, however, the result of a consistent expansionist policy until the reign of Elizabeth, when an aggressive Dublin administration led by Sir Henry Sydney (1569–76) succeeded in establishing a militant programme that eventually tied successive administrations to extending English influence by forcible means into areas hitherto beyond the reach of crown government.[1] Yet it was not until the end of Elizabeth's reign that the final contest for Irish sovereignty was fought. From 1594 until 1603, Hugh O'Neill, the Earl of Tyrone, led the last great Gaelic rebellion that shook the very foundations of English rule in Ireland and compelled the English government to commit financial resources that far exceeded the cost of military subvention in any of Elizabeth's continental wars.

The crushing success of English arms over rebel forces aided by Spain at the battle of Kinsale ultimately compelled O'Neill's unconditional submission to the Lord Deputy Mountjoy at Mellifont in county Louth on 30 March 1603 – six days after the death of Elizabeth. This military victory represented a necessary and primary phase in English domination over Ireland, but the second stage of political consolidation by judicial means was equally essential for England's lasting supremacy over the island. Thus the military victory of 1603 enabled English jurists and administrators to accomplish a variety of reforms that encompassed the defeat and break-up not only of native forms of political organization and landholding, but also of the Catholic religion and those elements of the social polity which adhered to it. The consolidation of the Tudor conquest that took place during the early years of James I's reign also set the

3

stage for the 'Protestant ascendancy' of the eighteenth century out of which emerged those familiar social, political and religious tensions that are the hallmark of twentieth-century Irish history. In any event, the death of the last Tudor monarch on 24 March 1603 ushered in a new era that produced changes as far-reaching in Irish history as the famine, the land war and the creation of the Free State.

In discussing this significant period, conventional scholarship has rightly stressed not only the political and military events that led to English hegemony over Ireland, but also the intellectual currents that influenced the formulation and direction of native policy. But in contrast with historians of colonial expansion by continental powers, Irish historians have yet to explore the role of metropolitan law as an agency in promoting and maintaining English rule in Ireland. This study focuses upon the juridical strategies employed by England during the first decade of the seventeenth century to lock a newly conquered country into permanent colonial dependence. Of the crown lawyers involved in the formulation of Irish policy and reform, the most important was Sir John Davies, whose career spanned sixteen years' service in Ireland, first as Solicitor-General, 1603–6, and second as Attorney-General, 1606–19.

More than any other English administrator, Davies realized that military force in itself did not provide an adequate basis for the economic and social exploitation of the newly conquered kingdom. To secure the long-recalcitrant country, Davies proposed the universal application of English law to the whole of Ireland in a way that would facilitate assimilation of the Gaelic polity and reduce the influence of the Old English descendants of earlier Anglo-Norman settlements that preceded the sixteenth century. To elucidate this and other complex and much neglected aspects of legal and administrative reform in Ireland in the wake of the Tudor conquest, this book discusses the role played by English law as an agency of colonialism in Ireland by reviewing select cases taken from Davies' *Reports*.[2] The study divides itself into four sections with the first concerned with the jurisprudential and biographical background to Davies' *Reports*, while the second deals with the impact of English law on the native community. The third part reveals the erosion of the privileged position of the Old English colonial community. A final section comments upon the significance of Roman law in Davies' *Reports*.

The argument of the book is fairly simple. This introductory chapter emphasizes the importance of Ireland in a developing jurisprudence of colonial expansion that would have a significant impact on the development of the British empire. Chapter two sketches out Davies' professional career as background to the third chapter, which outlines the structure and content of his *Reports* and examines the emergence of judge-made law as precedent. Part II, containing chapters four and five, focuses on the native community and details the role of the English judiciary in Dublin in assimilating Gaelic land tenures. Further commentary is devoted to the legal mechanisms employed to sequester the richest fishery in Ulster as an incentive to attract private capital to the plantation of Ulster. Part III concentrates on the colonial community and considers the consequences of the Tudor conquest for the Old English. Chapter six discusses how selective religious persecution by the courts eroded the privileged status and influence of the colonial community, and chapter seven explores the use of judge-made law to deprive the Old English towns of their considerable liberties and franchises acquired during previous reigns. Chapter eight analyses the attempts by the judiciary to reform the Irish currency in order to place the burden of the war debt on the shoulders of the colonial community. Finally, chapter nine in part IV concludes the study by examining Davies' employment of Roman law to provide the necessary precedents and legal principles to confirm and legitimize English rule in Ireland.

This study concentrates on the role of English law in consolidating the Tudor conquest, but it is necessary to concede that the common law never operated alone in the pacification of Ireland. English sovereignty had behind it the ultimate sanction of force, and the maintenance of an army in Ireland was indispensable in ruling the country as a conquered nation. Although the large forces necessary to subdue Tyrone's rebellion had been cut back at the end of the Nine Years War, there still remained at the end of 1603 some 9,000 troops in the country. That number was subsequently reduced in 1606 to a permanent establishment of 880 foot and 234 horse, but the Lord Deputy retained the right to levy a further 2,000 men without consultation with the English government.[3] By contrast to its task in the previous decade, the army's primary mission was not to guard against foreign invasion, but to maintain internal security throughout the country in small garrisons – most of them in Ulster which had, after all, been the heartland of Gaelic revolt during the last decade of the sixteenth century. This emphasis on internal security was not misplaced, and the army proved readily adapted to its new mission by its quick dispatch of Cahir O'Doherty's abortive uprising in early 1608.[4]

Still, the limitations of brute force must be recognized. Coercion could be used to intimidate or to subjugate the natives, but terror in itself did not give rise to co-operation between the native polity and the conqueror or establish the conditions necessary for the economic and social development of the country. In other words, the pacification of Ireland required an instrument other than military force to bring about an orderly administration under the supervision of a central government in Dublin. In the hands of Sir John Davies, that instrument proved to be the common law, which along with other elements of English judicial machinery became the major tool of a practical colonialism in Ireland.

Some historians might hesitate to use the term 'colonial' to describe the Irish situation at the beginning of the seventeenth century, yet Ireland did possess the characteristics of colonial and dependent status. These features included an obvious native problem and a divided settler community of Old English descendants of an earlier Norman conquest along with New English settlers and administrators who established themselves in various settlements planted during the sixteenth and seventeenth centuries.[5] Irish colonization has attracted attention from a variety of scholars and disciplines, ranging from those medieval historians who view English penetration into Ireland as an integral part of a wider scheme of European expansion stretching back into the twelfth century, to social scientists who see in Ireland a pattern of 'internal colonialism' that can be ranked alongside the extension of English influence into Wales and Scotland. Thus sixteenth- and seventeenth-century Irish history represents a kind of early modern 'nation building', an attempt to assimilate outlying Gaelic areas into a coherent state system.[6]

More recently a strongly revisionist historiography has emphasized other themes of the Tudor conquest by combining a more traditional political narrative with investigations into the mental world of policymakers in England and Ireland as the key to understanding the mechanisms of change that led to the conquest of 1603. In his most recent book Dr Brendan Bradshaw attributed the political transformation of Ireland from that of a 'medieval lordship' granted by the pope in the twelfth century to kingdom status conferred by the Irish parliament in 1541, not to aggressive designs of English policymakers in Westminster, but to a group of Pale reformers attempting to thwart the long-standing influence of overmighty Anglo-Irish magnates. In the minds of the Pale reformers this political metamorphosis paid the added dividend of committing the English monarchy to the political unification of Ireland under the crown. As a second step in this scheme, according to Bradshaw, the Dublin government under the deputyship of Sir Anthony St Leger sought an accommodation with the native population by assimilating the autonomous Gaelic lordships through an institutional mechanism known as 'surrender and regrant', whereby native chieftains would surrender their territories and accept the sovereignty of the crown in return for English titles and common law estates. As Professor Aidan Clarke noted recently, the liberal formula pursued during these years displayed the traits of colonial patterns elsewhere – the search for a system of collaboration with the natives and the attempt by the colonial community to manipulate official policy in order to serve its own interests.[7]

Bradshaw has astutely perceived the deeper implications of the liberal policy by analysing its intellectual origins. Rather than attributing the accommodations reached in the 1540s chiefly to political events, Bradshaw chose instead to assign the genesis of the liberal policy to the influence of European humanism. The Dublin administration, in Bradshaw's view, launched a scheme to reform Gaelic districts through a policy of education and persuasion rather than coercion. But the Reformation, argued Bradshaw, was responsible for the subsequent pursuit of a militant policy that shifted the locus of change away from the Pale reformers into the hands of English administrators whose policies were shaped, not by humanistic ideas of reform, but by the predestinarian ideas of Calvin. The new ideology also displayed features derived from Aristotle's views on government and society which stressed force of arms as the essential device to reduce the Irish to civility. This Protestant ideology of compulsion, according to Bradshaw, inspired the conquest and subjugation of the autonomous Gaelic lordships, the creation of plantations and the substitution of New English elites for the Old English in positions of favour and government in Ireland.[8]

Dr Bradshaw's emphasis on intellectual beliefs in the formulation of Irish policy has also attracted the attention of Professor Nicholas Canny, whose study of Sir Henry Sydney's deputyship from 1569 to 1576 discerned a significantly different conceptual design in explaining the Tudor conquest. Canny traced the origins of the new aggressive policy to a completely different intellectual context. As distinct from a Catholic-humanist ideology promoting reform by education and persuasion, or the converse Protestant and Aristotelian approach to change by coercion, Canny pointed instead to attitudinal currents in England and Europe arising from the complex of changes wrought by the Reformation, the 'price revolution' and the Spanish conquest of New Spain.[9]

According to Canny, these events conditioned European thinkers to form a new social perception, which displaced a static outlook on society in favour of an anthropological view of social development. Belief in an unchanging social order receded before an appreciation of the world's peoples as ranging from the primitive savagery of the Amer-Indians to the alleged civility and sophistication of contemporary Europe. English thinkers adapted this viewpoint to the Irish situation and concluded that the native Irish, like the Amer-Indians, were anthropologically inferior beings at a lower stage of social evolution than the English. Hence, in the words of Professor Canny, English policymakers in Ireland firmly believed 'that in dealing with the native population, they were absolved from all normal ethical restraints'.[10] Thus the germ of social Darwinism laid the basis for a violent conquest of the Gaelic Irish whose barbarism was frequently linked to that of the savages in America. In advancing this view Canny has added a new and different perspective to the conclusions of an earlier generation of Irish historians. In addition to patterns of colonial organization and finance, Irish native policy also served as a prototype for English subjugation of native peoples elsewhere, particularly in the American colonies.

The significance attributed by Professor Canny and Dr Bradshaw to the intellectual origins of the Tudor conquest has yielded fresh insights into a vital period of Irish history. Yet Canny's reliance on the transference of Spanish ideas to Ireland and the appearance of anthropological modes of thought disregarded a related and crucial topic that much exercised the Spanish intelligentsia during that period. This issue was, of course, the vexed debate concerning the legal rights and privileges of the conquerors and the conquered. Neglect of this juristic dimension in Canny's discussion of Spanish policy towards the Amer-Indians seems surprising since the literature generated by the lawyers to justify the conquest of New Spain achieved a volume comparable to that produced by the proponents of humanism, Aristotelianism or, as Canny has inferred, an emergent doctrine of social Darwinism.

In Europe both civil and canon lawyers had for several centuries discussed the issues of conquest and native rights largely as a result of medieval expansion into the Levant and Baltic regions.[11] This literature not only influenced Spanish juristic commentaries on the conquest of the New World, but also helped to shape the ideology of English expansion in Ireland. The origins of this continental legal tradition coincide with the eleventh-century revival of Roman law which became, after its acceptance by the church in the twelfth century, the learned law of Europe. Of particular interest to medieval canonists and civilians was the elaboration of conquest right as the paramount legal justification to validate titles to territories acquired by military force. European jurists discussed at length the legal effects of warfare, and agreed that conquest of a territory in a just war yielded full sovereignty to the conquering power.

In their extensive treatment of warfare and conquest right between Christians and non-Christians, the civilians and canonists evolved two approaches to define indigenous property rights in non-Christian territories. One of them constructed by Innocent IV in the thirteenth century recognized the validity of governments and property rights of non-Christians regardless of religious or political considerations. The other tradition, as outlined by Hostiensis, another thirteenth-century canonist, asserted that no legitimate *dominium* could exist without ecclesiastical approbation.[12] This meant that infidels and heretics lacked the capacity to exercise legitimate political control and ownership without approval of the papacy. Accordingly two legal viewpoints had emerged around 1500 to deal with the property and rights of native peoples in the expansion of Europe. The paradigm most favoured by ambitious rulers and governments was, of course, the Hostiensis model, which proved so useful to Spanish expansionists in the sixteenth century.[13] Indeed from the eleventh through the sixteenth centuries, the extension of European influence overseas, including Ireland, owed much to secular authorities acting on papal letters authorizing the secular arm to invade and conquer territories, on the convenient pretext that either the inhabitants or their rulers had somehow fallen foul of the Christian church and its civilizing role.[14]

Sir John Davies' selective approach to the Roman law allowed him to choose those aspects of conquest doctrine that would fit most easily within the intellectual framework of his own legal tradition. As propounded by Davies, the application of conquest right vested England with a public law title to Ireland. Based on the Elizabethan victory over Tyrone, Davies invoked the now familiar powers of conquest to justify the eradication of domestic Irish law as little more than a barbarous and lewd custom, with an eye to eliminating all competing claims to Irish dominion, foreign and Gaelic, that were contingent either upon the political authority accorded to Gaelic chieftains, or upon the papal donation of Ireland to Henry II in 1154.[15]

Davies portrayed this selective adaption of the civil law to his own legal tradition in the brightest possible light by invoking the national chauvinism characteristic of Jacobean lawyers. To mitigate the drastic powers conferred by conquest right, Davies made a distinction between conquest under a 'despotic monarchy or tyranny' as opposed to conquest under an English or 'royal monarchy'. Where despots ruled, as in 'Turkey or Muscovy', or even New Spain, conquest right vested the state with title to all lands conquered and occupied, reducing the inhabitants to 'villains or slaves as proprietors of nothing but at the will of their Grand Seignor or Tyrant'.[16] But under the milder governance of an English monarch, as Davies confided to the English Secretary of State, Sir Robert Cecil in 1606, a public law title to Ireland by right of conquest did not serve as a means to expropriate universally the personal estates of the Irish. Rather, in Davies' view, conquest first created what he called a 'lordship paramount'; this vested the state not only with a title to the whole of Ireland, but more importantly permitted the crown subsequently to confer rights of ownership to individual estates.[17]

Davies' main objective and most difficult problem was to reconstruct property rights in land, especially those held by customary Gaelic tenures derived from a political authority other than the crown. To facilitate the transformation of such titles Davies relied on the juridical teaching that property in the abstract sense represented a legal right acquired from the sovereign that enforced it. The defeat and subsequent departure of an old sovereign power, in this case the demise of Hugh O'Neill and his confederates, presented Davies with an opportunity to refashion all rights to real property in former Gaelic districts. In summarizing Chief Justice Ley's argument in the case of tanistry, Davies constructed a legal doctrine of considerable importance.

If such conqueror receiveth any of the natives or antient inhabitants into his protection and avoweth them for his subjects and permitteth them to continue their possessions and to remain in his peace and allegiance, their heirs shall be adjudged in by good title without grant or confirmation of the conqueror, and shall enjoy their lands according to the rules of the law which the conqueror hath allowed or established, if they will submit themselves to it, and hold their lands according to the rules of it and not otherwise.[18]

Davies and the Irish judiciary had thus created a legal formula subsequently adapted by English jurists in their discussions of native property rights during the period of rapid colonial expansion in the eighteenth and nineteenth centuries. According to the tenets of this formula, all laws and customs repugnant to the laws of the conquering power, particularly of landholding and succession, were either destroyed or subject to modification.[19]

The jurisprudence revealed by Davies' observations on native property rights demonstrates a distinctly English focus stemming from fundamentally different perceptions of property in the common law and in the domestic system of the brehon law. The common law, as one scholar has recently argued, stressed the individual over the family or extended kin group in landownership or occupation. English law, as distinct from brehon law, vested the individual with a variety of estates, interests and rights in land-fee simple estates, estates tail, life estates and leaseholds.[20] In what has been described as a lineage or clan-based society, Gaelic customary law vested property rights in the corporation of the extended kin group. In practice this meant that individual holdings of land in Gaelic districts were temporary and subject to periodic redistribution either by what contemporaries referred to as the custom of gavelkind or by a scheme of succession known as the custom of tanistry.[21] In discussing such tenures in Gaelic districts Davies concluded, rightly or wrongly, that 'all the possessions within these Irish territories (before the common law of England was established in this realm, as it now is) ran always either in course of tanistry or in course of gavelkind'.[22] It was this perception of Gaelic and Gaelicized Ireland that laid the foundation of native policy in Ireland during the first decade of the seventeenth century.

Gavelkind referred, of course, to the prevailing custom of inheritance in Kent in which lands descended to all legitimate male heirs in equal portions over the prevailing custom of primogeniture. In Ireland and in Wales, however, the custom referred to as gavelkind showed a marked deviation from Kentish practice. Apart from the aforementioned emphasis placed on the extended kin group as the unit of landownership, Irish gavelkind also excluded women from inheritance and allowed bastard males a portion or share of property alongside legitimate heirs.[23] In addition to such temporary rights in land, there also existed the custom of tanistry, which was in the strict sense a scheme of succession whereby the successor to a chief or king was nominated during the lifetime of the man to be succeeded. The office of tanist usually included lands and other privileges appendant to it, but Davies and other English jurists employed their own concepts of property to define the Irish custom as a kind of life trust in land for which there existed no ultimate proprietorship. As one legal historian has recently commented, English jurists were caught in the trap of *quia emptores*, a statue of 1290 which had the effect of concentrating all feudal tenures in the crown; consequently, English common lawyers in Ireland lacked the conceptual apparatus to posit a precise tenurial solution to accommodate native tenures.[24]

In order to incorporate such alien forms of property and landholding into the new state system whose sovereignty had been justified by conquest right, the Irish judiciary simply invalidated both gavelkind and tanistry by resolution of all the Irish justices acting in conclave. This extraordinary use of judge-made law became not only the instrument by which English lawyers sought to assimilate Gaelic tenures, but also contributed to the emergence of a doctrine of precedent in English jurisprudence. In practice, elimination of native custom by judicial fiat meant that prior possession might be respected, but unless accepted as lawful by the sovereign or the judiciary, Irish tenures had no validity against a superior common law title. In other words, legal sanction by the conquering power was necessary to validate or create rights over real property in Ireland.[25] The crown lawyers would thus allow the inhabitants to enjoy their lands, not according to Gaelic law, but according to the laws of the conqueror, regranting estates to natives under common law titles through voluntary surrender or through various commissions launched to repair defective titles.

The significance of Davies' application of conquest right to Ireland and the consequent elimination by judicial fiat of those aspects of native customary law that were either barbarous, unreasonable, absurd or lewd can be seen in subsequent litigation justifying English claims to distant lands during the formative years of the empire. As in the case of Ireland, territories acquired by conquest during the period of expansion in the seventeenth and eighteenth centuries were frequently inhabited by people of different cultures and races whose forms of political and social organization differed completely from that of Britain. Frequently in such areas it was not uncommon to find several racial groups and cultures existing within a single territorial unit. While the realigning of property rights by Britain in non-European territories has yet to attract the attention it deserves from historians and legal scholars, substantial evidence exists to show that Davies' imperial formula regulating the legal position of natives and their property rights in Ireland had set the pattern for colonial expansion elsewhere. As early as 1694 William Salkeld, an English Serjeant-at-Law, reported the case of *Blankard* v. *Galdy* referred from Jamaica to the King's Bench, in which the justices found it necessary to summarize the status of conquered kingdoms.

Where an inhabited country is found out and planted by English subjects, all laws in force here are immediately in force there; but in the case of an inhabited country conquered, not till declared so by the conqueror . . . That in Davies 36, it is not pretended that the custom of tanistry was determined by the conquest of Ireland, but by the new settlement made there after the conquest: That it was impossible the laws of this nation, by mere conquest without more, should take place in a conquered country, because for a time, there must want officers, without which our laws can have no force . . . also they held, that in the case of an infidel country, their laws by conquest do not entirely cease, but only such as are against the law of God; and that in such cases where the laws are rejected or silent, the conquered country shall be governed according to the rule of natural equity.[26]

This doctrine provided continuity for a colonial jurisprudence and for a strategy of imperial control over conquered territories. It was to appear again in an anonymous Chancery case reported by Peere Williams in 1722. According to Williams, conquest right not only vested the English monarch with a right and property in the conquered people, but also allowed the English state to impose or modify whatever laws deemed necessary to govern the conquered territory.[27] Writing later in the century, Sir William Blackstone incorporated the principles set forward by the Anonymous case of 1722 in his discussion of overseas plantations and colonies expanding the doctrine to cover territories acquired by cession as well as conquest.[28] The formula was corroborated by Sir Frederick Pollock's comments on the 'external conquests of the common law' in which English law was seen to regulate the legal systems of India, the Sudan and other territories within the empire.[29] Indeed, more recent research strongly suggests that the Davies formula became the basis for defining the status of native law and landholding throughout British overseas possessions.[30] According to a study on African territories subject to the crown, colonial jurists and administrators have regulated indigenous laws and customs in a pattern consistent with the Davies formula by allowing only those aspects of native law and custom that were not repugnant or incompatible with metropolitan law. Small wonder then that a scholar writing in 1977 on the formulation of native policy in Nigeria ascribed to English law the same power as the Maxim gun in subjugating Africa to colonial rule.[31] Davies' formula for Ireland – 'to give laws to a conquered people is the principal mark of a perfect conquest' – had established a paradigm for British expansion elsewhere.[32] In the wake of the Tudor conquest of Ireland, Davies' juridical stance on Gaelic property rights laid the basis for an imperial formula that was fundamental in the creation of the British empire.

2

Sir John Davies: a biographical sketch[1]

As a figure in late Elizabethan literary society, Sir John Davies' main attraction for scholars rests on his reputation as a poet and man of letters, rather than his career as a major legal official in Ireland during the Jacobean period. This emphasis on Davies' literary reputation owes its origin to Alexander Grosart's edition of Davies' prose and poetry which appeared in 1869.[2] Accordingly, Davies' upward mobility in Jacobean society has been ascribed not to an Irish career, but to larger poetic works written at the end of the sixteenth century – *Orchestra*, *Hymns to Astrea* and *Nosce Teipsum*.[3] While poetry doubtless played a role in gaining access to influential circles at court, Davies' little-studied professional career in Ireland (Solicitor-General, 1603–6; Attorney-General, 1606–19) must also be recognized as a significant chapter in a life that elevated the third son of a Wiltshire tanner to an appointment as Chief Justice of the King's Bench in England.

Davies was born in Tisbury, Wiltshire, and was christened in the parish church on 16 April 1569. His Welsh father, Edward Davies, had emigrated to England in the company of Sir William Herbert, the Earl of Pembroke, during the reign of Edward VI. The father later married Mary Bennet of Pitthouse, a small village located only a mile from Tisbury where he pursued, until his death in 1580, a successful career as a tanner. Following her husband's death, the widowed mother raised John along with four other children – two sisters, Edith and Mary, and two elder brothers, Edward and Mathew, who had both been born in 1566. Mathew was to precede John at Winchester and after his schooling received appointment as vicar of Writtle, Essex.[4]

John Davies was elected a scholar at Winchester in 1580, where he studied for four years until he reached the age of sixteen. As the literary scholar Robert Krueger has pointed out, Winchester sparked

Davies' interest in literature and placed him in contact with John
Hoskyns, Thomas Bastard, John Owen and other aspiring men of
letters.[5] From Winchester, Davies appears to have gone to Queen's
College, Oxford, but evidence concerning his university career is
somewhat contradictory. Matriculation rolls for Queen's record his
admission there on 15 October 1585, but the Carte Manuscript
'Notes' on Davies' life, compiled by his grandson Theophilus
Hastings, state that Davies studied at New College. The latter would
have been the more conventional choice for a Winchester scholar,
but Davies' expulsion from the Middle Temple in 1598 may have
occasioned a stay at New College.[6] At any rate Davies' residence at
Oxford lasted only eighteen months and it is doubtful if he ever
graduated. By 1588 Davies decided on a legal career and his entry
into the Middle Temple is fully recorded: 'Mr John Third son of John
Davies of Tisburie, Wiltshire gent and late of New Inn gent'.[7]
Davies apparently spent the time between leaving Oxford and
entering the Middle Temple in attendance at New Inn, the Inn of
Chancery associated with the Middle Temple, which made him
eligible for a reduced admission fee.[8]

Davies distinguished himself from the beginning of his legal
career and was called to the degree of the utter bar with the assent of
all the Masters of the Bench after the minimum seven years' residence.[9] The significance of this achievement is made clear by
comparison with the career of Davis' friend, Richard Martin, who
spent fourteen years as an inner barrister before being called to the
utter bar.[10] Nevertheless, Davies' legal acumen was offset by certain
defects of character, underscored by a flamboyant and tempestuous
personality. Sprinkled throughout the Middle Temple records of
this period are numerous references to Davies' general rowdiness,
and he was frequently disciplined for minor infractions of decorum.
On 25 November 1590, Davies, along with several others, was fined
for 'making outcries, forcibly breaking open chambers in the night
and levying money as the Lord of Misrule's rent'.[11] Within a year,
Davies found himself temporarily expelled, along with William
Fleetwood and Richard Martin, for committing similar offences
against fellow students. This unruly behaviour may have represented a kind of ritualized fraternal chaos endemic to the Candlemas
season. Middle Temple records for 1590–2, however, demonstrate
instances of disciplinary action against Davies at other times as
well.[12] One of these occasions inspired Davies' only recorded trip to
the continent. In 1592, Davies, along with William Fleetwood and

Richard Martin, journeyed to Leyden with letters of introduction from the antiquary William Camden to Paul Merula, the famous Dutch jurist.[13] Since Merula held the chair of civil law and jurisprudence at Leyden, it may be inferred that Davies was pursuing an early interest in the theory and practice of continental civil law.

After his return to England, Davies wrote to acknowledge Merula's hospitality in a letter dated 17 March 1592. He described his studies at the Middle Temple and enclosed an English law book as a token of his admiration for the Dutch jurist. In language unbecoming to a lawyer who has since acquired a reputation for insularity as ingrained as that of Sir Edward Coke, Davies explained his choice of a Latin edition of Fortescue's treatise on English municipal law by claiming that the barbarous character of the English legal vernacular would be unsuited for a cosmopolitan lawyer like Merula.[14] In a subsequent letter Davies complained of the tedium of studying English municipal law, and enviously remarked upon Merula's security in the ivory towers of Leyden where the 'musae nectar et ambrosiam omni ac abundantia apponant'.[15] Davies may have felt a nostalgic longing for the scholarly tranquillity of university life, but as the world of the Middle Temple drew him further away from the 'musae nectar', contact with Leyden ceased. The significance of the friendship, however, lies with Davies' interest in civil law which, as his *Reports* show, he would use with devastating effect in consolidating the Tudor conquest in Ireland.

From 1592 to 1598, Davies' life centred on the Middle Temple. During this period, nevertheless, his advancement in law was interwoven with his increasing success as a poet. Sometime during 1594 Davies completed the poems *Nosce Teipsum*, and *Orchestra*. In the same year Charles Blount, Lord Mountjoy, who was subsequently appointed Lord Deputy of Ireland, presented Davies at court.[16] Although Mountjoy's patronage may have resulted from an appreciation of the poet's talents, it is equally possible that the contacts had originated at the Inns of Court, for Mountjoy had been admitted to the Middle Temple on 20 June 1579.[17] At any rate, the connection with Mountjoy, whom Davies later described as his patron, proved fruitful. In 1594 Queen Elizabeth had Davies sworn as servant-in-ordinary and encouraged him in his legal studies at the Middle Temple.[18] In the same year he was part of the official party sent to the christening of Prince Henry in Scotland.

During the next few years Davies continued to write poetry and to read law; as we have seen, in 1595 he was admitted to the utter bar. But in 1598, an incident occurred which threatened to end his successful advance abruptly. Since the traditional interpretation of Davies' rise rests on the story of this event, it will be necessary to recount in some detail Davies' friendship with his fellow Templar, Richard Martin, the circumstances of its rupture and Davies' expulsion from the community in which he had spent the last decade.

Richard Martin was the colleague with whom Davies had travelled to Holland in 1592 after their joint suspension from the Middle Temple for misconduct. The poem *Orchestra* was dedicated to Martin, and Davies referred to him as 'mine owne self's better halfe, my dearest friend'.[19] John Aubrey described Martin as a 'handsome man, a graceful speaker, facetious and well beloved'.[20] Benjamin Rudyerd, another Elizabethan poet, portrayed him as:

Of face thin and leane of a chearefull and gracious countenance blackhaired tall bodyed and well proporcioned of a sweet and faire conversation to every man that kept his distance. Fortune never taught him to temper his own will or manhood. His company commonly weaker than himself put him into a just opinion of his own strength of a noble and high spirit as far from base and infamous strains as ever he was from want. Soe wise that he knew how to make use of his own subjects and they their own contentmant soe eloquent in ordinary speech by extraordinary practices and loss of too much tyme that his judgement which was good study could not mind it. He was very fortunate and discreete in the love of women, a great lover and complainer of company having more judgement to mislike their power to forbear.[21]

By contrast, contemporaries thought Davies an aggressive, indiscreet man with a penchant for showy behaviour. In 1607 the Earl of Tyrone, in an apologia written to James I justifying his flight from Ireland, angrily commented on Davies' defects in personality, portraying him as a man 'more fit to be a stage player than a counsaill to your highness'.[22] While some observers took note of the contrasts in personality between Davies and Martin, others remarked on the equally striking difference in their physical appearances. The most vivid illustrations of Davies' physique appear in two rather coarse selections taken from John Manningham's diary.

B. Rudyerd or Th. Overbury: He never walks but he carries a cloake bag behind him his arse sticks out so far.

Jo. Davys goes waddling with his arse out behind him as though he were about to make every one that he meets a wall to piss against.[23]

An equally graphic description may be found in Benjamin Rudyerd's poem 'Mathon', where Davies (Mathon) is depicted as a short, stout, pock-marked man with little to offer in the way of social graces:

Matho the dauncer with the maple face . .

Matho hath got the barr and many graces by studdying, noble men, newes and faces . .

> Mathon why shouldst thou think of common lawe,
> None can into an ordered method draw
> Since they rude feet, whose gate confusion wrought
> Weare by great paynes ordered dancing brought.[24]

These contrasts between Davies and Martin assist in understanding the events described in Benjamin Rudyerd's narrative of the Candlemas festivities in 1598, when both men competed for the coveted position of Prince d'Amour. During the annual Candlemas ritual the Middle Templars elected from their ranks this Prince d'Amour to serve as master of ceremonies. In 1598 Martin and Davies stood as the principal candidates, in itself an illustration of their popularity among their fellow lawyers. Davies narrowly lost this election, and Martin in the company of his supporters added to the injury by heaping abuse on his friend. Davies then made a spirited attempt to defend himself with an extemporaneous oration that was shouted down by the Middle Templars. Rudyerd, with rude allusions to Davies' squat stature and strange ambling gait, described him as inelegantly mixing metaphors borrowed from smiths and clowns.[25]

Unable to impress the revellers with his oration, Davies sought refuge in strong drink, but in his drunkenness succeeded only in casting lewd and offensive remarks at a number of ladies present at the festivities. His garish costume of orange taffeta, accentuating his defective physique, heightened his ignominy, according to Rudyerd. Davies was further alleged to have 'practiced factiously against the prince and earnestly stirred up enmity betwixt him and the Lincolnians'.[26] Undaunted, Davies made another attempt to regain the spotlight but again was stifled by a vicious and premeditated satire lampooning both his poetry and his social origins. Rudyerd stated that Davies, dubbed Stradilax in the drama, 'in great pomp with a left handed truncheon miscalled himself a lord no man gainsaying it or crying: God save your lordship'. An unidentified poet, 'Matagonius', then presented Davies with a shield 'wherein was drawn the monster sphinx; the word was Davus sum, non Oedipus, and saluted him by the name of Stradilax to the tune of the Tanner and the King'.[27]

In discussing this last incident, literary scholars have argued that the Middle Templars' prank represents a cleverly arranged piece of sixteenth-century class satire.[28] This conclusion was deduced from the Templars' choice of music which served to remind the prideful Davies of his humble social origins as the third son of a tanner. The mysterious iconography of the sphinx and the allusion to Oedipus are more difficult to analyse, but one scholar has concluded that the sphinx represents a standard seventeenth-century literary motif employed to show ignorance of self.[29] The classical allusion to Oedipus' solution to the sphinx's riddle symbolized the importance of knowing one's self, and of understanding the complexities of human nature. This elaborate, ingenious and obviously planned sneer must have dealt a devastating blow to Davies' ego.

Still smarting from this wave of insults, Davies constructed an equally staged, albeit more violent revenge directed against Richard Martin, the probable author of his torment. The following excerpt from the minutes of the Middle Temple tells what happened:

While the Masters of the Bench and other fellows were quietly dining publicly in the hall, John Davies one of the Masters of the Bar, in cap and gown, and girt with a dagger, his servant and another with him being armed with swords, came into the Hall. The servant and the other person stayed at the bottom of the hall, while he walked up to the fireplace and then to the lower part of the second table for Masters of the Bar, where Richard Martyn was quietly dining. Taking from under his gown a stick, which is commonly called a bastinado he struck Martyn on the head with it till it broke, and then running to the bottom of the hall he took his servant's sword out of his hand shook it over his own head (*super caput suum proprium quatiebat*) and ran down to the water steps and jumped into a boat. He is expelled never to return.[30]

Martin seems to have escaped with little or no damage, but the following anagram attributed to him amply shows his chagrin at having been betrayed by his friend:

Davis/Advis/Iudas/Martin.[31]

Since literary scholars have concentrated their attention on the novelty of Davies' attack on Martin, it should be noted that its style and execution show a surprising parallel to an incident at another of the Inns of Court. Between 5 February 1598 and 12 May 1598, Henry Colt committed a suspiciously similar offence against the steward of Lincoln's Inn.

With a revenge extraordinary in most outrageous and violent manner in the hall and the skreene, before the benchers were risen from the table, he did strike the said steward with a cudgell or bastinado upon the heade, giving unto him a most dangerous blowe, almost to the perill of his life . . .

And for other misdemeanours then by him committed, as in drawing his rapier, presently upon the said outrage done, in the court of this house, to yll example of others, intending as yt seemed thereby to have done some further outrage. He is therefore expelled the house.[32]

In view of this precedent, it would be difficult to represent Davies' transgression as an isolated incident, and Colt's activities at Lincoln's Inn may have served as inspiration for Davies' assault on Martin. The records of Lincoln's Inn also describe, on the same occasion, an incident in which a Mr Watts cudgelled the Pannyer-man over the head, an offence which he followed up by attempting to stab a Mr Holland, one of the fellows, with a dagger. Although one would normally consider attempted homicide with a dagger to be a more heinous crime than Davies' offence, it is interesting to note that Watts got off with a fine of £10.[33] The principal difference between the two assaults seems to revolve upon the question of decorum. Watts committed assaults out in the street or in the hallways of Lincoln's Inn, but Davies and Colt bastinaded their enemies during dinner hour before the watchful presence of their respective Inns of Court. A measure of official distaste over this lack of etiquette is illustrated in the epigrammist John Hoskins' allusion to Davies' assault:

Shall a soldier for a blow with his hand given in war to a captain, be disgraced, and shall a lawyer for the bastinado given in a hall of court to his companion be advanced? We that profess laws maintain outrage, and they that break all laws in this yet observe civility.[34]

The significance of the attack on Richard Martin lies in the role it has played in the myth of Davies' rise through literary patronage. According to tradition, Davies followed his disgrace with a period of extreme soul-searching and, out of sorrow and penance, purged himself of his former pride by writing the introspective *Nosce Teipsum* which brought him to the attention of James I. That is, the poem *Nosce Teipsum* has been seen as the source of Davies' re-admission to the bar and his subsequent legal career in Ireland, culminating in an appointment as Chief Justice of the Court of King's Bench in England.

The origins of this accepted view of Davies' rise lie in an apocry-phal anecdote invented by Anthony Wood, who misinterpreted several biographical details in the Carte Manuscripts. According to Wood, Davies accompanied Lord Hunsdon to Scotland at the death of Elizabeth to congratulate James I on his accession to the throne.

Introduced to Davies, James allegedly enquired as to whether he were 'Nosce Teipsum Davies'. Having received an affirmative reply, James embraced him and 'thenceforth had so great favour to him, that soon after, he made him his Attorney-General in Ireland'.[35] Wood's fallacious story later served as inspiration for Alexander Grosart's projection of Victorian moral progress on to Davies' career.[36] This virtuous chronology was subsequently endorsed by A. L. Rowse, who repeated Wood's account as a classic illustration of an Elizabethan political career launched through literary patronage.[37]

On all counts, this traditional story is false. Both the Carte 'Notes' on Davies' life and Rudyerd's description of the Candlemas revels clearly show that *Nosce Teipsum* was written before the violent incident with Martin. Nor can it be shown that Davies was at all penitent for his crime. A recently discovered manuscript poem attributed to Davies hardly indicates remorse.

Davies beinge committed to prison for a quarrel between him and Martin, wrote as ensueth.

> Now Davies for a bird is in
> But yet it is but for a Martin.[38]

That Davies returned to Oxford after his expulsion from the Middle Temple is confirmed by John Aubrey, who mentioned that Davies 'spent some more time there again then wearing only his cloak'.[39] The notion that he subsequently accompanied Lord Hunsdon to Scotland is, however, unfounded. It was not George Carey, Lord Hunsdon, but his brother Sir Robert Carey who took the news of Elizabeth's death to Edinburgh – Davies could not have gone to Scotland with a man who never even left England. It is possible that Davies did accompany part of James' progress south into England. In a letter written to Dudley Carleton on 30 March 1603, John Chamberlain commented on the flurry of activity surrounding the new king's progress and gave the names of various figures who had presented themselves for preferment, one of whom was 'John Davies the poet'.[40] Although Davies may have met the king at this time, there is no evidence to show that he received any immediate marks of royal favour. In the first month of his reign, James created 906 new knighthoods, 432 of which were bestowed on a single occasion on 23 July 1603. Davies was not included in this group. An entry in Manningham's diary records one sceptic's impressions of Davies' relations with the new monarch:

Jo: Davies reports that he is sworne the King's man, that the king shewed him great favour. Inepte. He slanders while he prayses.[41]

The Carte 'Notes' on Davies' life provide the solution to the problem of the timing of the mysterious patronage from the king. Davies did indeed meet James I, but not in the fictionalized encounter of 1603 created by Wood and Grosart. Rather Davies' association with James stems from the earlier journey to Scotland to attend the christening of Prince Henry, or as the Carte 'Notes' put it:

AD1594 when Prince Hen: was borne from whom Q. Eliz. was Godmother he went in the company of ytt Ambassye and when he kissed the King of Scots hand he was owned by him with the name of Nosce Teipsum Davies.[42]

The revision in the chronology of Davies' trip to Scotland and the reference to *Nosce Teipsum* in the Candlemas satire undermine the story that Davies' return to grace following his expulsion from the Middle Temple was based on some personality transformation enshrined in his poem, which had actually been written some six years before.

While the story is certainly apocryphal, it is true that Davies inclined towards using his literary talents to bring himself to the attention of influential men at court in the years following his disgrace. On the death in 1600 of Elizabeth Moore, the second wife of Sir Thomas Egerton, Davies sent the Lord Chancellor an autographed copy of *Orchestra* with an introductory sonnet designed to console the bereaved widower. In the attached letter, Davies reaffirmed his friendship with Egerton and added:

A French writer (whom I love well) speakes of 3 kindes of companions; Men, women and bookes; the losse of the second make you retire from the first, I have therefore presumed to send your lordship one of the third kind, which it may be is a stranger to your lordship. Yet, I persuade me, his conversation will not be disagreeable to your lordship.[43]

There is also evidence to suggest that literary talent helped in Davies' attempts to ingratiate himself with Robert Cecil. During January 1601 Davies wrote to Michael Hicks, Cecil's secretary, offering his literary services:

Mr Hicks: I have sent you here enclosed that cobweb of my invention which I promised before Christmas; I pray you present it, commend it, and grace it as well for your own sake as mine because by your nomination I was first put to this task, for which I acknowledge myself beholden to you in good earnest though the employment be light and trifling because I am glad of any occasion of being made knowne to that noble gentleman whom I honor and admire exceedingly. [44]

Within a year Davies composed another poem entitled a *Contention Betwixt a Wife, a Widow and a Maid* which was aired at Cecil's home. John Chamberlain mentioned the event in his diary, and referred to the poem as a 'pretty dialogue'. [45]

One need not look to the accession of James in 1603 to account for Davies' rehabilitation and subsequent rise. [46] As early as 1601 Davies' cause had been taken up by some of the most powerful men in the government. Literary efforts alone would have been scarcely sufficient to secure the attention of men such as Cecil and Egerton. Surely Davies' legal abilities and promise played a considerable role. At any rate, in June 1601 Davies openly petitioned Robert Cecil:

I hold it a necessary Duty to present my humble thanks to your lordship for the special favour you were pleased to show me, the last day at York house. Which though it hath not yet effected that good which your Lordship wisht it should, yet it reflectd much grace uppon me another way. For many that were present did valew me the better, when they saw so great and worthy a personage have such respect and care of me. My Lord Chief Justice pretended he could not end the business, because my adversary was absent. That lett is removed, for he is now returned to town and will not depart till the end of the terme .. I humbly beseech your lordship to cast one Sun-beame more of your favor uppon me in this behalf; which if it clear not my disgrace I will draw a clowd over me and so rest until I may overcome it either by time or by desert. [47]

Later in the same month Sir Thomas Egerton openly petitioned the Middle Temple on Davies' behalf:

The tyme that he hath been already sequestered from your house seemeth in mine opinion a sufficient punnishment, and the repentence which he hath shewed, a reasonable satisfaction for his offence. [48]

The collective patronage of Cecil, Egerton and others proved effective. As John Chamberlain noted a few weeks later, 'The Lord Chief Justice and Master Secretarie have taken great paines to compound the quarrel twixt Martin and Davies which they have effected to the satisfaction of both parts.' Only two and a half years earlier the Middle Temple had disbarred Davies 'never to return'. On 30 October 1601, in the presence of the Chief Justice, the Chief Baron of the Exchequer, several serjeants-at-law and the assembled members of the Middle Temple, Richard Martin publicly accepted his adversary's apology, and Davies was restored to the 'Societye amongst whom I have had my chiefest education, and from whence I expect my best preferment'.[49]

Following Davies' return to grace, the Middle Temple records make only brief mention of his activities. Davies never seems to have served as reader, or to have become a member of the Middle Temple bench – even after his appointment as Serjeant-at-Law. In fact, after 1601, there are only three references to Davies in the Middle Temple records, all dealing with room assignments. Nor apparently did Davies use his influence to gain admission for friends, or for that matter his relatives. One of the nephews, for example, was admitted to the Middle Temple in 1612, but Davies is not mentioned as a sponsor.[50] After 1601, then, it seems that Davies avoided participation in the daily affairs of the Middle Temple, although he did keep chambers there until 1610. The most important result of his re-admission to the bar was the right to practise law, but his reinstatement also helped to secure sponsorship for a seat in the English parliament of 1601. Shortly after his return to favour, Davies was elected MP for the borough of Corfe Castle. It is difficult to disentangle the patronage links that led Davies to a Dorset seat. Davies' association with Lord Mountjoy, who was implicated in the Essex plot of 1601, suggests a distant association with the unfortunate Essex. But in view of Cecil's role in securing Davies' return to the Middle Temple, it is more likely that Davies owed his parliamentary sponsorship to Secretary Cecil.

Davies achieved some prominence for his role in the debate over monopolies, an issue which dominated the business of the 1601 parliament.[51] The House of Commons, faced with the likelihood of paying out enormous sums to support the wars against Spain and Ireland, directed its discontent not at military disbursements, but against money wasted in granting monopolistic concessions to court favourites, who frequently gouged the public with excessive prices. Davies distinguished himself in the debates over these monopolies. The central question dealt with whether the House should seek redress by petition to the queen, or should pass specific legislation against monopolies themselves. Cecil expected the House of Commons to proceed by petition. The majority of members seemed to accept his influence, albeit reluctantly. Davies, however, proved an exception, hurling himself into a spirited oration that began with a series of legal precedents.

God hath given power to absolute princes, which he attributed to himself. And so, as attributes unto them, he hath given them Majesty, Justice and

Mercy. Majesty in respect of the Honour that the subject sheweth unto his prince. Justice in respect he can do no wrong. Mercy in respect he giveth leave to his subject, to right themselves by law. And therefore, in the 44 Ass. an indictment was brought against bakers and brewers; and for that by colour of license, they had broken the assize: wherefore, according to that precedent, I think it most fit to proceed by bill and not by petition.[52]

Secretary Cecil, obviously displeased by Davies' rhetorical display, delivered an eloquently reasoned speech reducing the dispute to two basic legal principles, the prerogative and the fundamental liberties of English citizens.

I am born an English-Man, and a Fellow member of this house. I would desire to live no day, in which I should detract from either.

I am servant to the queen; and before I would speak, give my consent to a cause that should debase the prerogative or abridge it, I would wish my tongue cut out of my head. I am sure there were law-makers before there were laws.[53]

After a few more brief speeches, the subject was referred to committee for discussion in the afternoon. But Cecil's rebuke did not prevent Davies from launching another assault on monopolies in the afternoon session.[54] While Davies succeeded in amusing the assembly, Richard Martin, his former adversary, took steps to soften the vehemence of this offensive speech. Martin apologized for Davies' verbal excesses, but cogently defended the substance of his friend's comments.[55]

A royal proclamation withdrew the more obnoxious monopolies, but Davies, undaunted, rose once again to speak. In response, the speaker queried, 'What need this new zeal?' Davies replied that he wanted the proclamation registered for as the 'Gospel is written and registered, so would I have that also: For good tydings come to the hearts of the subjects that is all.'[56] Then followed a series of speeches as to whether Davies' request constituted an insult to the queen, and 'Mr. Comptroller soundly rebuked Davies for his ironic skepticism; I think that he that moved this first question exceedingly forgot himself, and exceedingly detracted from her majesty.'[57]

Davies' behaviour in the debates over monopolies is illuminating for the clues it gives to his personality and methods. Certainly his actions belie the image of a sycophantic courtier conveyed by Wood and Grosart. His speech against monopolies, delivered in the face of those who were instrumental in restoring him to favour, reveals Davies as a tenacious and insensitively hard-headed adherent to causes – in short, a man of sharp-witted conviction. The proceedings of the parliament also show, incidentally, that by 1601, Davies and Martin were on friendly terms again, for they had collaborated in the battle against monopolies.

There is one last intriguing element to consider in Davies' rise in Jacobean society. In March of 1609 Davies married Eleanor Touchet, the fifth daughter of an English peer, George Baron Audley, who received an Irish title on 6 September 1616 as the Earl of Castlehaven. It is difficult to reconstruct the social context that enabled Davies to marry the daughter of a peer. Davies had perhaps met Eleanor while riding the Munster assize in 1606, but a more probable explanation lies, once again, in Davies' association with the Middle Temple. Although Audley was not a formal member of that body, he was a frequent guest, and is mentioned in Hutchinson's *Catalogue of Notable Middle Templars*.[58] One would ordinarily presume a marriage into the peerage to be socially advantageous, but Davies, like many an unwary suitor, found himself saddled with a set of in-laws whose emotional and mental stability left much to be desired. Almost immediately after the marriage, his father-in-law importuned Davies for political favours that included a request for 100,000 acres in Ulster. Audley's rapacity became notorious, and Lord Deputy Chichester found reason to complain of his proposal to the English privy council, at which he commented on the man's inherent meanness and general inability to support financially even a small estate in the Ulster plantation.[59] Then there was the unsavoury case of Davies' brother-in-law, Mervyn Touchet, the second Earl of Castlehaven, who though also listed as a guest of the Middle Temple could hardly be considered an asset to any professional body. In 1631, he was tried before the English House of Lords and executed for sexual offences that included supervising the premeditated rape of his wife and daughter, and the sodomizing of one of his servants. State's evidence was provided by the earl's wife and daughter.[60]

Nor was Davies' wife Eleanor exempt from the family's instability, and her seventeen-year association with Davies could hardly be described as blissful. Eleanor's defects of personality included a penchant for scriptural anagrams and prophesying. These skills, frequently cited in the domestic state papers, involved her in religious and doctrinal offences that eventually brought her to the attention of the High Commission. Such activities did not augur well either for married life or political ambition. Although the marriage produced three children, there were no surviving male heirs. Two sons, John and Richard, died before reaching manhood.

Richard died in infancy, while John, an idiot, drowned in Ireland, at what date is uncertain. A letter from Davies' friend Sir Robert Jacob, the Solicitor-General for Ireland, shows that the retarded son was alive in 1617.

Your lady is at her house in Chancery Lane and in very good health, and so are your children; and I am of the opinion that if your son Jack were now put into the hands of some skilful men, he might be brought to speak. For he is wonderfully mended in his understanding of late, for he understands anything that is spoken to him without making any signs, so as it is certain he hath his hearing, and then the defect must be in his tongue.[61]

On the evidence of this letter, we must assume that John died sometime between the years 1617 and 1619 when Davies terminated his Irish service. There was also a third child, Lucy, who eventually was married at the age of eleven to Ferdinando Hastings, the sixth Earl of Huntingdon. The whole of Davies' estate was to pass to Lucy, rather than to his widow, an illustration of the state of Davies' marriage. Although Eleanor's most notorious activities took place after Davies' death in 1626, there is an incident in the domestic state papers in 1622 that serves to preview her later behaviour. Evidently Eleanor had been badgering a Mrs Brooke and her daughter with her religious mania, and Mr Brooke reproached her for having 'abandoned all goodness and modesty', noting also that Eleanor was 'mad, ugly and blinded with pride of birth'. Moreover, Brooke informed her, if she did not cease her 'abuse of his wife and innocent child' he would 'scratch a mince pie out of her'.[62] He further assured Eleanor that he wished only the most terrible of curses upon her, and especially that she would 'remain ever what thou art'. The factual information surrounding this incident is incomplete, but a letter from John Chamberlain dated 1 July 1622 indicates that the controversy between Brooke and Eleanor had gained the attention of the Star Chamber.

There is a hot suit commenced in the Star Chamber twixt Sir John Davies' lady and the Lady Jacob about womanish brabbles, and an uncivil scurrilous letter written by Kit Brooke in his wife's behalf.[63]

This incident perhaps inspired Davies to burn Eleanor's prophecies, an act that can hardly be viewed as a disservice to the reading public. Eleanor was not amused, however, and predicted 'his doom in letters of his own name (John Davies: Jove's Hand) within three years to expect the mortal blow'. Davies' response was in keeping with his personality, 'I pray weep not while I am alive, and I will give you leave to laugh when I am dead.'[64] From that time until his death in 1626, Davies suffered the uncomfortable experience of staring across the breakfast table at a hopelessly insane wife dressed in mourning.

Eleanor lived to inflict herself on a second husband, Sir Archibald Douglas, who also made the mistake of burning her manuscripts, for which he was allegedly struck dumb and reduced to grunting like a beast. In 1633 Eleanor was indicted by the Court of High Commission for her prophesying, and there survives a curious anecdote which registers Eleanor's growing mental confusion. While appearing before the court, Eleanor claimed to be infused with the spirit of Daniel, whose presence she attempted to prove with an anagram composed from the letters of her own name: 'Eleanor Davies: Reveal O Daniel'. After great pains had been taken to show her the error of her ways, the Dean of the Arches contrived another anagram for Lady Eleanor which said: 'Dame Eleanor Davies – Never so made a Lady'.[65] The ensuing laughter from the members of that solemn tribunal threw Eleanor into a confused silence, and she was subsequently committed to prison. Within months Eleanor's daughter Lucy sought to lessen the severity of her sentence and petitioned the High Commission to remove her mother to another prison and appoint some 'grave divine to comfort her in her troubles of mind which lie heavy upon her, and for informing her in some points of learning and conscience'.[66] A fine of £3,000 and several months in prison did not diminish Eleanor's madness. By 12 July 1635, her reputation was such that Lady Alice Hastings wrote to her father, the fifth Earl of Huntingdon, to prevent her brother Ferdinando from bringing his mother-in-law to live with the Hastings family.[67] Not only did Eleanor attempt to inflict herself on her in-laws, but she also appears to have initiated litigation to contest Davies' will. According to J. R. Brink, Lady Eleanor claimed that Davies' Englefield estate in Berkshire was part of her jointure.[68] Hastings eventually won the case, but it is interesting to note, once again, that Davies deliberately excluded Eleanor from his will in favour of his daughter Lucy.

In 1636, Eleanor's activities finally landed her in Bedlam for defiling the Bishop Lichfield's seat with a so-called 'Holy water that proved to be a combination of tar, pitch, sink puddle and water and such kind of nasty ingredients'.[69] Similar offences brought her by 1640 to the Tower for prophesying the death of Charles I. She was rearrested in 1646 for her religious activities and remanded to the custody of the Hastings family where she appears to have remained until her death in 1652. There is, however, one more anecdote to show her inability to get on with others, even with those whose religious/political hysteria approached her own. From August to December 1650 Lady Eleanor had employed the impoverished Gerrard Winstanley to act as estate agent to harvest wheat. In 1650 Digger agents were active in the vicinity of Eleanor's home at Pirton, Hertfordshire, and it is likely that she and Winstanley had much in common. Eleanor's refusal to pay her new agent, however, demonstrates that even among Utopians, unpaid wages served to divide the community of the New Jerusalem.[70]

An assessment of Davies' disastrous marriage must take into account the question of his social position. Whether or not Davies reaped any benefits from his marriage to the daughter of a peer is, in view of the Audleys' history, problematical. Still one conjectures that this absence of marital bliss enabled Davies, like many a tormented husband, to develop a prodigious capacity for work. Whatever the source of Davies' industry, his many talents ultimately led, through a complex patronage network involving Devonshire, Cecil and Ellesmere, to his political appointments in Ireland – first as Solicitor-General in 1603, and then as Attorney-General from 1606 to 1619.[71]

For Davies' part, there is some question about whether he viewed his Irish appointments as anything but temporary exile. This sentiment was expressed in a letter written by Bacon to Davies on 26 December 1606, which instructed Davies to remain a 'laborer' in that state (Ireland) and not a 'plant'.[72] In fact shortly after his arrival in Ireland, Davies complained to Salisbury that:

I would Serjeant Heale might be banished hither, if it be trew that he has antedated the scire facias, I wish not this maliciously, like an ill angel that is fallen, and would have all others in as desparate a case as himself; but I fear a heavier punishment will light upon him, for I hope shortly to see this a rich and flourishing kingdom. This with my humble presentation of my duty and devotion to your Lp. I leave the same to divine preservation.[73]

Then once again in 1610 Davies petitioned Salisbury to secure an appointment elsewhere, by listing his personal achievements in securing a wide range of administrative reforms in Ireland.[74] These accomplishments, which included the constitutional assimilation of the autonomous Gaelic lordships to the crown, the reduction of medieval corporate liberties, the implementation of religious conformity and the mobilization of the Irish revenue, are detailed elsewhere in this volume. Certainly his Irish career served to secure rapid advancement. On 18 December 1603 Davies was knighted in Dublin by Lord Deputy Carey.[75] In 1612, while serving as Attorney-General for Ireland, he was created Serjeant-at-Law, and by 1613 he was financially secure enough to be included as one of the adventurers in the Virgina Company.[76]

Davies published in 1612 a *Discoverie of the True Causes Why Ireland Was Never Entirely Subdued Nor Brought under Obedience of the Crown of England until His Majesties Happie Reigne*, in which he attributed the shortcomings of English rule in Ireland to the failure to establish successfully a system of territorial rather than personal law.[77] Three years later Davies published his *Reports* elaborating step by step the innovative judicial measures he had employed to consolidate the Tudor conquest of Ireland.[78] Indeed Davies' legal skills and familiarity with Irish affairs earned him a high reputation with the king, and James himself picked Davies as the most competent candidate to become Speaker of the House for the scheduled Irish parliament to be convened in 1613.[79] Various letters and papers in the Carte Manuscripts show the degree to which Davies was personally responsible for planning the narrow Protestant majority of that parliament. The new boroughs arising from the plantations in Munster and Ulster returned 84 Protestants, leaving the government a narrow majority of 32. In the House of Lords, the Protestant episcopate, which outnumbered the twelve Catholic and four Protestant peers, gave the government a majority of eleven votes in the upper house. The Catholic Old English objected to the validity of the Protestant majority in the lower house by claiming that false returns had been made by the sheriffs, and that many other MPs were not even resident in their newly created boroughs. This conflict resulted in a contest for the speakership, where a deadlock election produced one of the most amazing episodes in Irish parliamentary history. Once the election appeared to be a draw, the recusant faction rushed the Speaker's chair and placed John Everard, a former Second Justice of the King's Bench, whom Davies had forced to resign for recusancy, into the speaker's chair. At this point, Davies' party simply placed the corpulent Attorney-General in Everard's lap while business was conducted until Everard was finally ejected by Davies' supporters.[80]

Within several years of the Irish parliament of 1613–15, Davies petitioned Buckingham to be relieved of office as Attorney-General for Ireland, and on 30 October 1619 he was replaced by Sir William

Ryves.[81] It is difficult to follow Davies' career consistently during the years from 1619 to 1626. During this period he probably composed his well-known abridgement of Coke's *Reports*.[82] He also published in 1622 a revised edition of his three major poems, *Nosce Teipsum*, *Astrea* and *Orchestra*, which contained a new dedication for *Orchestra* and a revised conclusion.[83] More significantly, Davies served in the parliament of 1621 as MP for Newcastle-under-Lyme, but unlike his earlier performance in the parliament of 1601, he failed to distinguish himself in the debates. In view of the outbreak of the Thirty Years War and a renewed attack on monopolies, this reticence is surprising. There does survive, however, one revealing speech which demonstrates the degree to which Davies' Irish experience had conditioned his view of the public law relationship between England and Ireland. In response to a bill calling for restrictions against the Irish cattle trade, Davies displayed his newly acquired planter mentality:

Sir John Davies saieth, that it is expressly in the Law Books set down, that Ireland is a member of the crown of England; That there was in Ireland also a patent of Alehouses, which, on the complaint of some principal men of that kingdom, the king did recall about two years since; and gave order to redress the same; That this kingdom here cannot make laws to bind that kingdom, for they have there a parliament of their own.[84]

Apart from Davies' appearance in the English parliament, he also rode the assize circuit between 1620 and 1626, and his speech to the grand jury at the York assize in 1620 represents a classic contemporary exposition of the jurisprudence on assize justice.[85] King Charles appointed Davies Chief Justice of King's Bench in 1626 to replace Randolph Crew as a result of Crew's refusal to declare the legitimacy of the forced loan. In view of Davies' treatise on the right of the monarchy to levy impositions without parliamentary consent, it is understandable that he was an attractive candidate for the job.[86] It is certain that Davies admired Charles and harboured great expectations for the reign of the young king. On 1 April 1625 he wrote to Henry, fifth Earl of Huntingdon, praising the virtues of the new monarch:

for the King desires that he and the Queen may be crowned together to save a double charge; which saving will be more than an entire subsidy. The young king doth already show many excellent tokens of a stout, a wise, and a frugal prince, and is like to restore the glory of our nation by his wisdom and valor.[87]

There can be little doubt that, had Davies lived, he would have been a similarly stout royalist in the civil war. On 26 December 1626

Davies prepared for his new judicial appointment by purchasing the robes of office, but an excess of food and drink took its toll and bore out the truth of Eleanor's prophecy. He died in a fit of apoplexy the night before he was to become Chief Justice – an act of God, wrote the English judge, James Whitelock, that prevented 'so inconvenient an intention to the commonwealth'.[88] At the funeral John Donne preached the oration, and Davies was subsequently interred in St Martin-in-the-Fields.[89]

3

Ireland and the origins of 'stare decisis'

In 1603, John Davies travelled to Dublin to assume his duties as Solicitor-General for Ireland. His appointment followed the defeat of Tyrone's rebel forces and the final subjugation of the long-recalcitrant kingdom. As one of the principal advocates of English policy during the next sixteen years Davies worked to consolidate and perpetuate this military conquest by a series of judicial decisions which transformed the legal and administrative structure of the island. In 1615 the Attorney-General presented a number of these judgements in his publication of the *Irish Law Reports*.[1] In format these *Reports* reflect the early modern reporting system at its most mature level. Like the reports of Plowden, Dyer and Coke, Davies' work departs from the yearbook tradition, giving full introduction to pleadings that focus on demurrers or special verdicts. Apart from several cases decided by resolution of the Irish justices, Davies' care in framing full case headings also allows the reader to identify easily the precise tribunal adjudicating each case. The *Reports* which were derived mainly from Davies' own work in the Dublin courts under-standably emphasize the pleadings of the Attorney-General or Solicitor-General. But either in his capacity as king's advocate, or in acting as private counsel before the Dublin courts, Davies was meticulous in divorcing his own opinions from those of other counsel and the court. Like Coke, however, Davies was not averse to using the *Reports* to emphasize his own arguments, and one should not discount a certain propagandistic element in tone and style.

A close examination of the *Reports* reveals two striking features of the litigation dealt with by Davies. One is the frequency of judicial resolutions, or collective decisions issuing from either the Irish or English judiciaries in conclave, and the other is that over half the cases deal with highly sensitive aspects of constitutional and administrative reform at issue in the first twelve years of James I's reign. In fact a thorough scrutiny of the *Reports*, in conjunction with the manuscript state papers and other sources, reveals nothing less than an intention on the part of the Dublin government to consolidate the Tudor conquest and extend the tenets of an uncompleted Tudor Revolution to Ireland, by using judicial resolutions to establish precedents whose authority would either obviate the need for further litigation or compel other tribunals to follow suit in adjudicating similar disputes. Thus the Dublin government set out to employ case law as authoritative policy guidelines in a variety of politically and constitutionally significant cases pending before the various Irish courts during the first decade of the seventeenth century. Nor, of course, can the English government be excused from complicity, for while most of the judicial resolutions issued from the Irish justices in the Privy Council Chamber in Dublin Castle, in some instances decisions were referred back to members of the English judiciary who ratified them with resolutions of their own decided in the Exchequer Chamber or in Serjeants' Inn in London.

The scenario of an English government deliberately using judicial procedures and mechanisms to consolidate its hold over Ireland in the early seventeenth century has never been fully explored and it is, perhaps, unexpected, given the more usual Tudor expedient of executing such sweeping changes by parliamentary statute. The explanation for this extraordinary use of judge-made law lies in a conjunction of circumstances peculiar to Ireland, notably the failure of the Irish parliaments to secure in the sixteenth century the statutory reforms that were the hallmark of the Tudor Revolution in England and the questionable reliability of an Irish judiciary comprised almost entirely of Old English descendants of the medieval Anglo-Norman conquest.

Certainly the changes wrought by collective resolutions in Ireland run counter to our understanding of the exalted role attributed to reform by statute law. Professor Elton has shown clearly enough the lofty status of English parliaments and the supremacy of statute law by his designation of parliamentary statute as the one 'omnicompetently sovereign' tool of legal constitutional change in Tudor England.[2] While few would dispute the accomplishments of Tudor parliaments in effecting the revolutionary secular and ecclesiastical changes in sixteenth-century England, the use of statute law in Ireland was far less significant. It is not an exaggeration to say that the firm execution not only of the Supremacy, but also of direct control by a central government based in Dublin, did not become an established fact until the early seventeenth century.

The comparative weakness of the role of statute law in Ireland had several causes, the most apparent being that effective English sovereignty during the major part of the sixteenth century penetrated to only a handful of port towns and to a fifty-mile radius around Dublin. Even within areas of English control, a parliamentary tradition on the English model was significantly less developed. In 1495 Poynings' Law restricted the Irish parliament's legislative initiative by proscribing all meetings of parliament without royal licence and setting forth a rule that all bills submitted for parliamentary approval required the prior assent first of the Lord Deputy and council in Ireland, and second of the king and his council in England. The purpose of this manoeuvre was to restrict a renegade Anglo-Irish Lord Deputy like the Earl of Kildare from using parliament for his own ends. In addition to Poynings' Law, the sixteenth century also witnessed the appearance of an Anglo-Irish opposition which, with a growing sense of national consciousness, frequently pitted itself against Irish policy formulated either by the monarch and the English Privy Council, or by English administrators in Dublin.[3]

While the scarcity of manuscript evidence does not allow a precise determination of the total number of sessions for each of the Irish Tudor parliaments, it is possible to demonstrate, by comparing the number of parliaments called in both kingdoms, the absence of a significant Irish parliamentary tradition. In England during the twenty-four-year reign of Henry VII, there were seven English parliaments as opposed to five in Ireland. During Henry VIII's thirty-seven-year reign, there were nine parliaments called in England, and again only five in Ireland – all of much shorter duration than their English counterparts. While Edward VI summoned two parliaments during his six-year rule, none was called in Ireland. Mary, in her brief four years' tenure of the English throne, called five English parliaments and one in Ireland. Her successor Elizabeth, during her forty-five-year reign, summoned ten parliaments in England, and only three in Ireland – all of very short duration.[4]

Given such statistics, it is perhaps surprising to learn that at one time during the sixteenth century there was an attempt to carry the Tudor Revolution to Ireland in a move that would have enhanced the role of an independent Irish parliament in the political relations of the two countries. As Dr Bradshaw has shown, Sir Anthony St

Leger, while Lord Deputy of Ireland (1540–7, 1550–6), evolved a programme critically dependent on the use of statute law, which envisaged a 'commonwealth' state appendant to the English crown and an active national parliament grounded in a consensus that extended to the Gaelic polity.[5]

This 'liberal' or 'commonwealth' solution was designed to repudiate first the notion of papal territorial sovereignty in Ireland, and to extinguish all autochthonous claims to sovereignty put forth by the independent Gaelic dynasts, by legislating an alteration of Henry VIII's title from feudal Lord to King of Ireland. As a second step in this revolutionary legislation St Leger attempted to extend both the royal title and the Supremacy throughout the island through a novel policy of surrender and regrant which in essence involved the feudalization of the Gaelic nobility who, in return, would acknowledge the king as their legitimate sovereign. Had this programme succeeded, Professor Elton's comments on the importance of statute law in determining constitutional change might be as applicable to Ireland as they were on the other side of the Irish Sea.

Unfortunately St Leger's liberal formula was scuttled by the complexity of the surrender and regrant programme and, more importantly, by the indifference of the king, who in 1540–1 was preoccupied with the proposed annexation of Scotland and with preparations for the coming war with France. In the end, only a handful of Gaelic dynasts subscribed to the surrender and regrant formula, a limitation illustrated by the fact that as late as 1603 no royal title could be found to the whole of Donegal.[6] The marginal results of the liberal formula meant the collapse of the national Irish parliament which, under the administration of St Leger, was the key to the programme's success. When St Leger was recalled in 1556, his efforts for reform through parliamentary statute were overruled by the radicalism of the Earl of Sussex and Sir Henry Sydney, who initiated a strategy that dominated the course of Irish history throughout the second half of the sixteenth century – conquest and colonization.[7] Thereafter the Irish parliament ceased to function independently and declined drastically in political importance – a fact evidenced by the transformation of the Old English consensus group that had subscribed to the commonwealth solution of 1540–1 into an opposition party in the parliaments of 1560, 1569–71 and 1585–6.[8] From the standpoint of 1603, it can be argued that it was an awareness of this opposition in Elizabeth's Irish parliaments, in combination with religious disturbances in the towns, that led the

English government to refrain from employing the parliamentary expedient in favour of the new and untried programme of reform by judicial fiat.

If the Irish parliament at the beginning of James I's reign was a less than perfect instrument for dealing with issues of constitutional significance, the hodge-podge of overlapping and conflicting jurisdictions which made up the Irish legal system provided an equally inauspicious mechanism for change. By the early seventeenth century, the Irish courts comprised a system of common law, equity and conciliar tribunals that paralleled those in England. Located in Dublin, the common law courts were the King's Bench, Common Pleas, the Exchequer and the Chancery. As in England, the King's Bench held jurisdiction over civil and criminal cases and exercised a reviewing jurisdiction over cases originating in the Common Pleas. The Court of Common Pleas, sometimes known as the Common Bench or Common Place, held jurisdiction over civil suits between parties where no crown interest was involved. The Irish Court of Exchequer, apart from its jurisdiction over revenue cases, also determined causes between subjects and exercised an equity jurisdiction.[9] The Irish Chancery Court, which emerged only during the sixteenth century, held extensive jurisdiction over cases of equity but also adjudicated common law cases: during the course of the sixteenth century, the Chancery Court absorbed the business of other tribunals and caused some jurisdictional friction with the common law courts. The increased significance of the Irish Chancery Court can be attributed to the fact that the whole of Ireland was only shired during the reign of James I. In the absence of an effective legal organization in many areas outside the jurisdiction of the royal writ, it was difficult to obtain impartial juries. In addition, the cumbersome and dilatory procedure of the common law courts led inevitably to Chancery's expanded jurisdiction.[10]

Apart from the central common law tribunals in Dublin, the activities of the conciliar courts must be considered. In addition to the Privy Council itself, which possessed a quasi-judicial function, these were the Irish Court of Castle Chamber and the provincial presidency courts in Munster and Connaught. The Court of Castle Chamber, which paralleled closely the development of the English Star Chamber, exercised jurisdiction over riots, unlawful assemblies, unlawful retainders and maintenances, embraceries of subjects, false returns by sheriffs, the failure of sheriffs to execute writs, the taking of money by jurors, perjury of jurors, forgery, slander, extortion of public officials, sedition, abduction, trespass and the enforcement of proclamations.[11] The installation of the conciliar courts in the provinces of Munster and Connaught owed its origins to similar institutions set up by Thomas Cromwell in Wales and the north of England as a measure to incorporate these areas into the state system.[12] Accordingly the provincial conciliar courts in Munster and Connaught, established by Henry Sydney in 1571, bear a strong similarity to the Council of Wales and the Council of the North. The purpose of these provincial conciliar jurisdictions with authority to exercise martial law and to hear civil, criminal and ecclesiastical causes was to extend the sovereignty of English law to those areas beyond the reach of the central courts in Dublin and to offset the authority of local dynastic interests.

In addition to the conciliar tribunals there existed at the end of the Nine Years War the court of the Tipperary palatinate, a liberty jurisdiction held by the earls of Ormonde from the time of Edward I.[13] From the surviving records of this last remaining medieval franchise, it is known that the court exercised, until its suspension by *quo warranto* proceedings in 1621, a comprehensive jurisdiction over all equity and common law cases, excepting the pleas of arson, rape, forestalling and treasure-trove that arose from within the boundaries of the palatinate. Since the jurisdiction of the Tipperary palatinate was exclusive of the common law courts in Dublin, only writs of error to the Irish Court of King's Bench could transfer litigation outside the venue of the palatine court.

The discussion of the major Irish law courts as they existed in 1603 inevitably simplifies and systematizes what amounts to a maze of judicial institutions whose jurisdictions frequently overlapped and sometimes conflicted with each other. It does, however, provide a useful outline of the Irish legal system as it existed during the early years of James I, and establishes the necessary institutional back-ground to discuss the personnel staffing the Irish bench and the circumstances that led to the wholesale replacement of judges of Old English extraction by those of English birth.

The term 'Old English' refers to the descendants of those Anglo-Norman settlers who had established themselves in Ireland before the sixteenth century. This group possessed extensive holdings of land which as late as 1640 amounted to one-third of the total profitable acreage in Ireland, mainly located in the most fertile regions.[14] The predominance of the Old English was particularly evident in the courts and had been encouraged from the reign of

Henry VIII when a body of local lawyers trained at the English Inns of Court was viewed as the ideal instrument for executing Reformation policy in Ireland.

Whether or not there even existed an institution to train the legal profession in Ireland is problematical. It has been claimed that the first Irish Inn of Court was established during the reign of Edward I. This institution, known as Collet's Inn, was probably a hospice that may have served as a meeting place for judges and barristers.[15] Dangerously housed outside the city walls, Collet's Inn was vulnerable to attack. In the early fourteenth century the wild Irish descended from the Wicklow Mountains to destroy the Inn and succeeded in massacring the unlucky residents in a midnight raid. In 1384, Sir Robert Preston, Chief Justice of the Common Pleas, assigned his house, subsequently known as Preston's Inn, to the body of lawyers residing in Dublin. During the early sixteenth century, for reasons which are not understood, Preston's descendants succeeded in recovering the Inn from the legal body, and it became necessary to secure a new dwelling place. Thereafter Henry VIII established another collegiate body called the King's Inn in a confiscated Dominican monastery. This institution, unlike its English counterparts, had no power to confer degrees, and a further statutory requirement, laid down in 1542, required all barristers practising law in Ireland to reside at least three years at an English Inn of Court.[16] Since implementation of the Irish Reformation involved the active participation and support of a group of Old English lawyers, it seems that the deliberate elevation of a local Irish legal profession trained at the English Inns of Court had an initial success. This policy also had pragmatic grounding in the unpalatable fact that it was difficult to attract competent English lawyers to Ireland.

During the second half of the sixteenth century, the support given by the Old English legal profession for the Supremacy did not extend to further innovations in religious doctrine, and almost all attempts to legislate changes in religion, particularly in the parliaments of 1569–71 and 1585–6, had to be dropped in the face of a determined Old English resistance.[17] To a hard-pressed English government that could ill afford the enormous costs of military subvention, toleration of Old English recusancy was a cheap price to pay for the preservation of whatever narrow foothold the English maintained in Ireland during the second half of the sixteenth century. Lacking both the will and the necessary statutory tools to enforce religious conformity, the English government never extended to

Ireland the practice of excluding Catholics from office, and the Irish judiciary continued, until the end of the Nine Years War, to be dominated by Old English lawyers.

In early 1603, however, a spontaneous uprising in the corporate towns, which directly implicated prominent members of the Old English legal community, brought home the fact that the adherence of the Old English to an outlawed religion was at odds with their privileged status of landed wealth and political influence on both the local and national levels. Inspired by the belief that James I intended to grant religious toleration in Ireland, the revolt of the Munster towns owed something to the economic chaos engendered by a debased coinage and to a desire to vindicate the extensive corporate liberties of the towns against potential encroachments by the crown. The active participation of two Old English lawyers in the city of Cork, Thomas Sarsfield and William Meade, the city's Mayor and Recorder, fuelled earlier complaints by English administrators that prominent members of the Irish legal profession were guilty of aiding and abetting the movement of the recusant clergy in the towns.[18] The revolt seriously challenged the assumption that an education at the English Inns of Court would provide a sufficient basis to ensure a loyalist outlook on the part of the Irish legal profession. More important, the accusations extended not only to the legal profession but to 'some officers of the King's Majestie in his several courts'.[19] Further complaints levelled against the judiciary and the Pale lawyers resulted first in the application of the Oath of Supremacy as a prerequisite to practising law before the Irish bar, and secondly in a wholesale purging of the Irish bench in favour of a judiciary comprised almost entirely of English rather than Old English lawyers.

As an example to both lawyers and judges, proceedings were initiated against John Everard, Second Justice of King's Bench, who had a reputation of being a 'notorious and obstinate recusant'.[20] Everard's subsequent refusal to resign was complicated further by the government's inability to find a suitable alternative. In the end, Everard was driven from office by direct order of the king. A pension of 100 marks and the generosity of the Earl of Ormonde combined to relegate him to the judicial scrapheap as justice of the palatine court of Tipperary.[21]

Everard's forced resignation was followed by a deliberate and ultimately successful attempt to pack the Irish bench with English Protestant lawyers. To aid this manoeuvre, it was deemed necessary to increase the number of justices in each of the common law courts.[22] In February 1607, the Dublin government added two more justices, increasing the total number of judges from seven to nine. In 1613 four additional judges were appointed, raising the total number of Irish justices to thirteen. By that time, only two judges, Sir Dominic Sarsfield, Chief Justice of the Common Pleas, and John Elliot, Third Baron of the Exchequer, were native born.[23] Sarsfield's appointment, in particular, to replace the vacancy left by the death of Nicholas Walsh was designed as a sop to Old English lawyers resentful of the new order. Sir John Davies, who was instrumental in securing Sarsfield's promotion, cynically commented that this 'will make the lawyers of this nation to see they are not disregarded, as now they seem to suppose'.[24] All other justices were practising members of the English bar, and by 1613 all the Irish judges, including Sarsfield and Elliot, were conformable in religion.

In view of the history of Irish parliaments in the sixteenth century, the packing of the Irish bench seems more than fortuitous. Since the style of law reform contemplated by Davies and the English government depended wholly on judicial resolutions, or more precisely majority decisions issuing from the Irish justices in conclave, the wholesale transformation of the Irish judiciary from Old English jurists to lawyers born and trained in England was a necessary prelude to overcome Old English provincialism and to ensure a view favourable to the use of judicial resolutions as binding precedent in cases of constitutional significance.

The existence of judicial resolutions, issued by the assembled Irish justices as binding precedent for all subsequent litigation involving like cases, may seem surprising to those who have accepted the view commonly held by legal scholars that *stare decisis* does not appear in English law until the nineteenth century. This doctrine as it is applied currently in the courts of Britain and the United States refers to the general policy of all courts to adhere to the *dicta* of prior cases decided by the highest tribunal in a given jurisdiction. A modern theory of precedent, scholars argue, cannot be found either in the yearbooks or the various early modern law reports because the citing of case precedent was construed by contemporary jurists to imply the existence of a custom or, more precisely, to elucidate some universally accepted principle or maxim that was beyond dispute.[25] In 1934, Holdsworth buttressed this argument by noting that the authority of reporters not officially appointed to the court of record was suspect and could be dismissed on the basis of inaccuracy. In other words, it was only the development of official court reporting in the nineteenth century and the abolition of the old central courts in favour of a judicature comprised of a High Court of Justice and a Court of Appeal in 1873 that allowed a strictly defined modern theory of *stare decisis* to emerge in the English courts.[26]

No one would dispute the application of this orthodox position to the vast majority of cases argued before early modern English tribunals, but the argument put forth by Holdsworth and others fails to take into account the emergence of the Exchequer Chamber for debate which W. J. Jones has recently described as one of the most important developments in early modern English administrative, legal and political history.[27] The Court of Exchequer, of course, had its own statutory jurisdictions, but as early as the fifteenth century, and increasingly during the sixteenth and seventeenth centuries, it appears that difficult matters of law in any of the common law courts might be referred to the Exchequer Chamber for discussion by all the justices of the King's Bench and Common Pleas together with the Barons of the Exchequer.[28] When agreement had been reached by the assembled judiciary, the decision was recorded in a certificate, referred back to the original tribunal and read before the court. Given the sixteenth-century avalanche of statute law and the consequent difficulties of applying statutes to litigation in the courts, it is not surprising to find justices willing to refer controversial legal issues to a convenient forum for debate, and even to subordinate their own minority views to the decisions of a more authoritative majority.[29] But it should be noted that the practice of referring to the Exchequer Chamber thorny questions on matters of public law placed the judges in the unique position of defining principles of constitutional law with an authority that clearly resembles the modern doctrine of *stare decisis*.

As Jones has shown, the habit of using collective resolutions to resolve litigation referred from the central courts (see for example the cases of Capel, Chudleigh, Slade, Shelley and Calvin) led in the 1620s and 1630s to the judges issuing decisions which, unlike the resolutions on issues referred from other tribunals, were divorced from any cases pending in the central courts.[30] These extra-judicial resolutions, which involved the English judiciary in the approval and formulation of controversial financial policy, were subsequently employed by the government in the development of Charles' forest policy, in the extension of Stannary jurisdiction, and finally in the controversy over ship money, when as early as March 1637, one year before Hampden's case, all the judges were in agreement over the government's right to collect this controversial levy. Jones has also argued that both types of resolution, those arising from cases referred to the Exchequer Chamber for debate as well as those derived extra-judicially, in so far as they were used to bind subsequent litigation, conformed very closely to a modern theory of precedent and exerted an authoritative influence over other tribunals.

It is interesting to consult the attitude of contemporary jurists towards the authority of resolutions arising from the Exchequer Chamber for debate. In the case of Alton Woods decided in 1601, the Lord Keeper admitted that it was necessary for him to rely upon the 'opinions of the said grave and reverend judges, without whom he could not proceed to judgement'.[31] The redoubtable Coke, in commenting on resolutions, asserted the importance of such decisions in 'maintaining the honor of the law and for the quiet of the subject in appeasing much diversity of opinion'.[32] Moreover, in his *Institutes* Coke placed the authority of judicial resolutions next only to statute law.[33] Similarly Coke's antagonist Bacon, in commenting on Calvin's case, went so far as to admit that even the Lord Chancellor would abide by the decision of all the judges.[34] In 1602, Chief Justice Popham elaborated a similar theme and maintained that judicial resolutions were 'to be a precedent for all subsequent cases'.[35] By the late seventeenth century Justice Herbert, in the trial of Sir Edward Hales, would claim that 'after any point of law has been solemnly settled in the Exchequer Chamber by all the judges, we never suffer it to be disputed or drawn in question again'.[36] Surely then to contemporaries, such weighty pronouncements of law must have appeared to carry the fullest authority.

So far this discussion of judicial resolutions has been confined solely to affairs in England. But it is obvious from Davies' *Reports* and the manuscript Irish state papers that judicial resolutions, similar to those pronounced by the English Exchequer both extra-judicially and for cases referred to it from the other courts, were employed in Ireland in the early seventeenth century with an effect so devastating as to bear out the awesome authority ascribed by contemporary jurists to such decisions. What has not been realized, moreover, is the degree to which the political application of judge-made law as binding precedent in England during the 1620s and 1630s was conditioned by Irish antecedents laid down in the early years of James I. Indeed the problems of ruling Ireland in the absence of parliaments during the early Stuart period foreshadow the political contours of Caroline England, and the exalted status accorded to the English judiciary in the 1630s can be seen much earlier in the role played by the Irish judiciary when it applied both types of resolution to politically controversial litigation in the central courts. In fact it is possible to infer from Davies' *Reports* that resolutions in Ireland, during the first decade of the seventeenth century, became the single most important instrument for executing legal-constitutional change in a manner that supports Jones' argument for a theory of modern precedent in England during the 1620s and 1630s.

Probably the most important and far-reaching application of judge-made law in Ireland was to the problem of assimilating the former autonomous lordships. The precise issue revolved around the identification of indigenous patterns of landholding and descent that were construed by Davies and other English jurists as a system of law lying outside the jurisdiction of the royal writ. By espousing Bodin's maxim that a 'king is not sovereign where others give law without reference to him', Davies endowed the autonomous Gaelic lordships and all tenures derived from Gaelic law with the full status of sovereignty.[37] In order to incorporate this allegedly sovereign and alien system of law and land tenure into the new state system, Davies envisaged a revolutionary two-part plan that would use extra-judicial decisions to proscribe the customary Gaelic forms of land tenure.

First Ireland and the Gaelic dynasts would have to accept the English common law without competition from the brehon law or, more precisely, such customary patterns of Irish land tenure and succession as 'gavelkind' and 'tanistry'. Next, the civil law doctrine of conquest, applicable because of the victory of 1603, would justify the eradication not only of the sovereignty associated with the domestic Irish laws, but also of all derivative foreign or Gaelic claims to Irish dominion that were contingent upon the papal donation of Ireland in 1155.[38] As a result of this second step, and as a significant departure from the liberal surrender and regrant formula applied by St Leger in 1540–1, a superior and therefore sovereign possessory right was to be lodged over all non-English tenures by applying two extra-judicial resolutions to void the customary patterns of Gaelic landholding and descent. The intent of these resolutions is obvious from Davies' correspondence of 1606 with Cecil and the English Privy Council, in which he confided that the Irish customs 'both of tanistry and gavelkind in this kingdom lately by the opinion of all the judges here adjudged to be utterly void in law, and they are so void, so shall they be shortly avoided and extinguished either by surrender or resumption of all the lands so holden'.[39]

The manuscript records show that these extra-judicial resolutions were used as 'binding precedent' in further disputes. In the famous case of tanistry argued before the King's Bench in 1608, the government settled, along lines laid down in the 1606 resolutions, a long-standing succession dispute involving two prominent Gaelic families in Cork, in which one party had revived a claim to the estate as tanist or heir apparent to lands that had been surrendered during Elizabeth's reign, in return for a common law estate.[40] In the infamous Cavan case in 1610, and in the disposition of certain types of ecclesiastical property in the north, these resolutions were also employed as a tool to invalidate native Irish titles that stood in the way of the Ulster plantation.[41] In this manner the extra-judicial resolutions reported by Davies, in so far as they bound subsequent litigation over similar cases, conform very closely to the modern theory of precedent Jones attributed to similar decisions rendered by the English judiciary during the 1620s and 1630s. Other litigation in the north illustrates further this novel power acquired by the Irish judiciary. During 1610 the Irish judges, in a manoeuvre to attract private capital to the Ulster plantation, voided by judicial resolution Sir Randall MacDonnell's claim to the Bann fishery. Thus by judicial fiat, on a case referred from the Irish Privy Council, the Irish judges secured the richest fishery in Ireland as an incentive to colonize the heartland of Gaelic revolt.[42]

As a second step in consolidating the Tudor conquest, Davies' *Reports* show that the English and Irish Privy Councils collaborated to employ judicial resolutions as a solution to the long-standing abuses associated with the corporate autonomy of the Munster towns. In this instance the spontaneous uprising by the southern towns in the spring of 1603 gave the government an excuse to deal with the unruly port towns along the lines consistent with the extra-judicial resolutions applied against the tribal system. As in the cases voiding the customary forms of Gaelic landholding and descent, the government embodied its action against the towns in three judicial resolutions to: (1) enforce religious conformity by validating a proclamation extending to Ireland the English penal laws passed by late Elizabethan parliaments; (2) eliminate extensive corporate liberties including appropriation of customs revenue; and (3) reform the national currency that eroded Irish trade and commerce. These resolutions, the first and second of which were decided by resolutions of all the judges in England, have yet to receive the full attention they deserve.

Let us take for example the application of judge-made law to the issue of religion. In this instance, the stringent application of English penal laws to Old English recusants, particularly the gentry, the legal profession and municipal officials, caused a constitutional furore that seriously troubled the Dublin government. What historians have failed to recognize is that it was a judicial resolution, rendered by the English judiciary based on principles suggested by the Irish judges, that staved off the aggressive assaults of the Pale lawyers who questioned the validity of extending English statutes to Ireland by proclamation and of enforcing religious conformity by using the Court of Castle Chamber as a spiritual consistory.[43]

In addition to the proceedings against recusants, it is also clear that the Dublin government interpreted the Munster disturbances of 1603 as an excuse to dismantle the extensive privileges of the port towns. In this instance Attorney-General Davies set up a test case against the corporation of Waterford which possessed extensive rights and privileges guaranteeing not only political autonomy, but also freedom to collect all customs duties normally due to the crown. This case, which was validated by a resolution rendered by members of the English judiciary in conclave at Serjeant's Inn in London, sustained a crown right to Irish customs duties and was subsequently endorsed by the king and employed as binding precedent against all the port towns.[44]

To these religious and jurisdictional applications of judge-made law, we may add the issue of finance. Both the manuscript Irish state papers and Davies' *Reports* make it clear that the Munster disturbances of 1603 were interpreted as an excuse to reform the Irish currency, which on account of a disastrous debasement in 1601 had all but paralysed Irish trade and commerce. In this case, the refusal of Irish merchants to accept the base coin was countered by another judicial resolution requiring a one-to-one valuation between the old sterling and newly minted base money. The case, involving an intent to repudiate the war debt, was subsequently used to bind further litigation to the judicial resolution recorded in Davies' *Reports*. As Davies himself claimed, 'several other cases on the same point were afterward ruled and adjudged in the several courts of record in Dublin'.[45] The resolution on the coinage, in combination with the resolutions that facilitated the assimilation of the Gaelic tenurial system, the sequestration of the Bann fishery, the enforcement of religious conformity and the destruction of corporate liberties, helped to achieve a centralized control of Ireland that proved impossible in the Tudor period. Together they represented a wholesale redefinition of the nature of English sovereignty in Ireland.

While the *Reports* and the manuscript Irish state papers detail fully the use of judicial resolutions as the preferred instrument of constitutional reform in Jacobean Ireland, there is further evidence to show that judge-made law continued to be used as the instrument of reform to secure a more efficient administration of both government and finance. Similar use of the judiciary can be seen in the administration of the Munster plantation, the mobilization of ecclesiastical revenue and in the application of wardships.

Like most sixteenth-century plantations in Ireland, the colonization of Munster was only a marginally successful enterprise. Inadequate surveys made titles uncertain and possession of the land was difficult to obtain. This uncertainty of title was further clouded by an official penchant for retaining natives, often with some measure of their own laws and customs, as tenants and labourers on colonized estates. In the case of the Munster plantation, this practice proved especially troublesome and confusion arose over the precise status of the attainted Desmond's undertenants, who brought continual suits against the Munster undertakers claiming that their tenure under Desmond exempted them as 'freeholders' from the attainder of their overlord. As late as 1611, Attorney-General Davies complained that the estates of the Munster undertakers continued to be 'sued and vexed by the Irishrie'.[46]

While information detailing the precise nature of this litigation is sparse, it appears from scattered manuscript evidence that difficulties arose over the ability of Desmond's litigious undertenants to avoid the findings of the escheator by denying, through a legal manoeuvre known as a traverse, the facts established by the office that found title for the crown. Since Jacob's *Law Dictionary* defines this manoeuvre as presupposing title in the person (i.e. Desmond's undertenants) who brought the traverse, it is not surprising to find Sir James Ware, Recorder of Dublin, complaining to the English Privy Council that the Irish judges were incapable of resolving the issue.[47] In the end, a direct plea from the Irish justices to the English judiciary resulted in a judicial resolution, rendered by the English judges, on the validity of the traverse in Ireland.[48] In the event the English judges scuttled the claims of the Munster 'freeholders' by resolving that the 'statute of 2

Edward 6 allowing a traverse and monstrans de droit' was not in force in Ireland. While it is beyond the scope of this study to measure the impact of this resolution on the administration of the Munster colony, it is possible to say that the decision had the significant effect of vesting presumptive title in the crown, thereby validating the original grants to the undertakers. Thereafter those who 'pretended title could only sue by petition as if the land was still in the King's hands'.[49] While the resolution's punitive intent towards those suing actions against the Munster undertakers is obvious, it is also clear that the resolution, in so far as it affected the Munster undertakers, was to pay added dividends by allowing the Irish Exchequer to levy retroactive rents on the undertakers.

Less significant than the resolution voiding the traverse was the further application of judge-made law to the problem of restoring the patrimony of the church. In this instance the Dublin government employed another judicial resolution to define the ambiguous status of ecclesiastical procurations, a charge previously levied in kind to support episcopal visitation. During the fourteenth century, such payments of food and drink were commuted to an annual cash payment payable to the local bishop or his representative. In the case of Ireland, the history of ecclesiastical procurations is more difficult to discern, but it is evident that after the Reformation, the Irish episcopate maintained its right to collect procurations, including those levied on religious houses prior to the dissolution. Then it appears that the government acquired the privilege of levying procurations through voluntary surrenders from the bishops, and then leased in fee farm many of the rectories to which proxies had been formerly collected as a reward for faithful service to members of the Pale gentry and to various government officials. Thereafter the crown never attempted to collect the proxies that had appertained to lands so leased.

When, during the early seventeenth century, the Dublin government attempted to resume collection of these proxies, litigation resulted, often involving prominent local officials. Once again the Irish judiciary appears to have found difficulty judging a controversial issue and referred the problem to the English judiciary for their resolution on the case. The question put to the English judges dealt with whether or not the unity of possession brought about by the resumption of the proxies by the crown extinguished the collection of all proxies formerly levied on parsonages granted by Elizabeth in fee farm.[50] In their reply the English judges confirmed by resolution the arguments put forth by Attorney-General Davies in the case of proxies argued before the Dublin Court of Exchequer in 1605.[51] Predictably the English judges resolved that the unity of possession resulting from the surrender of the bishop as ordinary to the king as 'supreme ordinary' did not extinguish the proxies and that the crown, notwithstanding prior alienation, could still levy proxies over lands leased in fee farm by Elizabeth. While it would be difficult to determine the extent of revenue obtained by virtue of the English resolution, it is interesting to note that the crown regranted many of these proxies to the 'Bishops of the diocese where they are due and on their successors forever', which demonstrates in a small way the manner in which extra-judicial resolutions could be applied in matters touching ecclesiastical revenue.[52]

There is one more graphic use of judicial resolutions to cite. In the general attempt to mobilize secular revenue, the Dublin government identified efficient administration of Irish wardships as a much neglected yet potentially lucrative source of revenue. As Dr H. F. Kearney has shown, the creation of an Irish Court of Wards in the early seventeenth century eventually yielded up to 25 per cent of the total national revenue.[53] There were, however, formidable barriers that stood in the way of this achievement. With no statutory requirement to register transfers of real property either in the Chancery or in the localities, the collection of rents and escheats was frequently evaded. Unlike the situation in England, it was also possible, until 1634, for A to grant land to B to the use of one or more third parties and their heirs. As a means to overcome this familiar device to avoid payment of the traditional feudal duties associated with wardship, the Master and Comptroller of the Irish Court of Wards in 1624 petitioned the English judges for a resolution over whether or not the 'heir of a cestui qui use' in fee farm or fee tail could be compelled to sue livery. The weight of the case was such that the king himself demanded a resolution, not only from the Irish judges but from the English judiciary as well.[54] In the event the English judges upheld payment of livery, anticipating, by nine years, formal passage of the Statute of Uses through the Irish parliament.

Additional examples of the use of judicial and extra-judicial resolutions in Ireland could be cited from the manuscript Irish state papers, but the cases discussed above illustrate that the Irish judiciary continued to apply judge-made law as a preferred instrument of legal reform long after the constitutional changes described by Davies' *Reports* for the period 1603–15.[55] The relationship between the use of judicial resolutions reported by Davies and the application of judge-made law in England during the 1630s is difficult to determine exactly. However it may not be coincidental that several of the Irish judges who participated in the extraordinary legal and administrative reforms launched by the Irish and English judiciaries during the period 1603–13 went on to acquire high positions on the English bench.[56] This connection, when considered with the fact that two of the cases reported by Davies involved the active participation of the English judiciary, suggests the possibility that Ireland served as a kind of testing ground for the controversial application of judge-made law which Jones describes in the Caroline period.

At any rate, the decisions reported by Davies certainly support Professor Jones' argument that an essentially modern theory of precedent did apply in the use of judicial resolutions in England – and as we have seen, in Ireland – during the decade preceding the outbreak of the civil war. While some legal scholars have argued that a theory of modern precedent was not clearly formulated or applied in the early seventeenth century, it is evident that the use of judge-made law in Ireland, alongside the examples cited by Jones, carried much of the weight of modern precedents and conformed very closely to the modern doctrine of *stare decisis*. In this sense, the cases of gavelkind, tanistry, the Bann fishery, customs payable for merchandise and the case of mixed money should be ranked alongside the cases of Calvin, Slade and Hampden as significant not only for the constitutional history of Ireland, but for that of England as well.

Part II

JUDICIAL ENCOUNTERS: THE NATIVE COMMUNITY

4

The cases of gavelkind and tanistry: legal imperialism in Ireland, 1603–1610

The previous chapter summarizing the contents of Sir John Davies' *Reports* introduced the role of judicial resolutions in consolidating the Tudor conquest of Ireland. The single most important example of the use of such resolutions was their application against the customary patterns of Gaelic succession and land tenure known as tanistry and gavelkind. The need for judicial action to void native forms of landholding and descent became clear to Davies when he analysed the barriers to English sovereignty in Ireland raised by the manner in which land was used and owned in the Gaelic districts. Like other administrators concerned with the legal status of the Gaelic polity, Davies saw the extension of common law tenures to the formerly autonomous Gaelic lordships as the most important pre-condition of the exercise of English sovereignty in Ireland. The decision to employ extra-judicial resolutions, or legal decisions divorced from litigation pending in the central courts, involved the Irish judiciary in the formulation of a policy that aimed at assimilating an alien scheme of law and land tenure into the new state system.

I

Davies' reflections on the problems posed for English rule by the existence of the autonomous Gaelic lordships are revealed in the *Reports* and the *Brief Discovery*. Davies concurred with Bodin's civil law maxim that 'a king is not sovereign where others give law without reference to him'. Precisely this situation, he argued, applied to large areas of Ireland up to his own day:

The Irishrie governed their people by the Brehon law, they made their own magistrates and officers, they pardoned and punished all malefactors within their several countries; they made warre and peace one with the other without controulment; and this they did not only during the reign of King

Henry II, but afterward in all times, even until the reign of Queen Elizabeth.[1]

In Davies' view, obstreperous Gaelic dynasts had always used their separate political institutions and landholding patterns, embodied in and legitimized by the domestic system of brehon law, to escape the jurisdiction of the royal writ and to assert independence from English rule.

The problem of Ireland's division into two societies, separated by a tenurial frontier, had begun with the failure of medieval governments to achieve a complete military conquest of the island. This view of Davies was shared by other jurists of his generation. It is easily detected in the briefs filed in the case of the Post-Nati (Calvin's case), long regarded as the definitive view of alien status at the beginning of the seventeenth century. Francis Bacon's discussion of Irish sovereignty in Calvin's case bore out Davies' interpretation of the limitations on English rule:

And hereof many ancient precedents and records may be shewed that the reason why Ireland is subject to the law of England is not ipso jure upon conquest, but grew by a charter of King John, and that extended but to so much as was then in the king's possession, for there are divers particular grants to sundry subjects of Ireland and their heirs, that they might use and observe the laws of England.[2]

The failure of the military efforts of Henry II and his successors meant that the English crown had never succeeded in exercising a sovereign possessory right or what Davies called a 'lordship paramount' to Ireland. English rule had penetrated only to those areas physically occupied under common law tenures.

England's tenuous hold on Ireland became evident during the fourteenth century when significant portions of the Anglo-Norman colonial community seemed to be adopting the customs, mores and laws of the native society. While recent scholarship has urged restraint in assessing the degree to which the Norman conquerors were assimilated into Gaelic society, the fact remains that the official policy – if such existed in late fourteenth-century Ireland – of assimilating juridically the native community had been abandoned in favour of a system of personal law to safeguard Anglo-Norman society from what had become a Gaelic revival.[3] This defensive effort, begun during the reign of Edward III, found its culmination in the legislation passed by the Kilkenny parliament in 1365. Known as the Statutes of Kilkenny, this controversial enactment proscribed in English areas, on pain of high treason, the use of Irish surnames, Irish law, the Gaelic language, fosterage of sons and inter-marriage with the Irish race.[4] In 1498, the Statutes of Kilkenny were to be renewed and in 1536 supplemented by equally strict and more specific proscriptions against Irish dress and customs within the Pale itself.[5] As late as 1534, George Cromer, Archbishop of Armagh and Primate of Ireland, was compelled to obtain a formal pardon for having used the brehon laws.[6]

Attempts to discover the nature of Gaelic customary law and social arrangements which threatened to overwhelm the small enclaves secured to English law have concentrated on the text of the ancient brehon law. Written during the seventh and eighth centuries, native Irish law has proved to be a less than perfect instrument in determining the structure of the Gaelic polity in the age of the Tudors. Even the ambitious nineteenth-century attempt to publish and translate the brehon laws has encountered severe criticism.[7] The translators had the habit, it seems, of pulling contextual meaning from gloss and commentary and transferring it to difficult textual passages without regard to wide chronological gaps between gloss, commentary and text.[8] Moreover, other obstacles beset the scheme to unlock the secrets of Gaelic society from its legal institutions.

Gaelic Ireland, unlike emergent national states in the early modern period, lacked a 'national' law promoted and enforced by a recognized and central authority. Irish brehons, or judges, settled legal disputes as arbitrators rather than officials of a court. These judges often employed the ancient brehon laws as a convenient set of legal maxims, a kind of 'pseudo-antiquarianism designed to impress the lay public'.[9] Outlining social conditions as revealed in the ancient law tracts and projecting these institutions as a 'national system' on to native society in the early modern period have led to the anachronistic notion that Gaelic Ireland had been changeless and rigidly controlled by ancient and immutable custom. As recent work has demonstrated, such generalizations ignore the continual replacement of dominant lineages, a feature hardly characteristic of a changeless or static society.[10]

Revisionist scholarship places greater reliance on English records as well as traditional Gaelic sources. The result of this approach has been to superimpose a feudal overlay on to the Gaelic polity at the end of the sixteenth century, thus dividing native society into two distinct groups: landed freeholders and landless unfree tenants dependent wholly on the will of their immediate overlords.[11] Thus

Gaelic Ireland at the end of the sixteenth century is seen as a two-tier feudal society in which a landowning class ruled over a landless tenantry subject to the whims of superior lords. In the most recent contribution to this genre, Kenneth Nicholls has modified the picture of a two-tier feudal society by demonstrating conclusively that the class of landowning lords in Gaelic Ireland consisted not of a large group of freemen or freeholders, but of a lesser group of local and regional lords of countries, as they were called, who held the remainder of the population, including their own kinsmen, in absolute subjection.[12]

Nicholls' assessment of Gaelic and Gaelicized Ireland during the fifteenth and sixteenth centuries also envisages a clan-based society consisting of patrilineages functioning through a complex of rights, duties and exactions imposed by one group over others, as independent or autonomous political units. Within a political unit comprised of dominant and subordinate lineages, each member theoretically possessed as a mark of his status an honour price or *eraic* that varied, like the early Germanic *wergeld*, according to an individual's social rank. In theory, political power within a Gaelic district resided in a leading family unit, the chief of which was elected by a four-generation family grouping descended from a common ancestor from great-grandfather down to grandfather, father and son. This grouping, called the *derbhfine*, was the legal family that theoretically determined succession to a chiefry.[13] Aggregate or composite groups of lineages were frequently bound by kinship or clientage under the suzerainty of a captain, lord or chieftain. In the north of Ireland, by far the most Gaelic part of the island at the end of the sixteenth century, such groupings within Tyrone included the septs or corporate lineages of O'Cahan, MacMahon, O'Reilly and Maguire and in Tyrconnell, the MacSweeneys, the O'Dohertys and the O'Boyles. Where there existed a superior lord, the head of each political unit was usually a chieftain allied with his immediate overlord, variously referred to as *tighearna* (lord), *ceann phobail* (head of territory or people) or in Ulster, *urriagh* – an apparent contamination of the Gaelic word *uir-ri*, meaning literally 'vice-king'.[14]

The sixteenth-century Irish polity that England attempted to subjugate and rationalize through its common law was a complex entity. The economic arrangements that governed the relationships between the head of a country and his dependent chieftains were determined by the chief lords who imposed tributes on their client septs. The nature of these tributes varied widely, but usually took the form of subsistence and labour services aimed at providing support and entertainment for a lord, his armed followers and servants. Failure of client septs to render such tributes, often onerous, allowed a lord or chief to convert such unpaid exactions into pledges to the land on which they had been charged. While in theory such a pledge or mortgage was redeemable, more often it was impossible to retrieve, particularly if the land fell out of the possession of the pledging sept for any length of time. In such a case the lord might very well treat the pledged land as his own inheritance and pass it on to his own lineage. In addition to the lord's ability to take over land for which the occupiers were unable to render tribute he also had the right to utilize waste or unoccupied land from which he could not draw tribute. As Nicholls again has shown, both means of occupation demonstrate an active market in land as characteristic of Gaelic Ireland in the sixteenth century. In the wake of the Tudor conquest, metropolitan lawyers came to regard client septs with subordinate interests in land as 'freeholders', while the rights of a captain or chief were regarded as no more than a rent charge.[15]

Apart from the landed interests of social elites, there were other social categories that included bards, brehons, chroniclers, artisans, scholars and a military caste of mercenaries or *galloglaigh*, many of whom held lands from their immediate lord or patron, exempt from tribute or exactions.[16] In some instances military men may have acquired lands of their own through unredeemed pledges or through the occupation of vacant or unclaimed property. By far the most numerous element of the population, however, was landless tenants whose status, free or unfree, has been the source of some dispute and confusion not only to contemporaries, but also to modern scholars of Irish history. For Sir John Davies, who rode numerous assizes in Gaelic districts during the first decade of the seventeenth century, the treatment accorded by the Gaelic nobility to landless undertenants and others dependent on their will was little better than that accorded to a hereditary serf, bound to the land as a mere chattel or appurtenance.[17]

The results of centuries of divided rule in Ireland could be seen in the peculiar legal status accorded to Gaelic natives in Ireland. Their condition, as revealed in Davies' works, involved a number of legal disabilities quite similar to those pertaining to aliens.[18] In civil litigation, for example, Irish widows were frequently disabled in securing dower and were excluded from suing real or personal actions in the central common law courts. In fact, natives living within reach of the royal writ were forced to purchase charters of denization as a pre-condition to owning land or suing actions in the Dublin courts. In other words, unless litigants enjoyed the privilege of English law accorded to the 'five bloods' (the royal families of O'Neill of Ulster, O'Melaghlin of Meath, O'Connor of Connacht, O'Brien of Munster and MacMurrough of Leinster) they suffered the effects of a peremptory plea of Irishry which dismissed the case from court, unless they possessed a charter of denization.[19] Sir John Davies, who had himself issued a general proclamation of denization to tribal undertenants in Ulster during March 1605, fully recognized the legacy of an uncompleted medieval conquest.

English jurists like Bacon and Davies were concerned about the legal consequences that resulted from 'alien' status ascribed to the Gaelic polity. In their search for a solution Jacobean lawyers and administrators, like their late Elizabethan predecessors, identified Irish customary forms of shared inheritance and succession as the most important obstacles preventing full assimilation of the autonomous Gaelic enclaves into the state system. In Gaelic or Gaelicized districts native customary law vested ultimate proprietorship over land in the extended kin group. Individual allotments of land were temporary and subject to periodic redistribution in what English observers familiar with Kent and Wales called the 'custom in nature of gavelkind'. But native custom differed in special ways from Kentish and Welsh gavelkind. Characteristic features of the Irish custom were the exclusion of women from inheritance and the right of bastard males to a portion or share of property alongside legitimate heirs.[20]

The distribution of individual shares among the Irish natives varied from place to place, but according to Davies and others, a major emphasis was placed either on the senior (*sinnsear*) or clan head (*ceannfine*) to allocate portions of land to individual members of the sept – usually, though not always, on the death of one of the co-heirs. Basically there were two main types of division: (1) the younger co-heir made the division in which all shared equally; (2) the chief made the division and reserved the best share for himself resulting in an unequal division.[21] While such practices were by no means universal, the emphasis placed on the eldest co-heir or clan head caused many English observers to identify shared inheritance by gavelkind with that of succession by right of tanistry.

As distinct from English practice, Irish succession devolved through the male or agnatic descendants of a common great-grandfather to the 'most worthy' male member of the extended kin group. This scheme of succession, known to contemporary English observers as the custom of 'tanistry', derived from the technical Gaelic term *tanaise rig*, meaning second or next to the king.[22] The custom originally referred to the practice enshrined in eighth-century Irish law whereby the successor to a chief or king was nominated during the lifetime of such a leader. The advantage of 'tanistry' as a lateral system of succession, peculiar to societies where agriculture is extensive rather than intensive, lies in the avoidance of the uncertainties associated with minority or regency government.[23] To many English observers in the sixteenth century, tanistry became synonymous with succession through seniority by the 'eldest and worthiest' member of the extended kin group – a euphemism for succession by *forte maine* which frequently plunged rival factions or groups into violent civil strife.[24] Since the office of 'tanist' usually included appendant lands and other privileges, English jurists chose to define the custom as a kind of life trust in land in which there existed no ultimate proprietorship.[25] The instability of succession by tanistry and the frequency of land distribution associated with the Irish variant of gavelkind allowed critics like Davies to argue that the limited tenancy associated with these Irish customs prohibited the intensive exploitation of land and deterred formation of a stable body politic.[26]

To some English observers the inability of Gaelic law to systematize a political order more definite than the temporary authority associated with elective succession meant that the possessory rights conferred within the framework of the Gaelic tenurial system were only as permanent as the political authority from which they devolved. This inability to abstract political institutions and proprietary rights more lasting than the limited tenure associated with a life trust emanating from the corporation of the extended kin group struck English spokesmen as a liability that prevented the absorption of autonomous Gaelic areas into the state system. In such a view the tenurial system in Ireland had a significant impact on the failure of the 1540–1 constitutional revolution in effecting a lasting penetration into the autonomous Gaelic lordships.

In commenting on the refusal of substantial sections of the Gaelic polity to abide by the political engagements laid down by their forebears in the 1540s, the poet Edmund Spenser noted in 1597 that the descendants of those who had subscribed to the royal title and supremacy under St Leger's liberal formula of surrender and regrant explained their relapse to Gaelic practice by reference to the rules of 'tanistry'.

Eudoxus: Doth not the act of the parent in any lawful grant or conveyance, bind their heires forever thereunto? Shall it not tye their children to the same subjection?
Irenaeus: They say no; for their auncestors had no estate in any of their lands, seignories, or hereditaments, longer than during their own lives, as they alledge, for all the Irish doe hold their land by tanistry; which is say they no more but a personal estate for his lifetime, that is tanist, by reason that he is admitted thereunto by election of the country.[27]

Writing ten years later, Fynes Moryson, secretary to Lord Deputy Mountjoy, made a similar but more succinct observation, noting that the heirs of any 'chiefs or lords of countries' who had made surrenders of their lands under St Leger's scheme, or under subsequent attempts to assimilate the autonomous Gaelic lordships, 'baldly say that he held his lands by the tenure of tanistry only for his life, and so will not be tied to any of his acts'.[28] This alleged refusal by Gaelic leaders to ascribe any permanence to the covenants of their predecessors is easily documented by examples drawn from the O'Neill lordship.

In the general attempt to substitute English for Gaelic tenures during the 1540s, the St Leger government convinced several of the principal Gaelic dynasts to surrender their lordships in return for a heritable estate valid according to English law. One such dynast was Con O'Neill, newly created Earl of Tyrone, who endeavoured to stabilize the scheme of succession in his region at the expense of the rightful heir, Shane O'Neill. In the end, Con's arrangements to substitute an illegitimate son, Mathew, into the place of Shane, who would have inherited by the strong hand, threw the whole of Ulster into turmoil. In 1558 Shane killed Mathew, but Mathew left two sons, Brian and Hugh Roe, to whom the title descended by English law. In 1561 Turlough Luineach, a kinsman of Shane, murdered the elder son Brian, leaving young Hugh, who was too young to threaten Shane, as rightful heir under English law. Shane then manoeuvred himself into election as the O'Neill and successfully pleaded his own case before Queen Elizabeth who in 1562 conceded official sanction on Shane's leadership in Tyrone as tribal chief under Gaelic law. Commenting on this episode, Dr Canny has remarked that the case of the O'Neill lordship was fairly typical of the surrender and regrant formula pursued by St Leger in 1540 – a fact underscored by the case of Donegal for which no crown title could be found until 1603.[29]

In addition to the presumptive sovereignty associated with the Gaelic customs of 'tanistry' and 'gavelkind', the medieval legacy left by the twelfth-century donation of Ireland by Pope Adrian IV in the bull *Laudabiliter* clouded further the constitutional relationship between the colony and the independent native lordships. In the charged atmosphere of the sixteenth century, several independent Gaelic dynasts exploited the alleged theory of papal sovereignty over Ireland either in deploying the forces of Catholic Europe in Ireland by offering an 'Irish crown' to a foreign monarch, or in legitimizing the independence of their own laws and institutions.[30] Hindsight makes it easy to deny any significance to the attempts by various continental princes to assert legal claims to Irish dominion, but it should be remembered that to contemporary English policymakers and legal advisers confronted with the problem of native Irish lords asserting autochthonous powers over their Gaelic enclaves, foreign designs on Ireland, poorly conceived and executed as they were, represented something more than mere nuisance.

This concern can be detected in the literature of various English jurists and polemicists who strenuously denied validity to papal temporal jurisdiction in Ireland. An anonymous contribution to the *Book of Howth*, for example, maintained an antecedent claim to Irish dominion, because English rule in Ireland owed its origins to King Arthur and not to the Pope.[31] Sir Edward Coke, a man always partial to Anglo-Saxon myth, developed a similar theme. Coke, however, relegated Arthur to a marginal note and justified an English title to Ireland by citing a rather spurious Anglo-Saxon charter reporting a dubious conquest of Ireland by King Edgar.[32] The appearance of an elaborated theory of conquest to justify English rule in Ireland, discussed earlier in this volume, provided legal thinkers like Coke, Ellesmere and Davies with an ultimate justification for dominion in Ireland that could withstand any other claim to Irish sovereignty, either through the so-called papal donation of 1155, or through the presumptive sovereignty associated with independent Gaelic lordships.[33] Yet, despite the end of the Nine Years War and the subjugation of the last great Gaelic lordships, it is important to see that as late as 1608 references to papal jurisdiction in Irish affairs continued to occur. One of these allusions involved the deposition of John Leigh, High Sheriff of Tyrone, who complained:

Another matter of note is that the permitting of some of the naturals in every quarter of that country to bear the title of officials for the Bishop, is a great inconvenience and hurt to the establishment of the king's laws and courses of justice amongst the barbarous people for these kind of fellows under color of their authority from the Bishops take upon them to decide all private controversies committed between party and party in the nature of Breghans or judges according to the rules of the Popish canons.[34]

Leigh's declaration clearly highlighted the conflict between Reformation England and Gaelic legal/political institutions. To those chieftains sophisticated enough to view their own customary law as legitimate, the legal status of their territories represented a form of autonomy independent from the jurisdiction of the English crown. This view was widely held during the Nine Years War, and can be perceived in Hugh O'Neill's plan to extend his authority over the whole of Ulster in what may have been a prelude to an intended resurrection of the 'high kingship' of Ireland.

It is well known, for example, that Tyrone maintained two agents, Peter Lombard of Waterford and Edmund MacDonnell, Dean of Armagh, at the courts of Rome and Spain to solicit foreign support. In 1595 the Gaelic nobility even dared to offer the Irish crown to the Spanish king, an event that probably inspired Lord Deputy Fitzwilliam in 1597 to connect the tenurial and political structure of Gaelic society with the designs of foreign monarchs in Ireland:

The rebels pretend to recover their ancient land and territory out of the Englishman's hands and for the restoring of the Romish religion and to cast off English laws and government and to bring the realm to the tanist law acknowledging Tyrone to be Lieutenant to the Pope and king of Spain.[35]

Fitzwilliam plainly linked international aspects of law and jurisdiction with problems in assimilating Gaelic society. This recognition of a public and international law dimension to the Irish problem furnishes the necessary background to examine Davies' controversial assessment of alien status which he ascribed to Gaelic patterns of landholding and descent operating outside the jurisdiction of the royal writ.[36]

II

Ireland's medieval legacy arising both from the papal donation and from the autonomy accorded to those areas subscribing to Gaelic customary law is readily evident in the Treaty of Mellifont which ended the Nine Years War on 4 April 1603. In this treaty Hugh O'Neill, Earl of Tyrone, agreed to abjure all dependency on foreign potentates, in particular the king of Spain, to forswear the title of O'Neill, to terminate all 'challenging or intermeddling with urriaghts', to renounce all 'claims and title to any land but such as shall be now granted by his Majesties' letters patent', and to assist the abolition of all 'barbarous customs contrary to the laws being the seeds of all incivilitie'.[37] In return, the English government exercised a restraint that was surely remarkable, the more so in view of its response to previous rebellions in Ireland. Whereas earlier disturbances entailed extensive confiscation and plantation of rebel estates, in 1603 O'Neill, O'Donnell and other leaders of the Nine Years War found themselves restored to much of their former property and decorated with new titles of nobility.

These amicable and auspicious policies were short-lived. Within a year, reports began to drift in to the Irish Privy Council that the Ulster nobility was deliberately exploiting the liberal tenets of the Mellifont agreement in order to establish full possession over vast areas that may even have exceeded the personal demesnes allowed to them under Gaelic law before Tyrone's rebellion. In Tyrconnell, for example, Rory O'Donnell succeeded in convincing his former subject *urriaghs* to surrender their estates to himself, thereby acknowledging him as owner in fee simple of all Tyrconnell – conditions very similar to those enjoyed by his predecessors under Gaelic law during the Nine Years War. Fynes Moryson, secretary to Lord Lieutenant Mountjoy, discovering the mechanics of O'Donnell's subterfuge, wryly commented that O'Donnell retained a Pale lawyer to convince the men of Tyrconnell that they had, in the absence of a specific pardon for their complicity in the Nine Years War, no lawful estate in their property.[38]

To the east in Tyrone, similar events seemed to indicate another attempt to return to the old ways. O'Neill, however, relied less on O'Donnell's legal chicanery than on his own abilities as a statesman to restore his old position.[39] Tyrone's negotiating skills are clearly revealed in the land settlement formalized by the English Privy Council at Hampton Court during the month of August 1603.[40] In accordance with the general principles laid down by the Treaty of Mellifont, Tyrone convinced the Privy Council to restore the same estate allowed to him by Elizabeth in 1587 – a grant which confirmed the earl in possession of all lands, tenements and hereditaments held by his grandfather, Con Bacagh O'Neill, at the time of his surrender and regrant in 1542.[41] It should be noted, however, that Tyrone subsequently interpreted this to mean:

The country of Tyrone and all his interest and command over the lords and chieftains of countries within the province of Ulster in Ireland, who held of him and were subject to his taxes.[42]

The only property that the English Privy Council at Hampton Court exempted from the earl's control was the allocation of 300 acres to each of the forts at Charlemont and Mountjoy, and further grants of territory ceded to Henry Oge O'Neill and Turlough McHenry of the Fews. Henry Oge's territory, located north of the Blackwater, stood in the heart of Tyrone's land, and the loss must have been difficult for the earl to accept. The Fews, a forested area in Armagh bordering the Pale, was granted to Turlough McHenry to safeguard the government's line of march into the formerly autonomous O'Neill lordship. As Canny has pointed out, however, the loss of these territories to Tyrone's overlordship cannot be termed excessive.[43] Thus, despite the crushing defeat dealt by English forces to Gaelic dynastic ambitions in the Nine Years War, events in both Tyrone and Tyrconnell allowed not only O'Neill and O'Donnell, but also the rest of the tribal leadership (O'Dogherty, O'Hanlon and O'Neill of the Fews) to appropriate to themselves in fee simple the counties of Donegal, Tyrone, Derry and Armagh.[44]

Irish historians have traditionally attributed responsibility for this lenient policy to the Lord Lieutenant, Charles Blount, who, as Baron Mountjoy and Earl of Devonshire, sat as member of the English Privy Council and resided then in England. Whatever its origins, official Irish policy as enshrined in the Treaty of Mellifont and in the land settlement at Hampton Court was to undergo complete change within a year's time, and the munificence accorded to Tyrone and Tyrconnell soon hardened into an attitude that approached hostility.[45] The reasons for this change may in part lie in Mountjoy's growing alienation from Cecil and the English Privy Council. This estrangement stemmed from Mountjoy's shady association with the Essex plot and from his scandalous marriage to Essex's sister, Penelope Rich, which resulted in a noticeable cooling of relations with Robert Cecil.[46] By late 1605, Mountjoy's proposed marriage to Penelope led to his virtual disgrace at court, which suggests that the formulation of Irish policy had, for some time, shifted from Mountjoy's hands. While it is difficult to determine the precise *locus* of Irish policy, the comments of P. M. Handover,

Robert Cecil's biographer, are worth consideration.[47] To Hand-over, Cecil's foreign policy, particularly *rapprochement* with Spain, depended entirely on the pacification of Ireland. Cecil, she argued, was prominent in dictating Irish policy, and this assessment is supported by Sir Roger Wilbraham, who preceded Sir John Davies as Irish Solicitor-General. Writing on the eve of Cecil's death in 1612, Wilbraham noted that Cecil alone exercised responsibility for Irish affairs. Wilbraham's testimony certifies the change in policy towards the Gaelic leadership in Ulster, and Sir John Davies, who owed much to Cecil, stated frankly in November 1606 that it was Cecil, on advice provided by himself, 'who moved the king to write special letters to the Earl [Tyrone] and other lords of the North requiring them to make a competent number of freeholders in their several countries'.[48]

This new defensive strategy, formulated by Cecil and Davies in order to install a pattern of freeholders limiting the power of Tyrone, Tyrconnell and other chiefs in the north, emerged as a result of Davies' extensive investigations of Gaelic society. By April of 1604 Davies had begun to complain to Cecil that the demesnes granted to the Gaelic nobility were excessive, comparing Tyrone's hold over tenants to that of the Earl of Warwick over his barons during the feudal anarchy of Henry VI's reign. Davies concluded that Tyrone's usurpation in Ulster had allowed O'Neill, like the Earl of Warwick, to make 'war against the state of England and make his barbarous followers think they had no other king than Tyrone, because their lives and their goods depended upon his will'.[49]

This assessment subsequently led Davies to apply the controversial theory of alienage to the Gaelic Irish living within the compass of the royal writ. According to Davies such persons were:

Not reputed free subjects nor admitted to the benefit of the laws of England until they had purchased charters of denization. Touching their denization they were common in every king's reign since Henry II and were never out of use till his majesty that now is come to the crown.[50]

Within a year Davies' use of alien theory resulted in a general proclamation of denization, granting the benefits of English law to all undertenants and former 'freeholders' residing in Ulster. This same proclamation further curtailed the powers of the Gaelic nobility by reinterpreting the land settlement of 1603. The proclamation declared that the letters patent issued to Tyrone and Tyrconnell and other chieftains, 'notwithstanding the said general words therein conveyed', did not transfer to the lords the lawful freeholds

of inheritance that had formerly belonged to various tribal undertenants in accordance with the customs and traditions of Gaelic land
law.[51]

The government supplemented this directive by authorizing a
commission on 19 July 1605 to investigate the patterns of land tenure
in Ulster. The commissioners restricted themselves to reforming
civil defects due to an absence of freeholders in Gaelic areas.[52] But as
a consequence of this commission the English Privy Council,
advised by Davies who had returned to England, informed Lord
Deputy Chichester and the Irish Privy Council that it had never been
their purpose to grant the whole of Tyrone and Tyrconnell to
O'Neill and O'Donnell. The commissioners were thus empowered
to accept voluntary surrenders of Gaelic estates in return for
common law tenures. To supplement this directive, the Irish Chancery warranted a special commission to determine the number of
freeholders within the various tribal jurisdictions in Ulster, and to
accept surrenders of Gaelic estates held by titles not derived from the
common law. These special commissioners were to take particular
care in accepting surrenders of 'tanist' lands, stipulating that such
lands could only be surrendered and regranted in the presence of the
Lord Deputy and four members of the Irish Privy Council.[53]

Despite the scope of these commissions for the surrender of
defective titles and 'tanist' lands, the achievements of this expedition
into the north were not altogether encouraging. In Tyrconnell they
had some success. Here Davies and the commissioners compelled
O'Donnell to restore the rights of the MacSweeneys and the
O'Boyles. The government also undercut the O'Donnell lordship
by allocating 12,900 acres in the vicinity of Lifford, considered by
O'Donnell to be the only 'jewel' left in his lordship to Sir Neill Garve
O'Donnell, a rival claimant.[54] For O'Donnell, whose position in the
north was rapidly crumbling, the loss of income and prestige arising
from these awards to his rival must have been overwhelming. In
Tyrone the commissioners were less successful. Various cadet
branches of the O'Neill family along with other septs subordinate to
Tyrone's rule did present petitions claiming rights to freehold, but
O'Neill outmanoeuvred them by presenting his immediate kinsmen
as freeholders instead. As an interim measure the commissioners
accepted this arrangement but deferred making a final settlement
until a later date.[55] After a year, in 1606, the government authorized
another commission whose purpose was to determine which freeholds had been unlawfully expropriated and mistakenly assigned to

the various Gaelic chiefs in Ulster. This 1606 commission was different from its predecessor.[56] Sir John Davies conspired with the Irish judiciary to modify the proclamation of denization conferring the protection of English law on the inhabitants of Ulster with the issuance of two extra-judicial resolutions voiding the customs of 'gavelkind' and 'tanistry'. Davies' *Reports* and scattered manuscript references make it clear that the Dublin government viewed these resolutions, at the outset anyway, as a constitutional mechanism to facilitate the surrender of Gaelic holdings in return for common law estates. In turn, these common law tenures would strengthen the tenancies of tribal underlings as freeholders against the claims of superior chiefs like Tyrone. In so far as this strategy affected the lesser tenancies held by the Irish custom of 'gavelkind', Davies' report on that resolution maintained:

This resolution of the judges, by the special order of the lord deputy was registered among the acts of the council; But there this provision was added to it, that if any of the meer Irish hath possessed and enjoyed any portion of land by this custom of Irish gavelkind, before the commencement of the reign of our lord the king who now is, that he should not be disturbed in his possession, but be continued and established in it.[57]

For the resolution voiding the custom of tanistry, no record survives of the judges' deliberations but the intent, as described by Davies to Salisbury concerning the 1606 commission for Ulster, was clear. The Irish customs:

both of tanistry and gavelkind in this kingdom lately by the opinion of all the judges here adjudged to be utterlie voide in law, and they are so voide, so shall they be shortly avoided and extinguished either by surrender or resumption of all lands so holden.[58]

These extra-judicial resolutions voided the Gaelic tenurial system, and a commission on defective titles validated Gaelic estates with common law titles. The government thus acquired the instrument to modify the overliberal grants allowed to the Gaelic leadership in 1603. The strength of these judicial weapons became apparent when the commission began to investigate the nature of landholding in three other Ulster counties, Monaghan, Fermanagh and Cavan. In Fermanagh Davies reported to Salisbury that 'far from Maguire [the chief] owning all, he possessed only in right of his cheefry, certain demesnes in various places and a cheefry or right to levy contributions or taxes in the rest'.[59] Similarly a jury in Cavan reported that:

There is first a general chieftain of every country or territory, which hath some demesnes and many household provisions yielded unto him by all the inhabitants; Under him every sept or surname hath a particular chieftain or tanist, which has likewise his peculiar demesnes and duties and their possessions go by succession or election entirely without any division; but all other lands holden by the inferior inhabitants are partible in the course of gavelkind.[60]

In the Leinster assize in the autumn of 1606 Davies discovered similar patterns of landholding, and he stressed to Salisbury that the system of demesnes and freeholds was 'alike throughout the former Irish districts'.[61] Against the backdrop of the renewed commission for defective titles and the surrender of tanist lands in 1606, it appears that the commissioners used the above-mentioned decisions in Fermanagh to divide the tribal demesnes equally between rival Maguire claimants and to redistribute the remainder of the county to various other freeholders. In Cavan, which was adjudged to be crown property, replacement of Gaelic tenures by common law estates proved simple enough, and the commissioners found little difficulty in appointing sufficient freeholders there. In Monaghan, a somewhat different approach was employed. There the commissioners resorted to a settlement laid down by Lord Deputy Fitzwilliam in 1591, confirming an earlier scheme to redistribute the lands of the MacMahons among various freeholders as the commissioners themselves saw fit.[62]

The effect, therefore, of the extra-judicial resolutions eliminating tanistry and gavelkind was to create a large class of freeholders in Fermanagh, Cavan and Monaghan, or as Davies described the policy to Salisbury, to 'cut off the three heads of that Hydra from the North, namely McMahon, McGwyre and O'Reilly'.[63] Within the precincts of Tyrone the impact of these extra-judicial resolutions is more difficult to assess. But Davies' lofty appraisal of the 1606 settlement, that it has prevented 'the error which hath formerly been committed in passing all Tyrone to one and Tyrconnell to another and other large territories of O'Dogherty and Randal McSorley without any respect of the king's poor subjects who inhabit and hold the lands under them', indicated that Tyrone was in for trouble.[64]

Davies kept careful watch over Tyrone's attempts to thwart the extension of crown government within his lordship. Ever suspicious of events in Ulster, Davies severely criticized Tyrone's interpretation of the land settlement at Hampton Court. Tyrone's version, said Davies, allowed the earl 'like the Turk or Tartar to have all in possession, and consequently all the tenants of that county to be his slaves and vassals'.[65] To safeguard the north from these encroachments, Davies sought to delineate the metes and bounds of Tyrone's districts and found in Donal O'Cahan, Tyrone's son-in-law and former *urriagh*, a likely volunteer in a plan to limit O'Neill's extensive claims to freehold. For several generations, the chiefs of the O'Cahan sept had possessed the traditional right to preside over the investiture of the O'Neills; moreover, O'Cahan's country held strategic significance since it guarded the northern approaches into Tyrone's territories. In addition, for several years a mounting hostility had developed between O'Cahan and Tyrone. Towards the end of the Nine Years War, O'Cahan had deserted Tyrone's cause in return for a promised crown title to his lordship, a treacherous move that must have hastened the decline of Tyrone's military fortunes. Pending final termination of the Nine Years War, the government had granted a custodianship, or temporary *usufruct*, to O'Cahan as an interim settlement. In the wake of agreements laid down at Mellifont and Hampton Court during the spring and summer of 1603, the government reneged upon its agreements. Thereafter O'Cahan was forced to enter into an uneasy arrangement with Tyrone whereby O'Neill received one-third of O'Cahan's territory and an annual rent of 160 cows. Since this agreement appeared to violate one of the fundamental provisions of the Treaty of Mellifont, that Tyrone 'terminate all challenging or intermeddling with the urriaghts', Davies seized on a ready and useful tool with which to cut Tyrone down to size.[66]

Davies capitalized on another tenurial dispute in Tyrone involving O'Neill and George Montgomery, Bishop of the northern sees of Derry, Clogher and Raphoe. Like the dispute over O'Cahan's territories, the disagreements with Montgomery dealt with the status of Gaelic ecclesiastical tenures within Tyrone's district. In this instance, Montgomery attempted to expand his pluralistic livings by laying claims to all *termon* and *erenagh* property within his jurisdiction.[67] O'Neill seems to have had similar trouble with the Archbishop of Armagh who also pressed suits against the earl before the Irish Privy Council. In reality, however, possession of these lands resided with the septs of the hereditary tenants, known as *coarbs* and *erenaghs*, who lived on church lands and held their tenures by 'tanistry' and 'gavelkind', rendering annual rents and hospitality to the local bishop. Montgomery, conscious of the notorious poverty of the Irish *ecclesia*, righteously argued for the patrimony of his church, while Tyrone, who saw in Montgomery's actions a design to introduce more freeholders within his lordship, claimed these ecclesiastical tenures as parcel to his own demesne.[68]

These disputes involving O'Cahan and Montgomery encouraged Davies' inclination to investigate the historical background to O'Neill's claim to the whole of Tyrone. In reaction, the earl sent a petition to Salisbury and the English Privy Council, stating his own understanding of the Mellifont agreements. According to Tyrone, the lands of all subordinate septs rendering tribute to him under the Gaelic system were his in demesne. Davies argued the contrary, focusing attention on the land settlement laid down at Hampton Court in August 1603 when Tyrone had renounced all 'claims to land and authority not granted or conferred unto me by the late queen'.[69] Davies then called attention to the 1587 royal patent establishing Tyrone in his lordship. That patent had granted to O'Neill the same estate held by his grandfather, Con Bacagh O'Neill, at the time of his surrender and regrant in 1542. But, argued Davies, the express words of Con O'Neill's patent stating that his son, Mathew, should receive 'all the castles, manors, and lordships which he formerly possessed' did not convey the whole of Tyrone, a fact witnessed by two jury inquisitions carried out as a preliminary formality to issuing the 1587 patent.[70] Davies having 'drawn the case more exactly out of the records themselves', concluded that neither Montgomery, O'Cahan nor Tyrone had any title to the lands in dispute.[71]

This daring assertion was based on two highly interesting jury inquisitions taken during June of 1587 to determine the metes and bounds of Tyrone's lordship. The jury had found that Hugh was justly entitled to his lordship by virtue of his grandfather Con's surrender of 1542. But, the jurors decided, the boundaries of O'Neill's lordship did not include O'Cahan's country in Coleraine, or those parts of Clandeboy that included the vast forest of Glanconkein or the area known as Killetragh, an extensive territory bordering the north-west extremity of Lough Neagh.[72] With respect to the disposition of various abbeys and other forms of ecclesiastical property at the time of Con's surrender, the jurors had anticipated the arguments put forward by Bishop Montgomery twenty years later, explaining that religious foundations within Tyrone paid only rents to O'Neill and were not parcel to his demesne. As a conclusion, Davies ruled that neither O'Cahan, Tyrone nor Montgomery had any title:

to the freehold or inheritance of the country, or territory in question but that it now is and ever hath been vested in the actual possession of the crown since the eleventh year of Queen Elizabeth.[73]

All lands not parcel to the demesne lands set out in Con Bacagh O'Neill's patent, said Davies, belonged beyond any 'color or shadow of doubt' to the state by virtue of the attainder of Shane O'Neill in the Irish parliament of 1569–71.

Apart from O'Cahan and Montgomery, Davies' scholarly forays into Tyrone's and Con O'Neill's patents also revealed the existence of a substantial number of small freeholders occupying land by Gaelic tenures who owed only rents to Tyrone. With the abolition of 'tanistry' and 'gavelkind' by judicial fiat, Davies had acquired the institutional leverage to convert these holdings into common law tenures and thus not only reduce the earl's prerogatives, but also extend local government and English law to areas previously subject to the whims of tribal leadership. Confronted with litigious disputes on all sides, Tyrone complained bitterly of these vexatious proceedings contrived to dispossess him of his lands.

Harried by the state, Tyrone took matters into his own hands and violently distrained cattle from O'Cahan. To settle the dispute, the Irish Privy Council called both men to Dublin to present their respective grievances. Tyrone, in a fit of anger, recklessly tore O'Cahan's petition to shreds in front of the Lord Deputy. The earl complained of Davies' effrontery on the same occasion, quoting the Attorney-General as having remarked that he would never 'serve the king if I had not lost all the land of Iraght-I-Cahan and much more of that I hold and thought myself most assured of'.[74] By July 1607, the O'Cahan affair approached breaking-point. Davies, for his part, proposed submitting the case to the English justices for their collective resolution. In the end Davies was pre-empted by James I, who authorized Chichester to refer the various disputes over Tyrone's estates to Westminster for the 'sentence of their sovereign'.[75]

Tyrone at this point appears to have lost his nerve. Unable to weather the obvious hostility of Davies and others within the Irish government, the earl grew apprehensive over his future in a thoroughly Anglicized Ulster and retired to an ignominious exile on the continent. On the night of 3 September 1607, O'Neill, O'Donnell and ninety of their followers boarded ship at Rathmullen and sailed, never to return to Ireland.[76] Combined with the failure of Sir Cahir O'Dogherty's hopeless and pathetic attempt to lead a revolt in Ulster during the month of April 1608, the flight of the earls left a vacuum so vast as to open up the whole of Ulster to confiscation and plantation. Davies had been instrumental in assimilating Gaelic tenures into the new state system ruled only by the sovereignty of the common law. The judicial resolutions against tanistry and gavelkind, previously employed as a constitutional mechanism to absorb an alien system of law and land tenure, were now to be transformed into a tool of confiscation that paved the way for one of the biggest plantations in Irish history.

III

Colonization of the north followed in the wake of Tyrone's departure from Ireland. Plans for such a settlement had been meditated for some time. As early as 1604 James I had expressed some interest in planting Irish freeholders and English servitors around key military posts. Again in 1606 James had been reported to favour a plantation in Cavan, except that any English or 'foreign settlement should be confined to church land which the Irish seldom claimed, so as not to create the impression that there was a general attempt to displace the original inhabitants'.[77] At least until O'Dogherty's rebellion in the summer of 1608, however, no specific scheme for a general plantation had been presented. Chichester himself suggested only a limited settlement of the demesnes belonging to the departed Gaelic leadership, thus leaving the newly created freeholders in possession of their lands. But O'Dogherty's rebellion itself did result in more thorough plans for colonization that included not only the four counties of Tyrone, Armagh, Derry and Donegal, but also the counties of Fermanagh and Cavan.[78] At this time the Irish government had decided to throw all caution to the wind in favour of a general plantation. The most enthusiastic supporter of the venture, Lord Deputy Chichester, commented:

If my endeavors may give any help and furtherance to so glorious and worthy a design, besides my duty and obedience to your majesty, my heart is so well affected unto it, that I would rather labor with my hands in the plantation of Ulster than dance or play in that of Virginia.[79]

Once again, the immediate obstacle of finding title to the escheated lands had to be overcome. In these altered political conditions, the judicial resolutions voiding the customary patterns of Gaelic succession and partible inheritance assumed a totally different role. The first application of these decisions had served as a constitutional means to limit the powers of the Gaelic nobility, but now the 'flight of the earls' allowed the government to use the same extra-judicial resolutions to confiscate estates for which no crown title could be found. This new strategy to employ the extra-judicial resolutions against the customs of 'tanistry' and 'gavelkind' as a tool of confiscation resulted from the shortcomings of the more traditional measures of attainder, or revived medieval titles to confiscate native estates.

Of the six northern counties, Armagh, Tyrone, Derry, Donegal, Fermanagh and Cavan, all save the last two were easily brought into the government's net. To foil the landholders in Armagh, Tyrone and Derry, Davies fell back upon the attainder of Shane O'Neill which had established crown title to the land in these three counties.[80] Donegal, however, proved a bit more difficult, because 'until the first year of his Majesty's reign, the county was always a mere Irish country, not governed by the common nor statute law, nor subject to the ordinary ministers of justice, for the king's writ did never run there'. Here Davies contrived another expedient. Referring to a patent issued in the first year of James I, Davies relied upon the pretext that the crown had conveyed the whole of Donegal to Rory O'Donnell in fee simple, and hence must all devolve back to the crown by virtue of O'Donnell's attainder.[81]

Problems did arise with the freeholders' estates so laboriously created by the commissioners during the summers of 1605 and 1606 in Fermanagh and Cavan, as well as with the *termon* and *erenagh* property within each of the several counties. But the inquisition carried out by Davies and the commissioners in these counties in 1606 had demonstrated the freeholders' potential vulnerability.

But forasmuch as the greatest part of the inhabitants of that country did claim to be freeholders of their several possessions, who surviving the late rebellion had never been attainted, but having received his majesty's pardon, stood upright in law, so as we could not easily entitle the crown to their lands, except it were in point of conquest, a title which the state here hath not at any time taken hold of for the king against the Irish; which upon the conquest were not dispossessed of their lands, but were permitted to die seized thereof in the king's allegience, albeit they hold the same not according to the course of the common law, but by the custom of tanistry, whereby the eldest of every sept claimed a chiefry over the rest, and the inferior sort divided their possessions after the manner of gavelkind.[82]

Only now with the departure of the Gaelic nobility, the abolition of 'tanistry' and 'gavelkind' by judicial fiat served to dissolve the network of freeholders fabricated by Davies and the commissioners of 1605 and 1606.

Oddly enough, the first test of the extra-judicial resolution against tanistry arose from litigation referred to the Court of King's Bench from county Cork. Why Davies and the Dublin government chose this particular suit as a test case is unclear. Davies' earlier statement to Salisbury that the scheme of demesnes and freeholds in Gaelic districts was universally the same suggests that the Attorney-General was unsure of the authority of an untried extra-judicial resolution and desired to test the abolition of tanistry by judicial fiat in a trial before a jury more sympathetic to crown policy than an Ulster jury. Davies' intention to promote a favourable decision is further suggested by the timing of the case referred from the Munster Presidency Court to the Court of King's Bench which conveniently fitted the need for an authoritative decision to undercut the 'freeholders' in Fermanagh and Cavan. Whatever the reason for playing up the case in county Cork, the Irish judges relied upon the judicial ruling concerning the abolition of tanistry in 1606 as a precedent to guide judgement in the case of tanistry in 1608.

The famous case of tanistry began as a forcible ejectment from a common law estate containing the castle and six ploughlands of Dromaneen in Duhallow, county Cork. The dispute arose between the plaintiff, Murrough MacBryan, and the defendant, Cahir O'Callaghan, on 4 March 1604 and appeared first in the presidential court of Munster.[83] Like the provincial courts in England, the Munster Presidency Court was empowered to examine titles to land as a preliminary step to a common law action that would subsequently be referred to the central common law courts in Dublin. The purpose of this possessory proceeding was to provide a temporary settlement over disputed titles to prevent violent disseisins or breaches of the peace. In the case of tanistry, the Presidency Court of Munster then referred the case to be tried by *ejectio firmae* in either the King's Bench or Common Pleas in Dublin. In the event these interim arrangements proved unsatisfactory; the decree book of the Court of Castle Chamber shows that the litigants were fined for forcibly ousting John Barrie, Sheriff of Cork, from the castle with an armed mob of over two hundred persons.[84]

The reasons for the extraordinary passions generated by the case become evident if we examine the pedigree of the litigants and the numerous counterclaims to the contested estate. From various manuscript sources, it is possible to identify the litigants with some certainty and to sort out the welter of claims to the castle and six ploughlands in Duhallow. Both the plaintiff Murrough MacBryan and the defendant, Cahir O'Callaghan of Publicallaghan, belonged to local families who had paid allegiance to the chief of Clan Carty. In turn, the Clan Cartys were subject to the MacCarthy Mór, principal dynasts of Munster, who, at the end of the sixteenth century, were loyal to the government. The case was litigated before the Court of King's Bench for over three years and was argued several times. The extraordinary time taken by the dispute is explained by the convoluted series of land transfers that formed the factual basis of the case itself.

According to Davies' *Reports*, the controversy had its origin with Donough MacTeige O'Callaghan, chief of his name, who was:

> seised of the seignory or chieftainship of Publicallaghan, and of the land aforesaid, according to the custom and course of tanistry; and being so seised, had issue Conogher O'Callaghan; Conogher had issue a son and daughter; Teige and Eleanor; Teige had issue Donough MacTeige the Younger; Eleanor was married to Art O'Kiefe and had issue Manus O'Kiefe.[85]

Sir John Davies, Attorney-General, was counsel for the defendant, while Richard Bolton, Recorder of Dublin, and John Mead, a Munster lawyer, represented the plaintiff. Contending that tanistry existed time out of mind, Bolton and Meade argued on MacBryan's behalf that the custom of tanistry was good in law by prescriptive right, as was partible inheritance in Kent and Wales.[86]

Davies, in outlining the case for the crown, employed his practical knowledge of the workings of Gaelic land law to point out that the rules of Gaelic succession were not only technically different from those of Kent and Wales, but also, by virtue of their instability, prejudicial to the king's peace. Moreover, Davies argued, the custom of tanistry represented little more than a temporary life trust in land inimical to the canons of English descent. More precisely, land could not be appended to an office unless the successor was a corporate person, as was the case with an ecclesiastical prebendary, which a tanist was not. Since a tanist came to office by way of election, freehold was held in suspense. Hence there was no fee simple, because succession by tanistry denied Littleton's canon that 'que de chescun terre il y ad fee simple'.[87] Therefore, the 1593 surrender made by Conogher of the Rock as tanist for a common law estate was void because he had, as a tanist, nothing to surrender. The effect of Davies' arguments was to apply a drastically different gloss upon the statute 12 Elizabeth c. 4, which had enabled 'tanists' to surrender their estates in return for a regrant under a common law title.[88]

On the specific pleadings of the case, the judges of the King's Bench failed to reach a decision and the litigants came to an agreement dividing the disputed property between themselves. But on the larger issue of the validity of tanistry, the judges produced a resolution that had far-reaching implications. In Davies' words, it was 'resolved by the court, that the said custom of tanistry was void in itself, and abolished when the common law of England was established'.[89] The impact of this pronouncement was profound for two reasons. First, the judges' decision to void the 1593 common law surrender and regrant to Conogher of the Rock rendered insecure the titles of all *de facto* lords who, like Conogher of the Rock, had acquired their estates against all notions of equity and fair play by the strong arm.[90] Second, the decision of the judges in 1608 to adhere to the extra-judicial resolutions voiding the custom of 'tanistry' in 1606 also provided the Irish government with a handy tool to eliminate Gaelic tenures in Ulster.

The punitive abolition not only of tanistry, but also of gavelkind, can be seen in further litigation involving the Ulster plantation. On 5 June 1610, when Sir Arthur Chichester received the king's warrant to form a commission for establishing planters in possession of their estates, the freeholders in Cavan, 'who bordering on the Pale had learned to talk of freehold and estates of inheritance', decided to make a fight of it.[91] When the proclamation for removal of the natives had been announced in the public sessions house, an unidentified Pale lawyer challenged the decree, asking to traverse the office that had found title for the crown. He further claimed that the Cavan 'freeholders' did indeed have estates of inheritance that were not forfeited by the attainder of their chief, and that the Cavan men might have the benefit of the king's proclamation of denization of 1605, which had promised undisturbed possession of their lands.[92]

Realizing that the eyes of Ulster 'were turned upon this country', Davies rose to the occasion, remarking at first that he was:

glad this occasion was offered of declaring and setting forth his Majesty's just title, as well for His Majesty's honor (who being the most just Prince living, would not dispossess the meanest of his subjects wrongfully to gain many such kingdoms) and for the satisfaction of the natives themselves and of all the world.[93]

But in the remainder of his response Davies argued that the 'Cavan freeholders cheefries were ever carried in a course of tanistry which hath lately been adjudged no estate in law' and that 'their inferior tenancies did run in another course of gavelkind', which 'by the opinion of all the judges in the kingdom is adjudged and declared void in law'. Davies concluded, in other words, that the Cavan freeholders had no basis for their claim of traverse.[94] Furthermore, if they had no estate in the land they possessed, 'the proclamation which receives their lands into His Majestie's protection does not give any better estate than before'.[95] Like the arguments used in the case of tanistry, Davies held that the absence of any kind of lawful English tenure disallowed the Cavan freeholders from bringing any legal action before the assize judges or the central common law courts in Dublin – a situation that parallels very closely the dilatory exception of Irishry mentioned by Professors Murphy and Hand in their discussion of Irish alien status from the fourteenth to the sixteenth centuries. Only now with the abolition of Gaelic tenures and the creation of what Davies called a 'lordship paramount' arising from the Tudor conquest, the medieval and racial exception of Irishry was replaced by a tenurial exception of tanistry and gavelkind.

As an instrument of metropolitan control, this tenurial exception was not confined to the Gaelic polity. It will be recalled that one of the main disputes leading to the departure of O'Neill involved Bishop George Montgomery's claim to most of the *termon* and *erenagh* property in Ulster. Montgomery's rapacity in the title-finding commissions of 1608 and 1609 attained notoriety, and the bishop went so far as to scuttle the commission of 1608, because the commissioners failed to set aside these Gaelic ecclesiastical tenures for the church.[96] But in the subsequent commission to investigate titles in Ulster in 1609, the commissioners discovered that *termon* and *erenagh* tenures were not the proper demesne of the church and were in fact held by the course of gavelkind and tanistry. Indeed, Davies' abstract of the king's title to the escheated lands in Ulster shows that the judicial resolutions against gavelkind and tanistry played a role in recovering these Gaelic ecclesiastical tenures, and to the chagrin of Montgomery, some 60,490 acres lapsed to the crown.[97] While much of this was later granted to the church, it is important to see that the extra-judicial resolutions against tanistry and gavelkind allowed Davies to affirm the state's right to arrogate rights of disposition over all secular and ecclesiastical property in Ireland.

Application of these resolutions to support a massive confiscation of the northern counties has engendered a lush array of opinions concerning Davies' native policy during the first decade of the seventeenth century. Not surprisingly, Davies has fared poorly with a distinctly nationalist historiography which says, in effect, that the Attorney-General sought to generalize a national system from local observation. This interpretation emerged in the early seventeenth century when Geoffrey Keating, the famous Gaelic scholar, condemned Davies for not judging the Gaelic system on its own merits rather than that of the common law. This imposing verdict has been substantiated by more recent research: K. W. Nicholls, for example, has demonstrated numerous variations of tribal organization and descent patterns that are in fact at odds with Davies' *Reports*.[98] Similarly, other students have embellished this argument by borrowing from the Teutonic myth of collective ownership, implying that the pre-conquest Celts, unsullied by the corruptive influence of private property, were defiled by contact with English law and society.[99] This view has, in turn, encountered an antithesis which sees the destruction of Gaelic society as the inevitable triumph of natural selection over an inferior species of law. Accordingly, the dictates of social Darwinism, as expounded by D. Mathew, determined the victory of Renaissance civilization over Gaelic barbarism.[100]

Against this formidable battalion of scholarship, it would be difficult to vindicate Davies' understanding of Irish society. Yet, valid as these criticisms may be, they involve technical questions of Gaelic law and language with which Davies was probably unconcerned. Nor can it be said that Davies was ever interested in an equitable conflation of the two laws. As we have seen, the extra-judicial resolutions against 'gavelkind' and 'tanistry' arose from Davies' juridical and constitutional perceptions of alien status ascribed to the Gaelic Irish. Davies' legal legerdemain was brilliant in scope, and was astutely designed to limit the powers of the tribal elite by stabilizing a system of freeholds within Gaelic districts. As we have also seen, in the wake of the mysterious flight of the earls in September 1607, the abolition of 'tanistry' and 'gavelkind' by judicial fiat served as a device to circumvent native rights in land whenever the more usual methods of attainder and revived medieval titles proved unsatisfactory. The cases of 'gavelkind' and 'tanistry' were indeed employed in a conscious programme of legal imperialism, but not, as the critics allege, as an entirely punitive measure aimed at the complete destruction of Gaelic society. As Kenneth Nicholls has recently shown, the Irish Court of Chancery adjudicated cases of Irish partible inheritance as late as 1622.[101] Moreover, in subsequent plantations in Wexford, Longford and Leitrim, a great deal of equity was shown when the government granted to natives, in what appears to be a rule of thumb, two-thirds to three-quarters of their lands formerly held by Gaelic forms of tenure.[102] Further references to Irish partible inheritance and elective succession may be found in a number of commissions established to enquire into the state of landholding in Wexford, Longford, King's and Queen's counties more than ten years after the litigation recorded by Davies in his *Reports*.[103] There also exists, among a number of other proposals, a bill intended for the parliament of 1613 calling for the extirpation of 'tanistry'. That no such bill was ever passed testifies to the strength and usefulness of judicial resolutions, and to the willingness of the government to deal with Gaelic tenures equitably before the Privy Council, the Court of Chancery, or through various commissions of defective titles.[104] The government could apply these decisions as cases arose in order to augment the more traditional forms of forfeiture in the Ulster plantation, obtaining at the same time the much coveted security of land tenure absent during previous Irish plantations. Davies' achievement is clear: the constitutional assimilation of an alien form of land tenure and the securing of good title for a plantation of 'propertied men' whose future success would leave a permanent mark, for better or worse, on the political map of Northern Ireland.

Appendix: Background to the case of tanistry

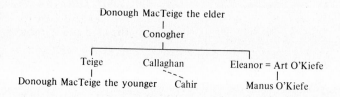

Donough MacTeige the elder
|
Conogher
|
Teige   Callaghan   Eleanor = Art O'Kiefe
| |
Donough MacTeige the younger   Cahir   Manus O'Kiefe

From this genealogy and various manuscript sources, it is possible to unravel the claims and counterclaims to the disputed property.[105]

(1) Sometime before 1574, Conogher and Teige died while Donough MacTeige the elder was still alive. This probably influenced Donough to attempt to keep the estate in the family by circumventing the Irish pattern of lateral succession.

(2) As a result, Donough MacTeige, in 1574, settled the land by a common law feoffment to his second grandson Callaghan for life, remainder to Donough MacTeige the younger for life, remainder to the heirs male of the body of Donough MacTeige the elder.

(3) Donough MacTeige the elder died in 1578 and a year later Callaghan, the first life tenant, was drowned. He left no legitimate issue, but there was a bastard son, Cahir O'Callaghan.

(4) Donough MacTeige the younger succeeded as a second life tenant, but died in 1584 without heirs. Since both Callaghan and Donough MacTeige the younger died without issue, neither estate tail took effect and the land then passed under the ultimate remainder to Eleanor O'Kiefe.

(5) The idea of a woman succeeding to the family estate may have been contrary to local forms of Gaelic succession, and a distant relative, Conogher O'Callaghan, known as Conogher of the Rock, seized and occupied the property in accordance with the custom of tanistry.

It was with the entry of Conogher of the Rock into the estate that complications began to set in. By Irish statute 12 Elizabeth c. 4, all persons holding land by Irish custom were empowered by the authority of the statute to surrender their estates in return for a regrant under a common law title.

(1) In 1593 Conogher of the Rock made a surrender of the afore-mentioned estate and received a regrant in fee simple, which he then enfeoffed to one Fagan, who in turn enfeoffed to Brian MacOwen McSweeney. Brian MacOwen McSweeney then made a lease to his son Murrough MacBryan.[106]

(2) Then it appears that the heirs of Donough MacTeige the elder decided to resurrect their rights. Art O'Kiefe and Eleanor were dead, but Manus O'Kiefe entered on the land and transferred to Cahir O'Callaghan, the bastard son of the Callaghan who was drowned.

(3) The case was brought to trial by action of ejectment before the King's Bench between Murrough MacBryan, the plaintiff, and Cahir O'Callaghan, the defendant. At issue was the title of Murrough MacBryan based on Conogher of the Rock's claim as tanist, and of Conogher of the Rock's title based on the surrender and regrant of 1593. Cahir O'Callaghan's title rested on the settlement made by Donough MacTeige the elder in 1574.

5

The case of the Bann fishery

Gaelic patterns of landholding at the beginning of the seventeenth century constituted a barrier to the exercise of effective English sovereignty in Ireland. The Tudor conquest, however, enabled the government to eliminate tribal patterns of descent and partible inheritance by judicial resolution, thus extending English law throughout the island. Judge-made law likewise served as the tool for establishing English tenures throughout the former autonomous Gaelic lordships. This new departure launched by the proclamation of denization in March 1605 resulted in a series of investigations into patterns of landholding in Ulster that reduced significantly the large tracts of land allocated to the Gaelic leadership by the settlement made at Hampton Court during August 1603. The government concentrated this campaign against the earls of Tyrone and Tyrconnell, and Davies' *Reports* also record its efforts to disrupt the estates of Sir Randall MacDonnell.[1]

Like the northern earls, this renegade Scottish chieftain fared well in the land settlement of 1603, repossessing much of his family's traditional estate comprising the territories known as the Rout and the Glens in the present county of Antrim, running along the coast from Larne to Coleraine. This grant, exceeding 300,000 acres, owed much to the personal influence of the new Scottish king, James I, as well as to the personal acumen of Sir Randall himself. James VI of Scotland had openly supported the MacDonnells during the Nine Years War in their rebellion against the English government. James had done this partly in order to monitor affairs in Ulster, and partly to play off the Irish branch of the family against the rebellious Scottish MacDonnells inhabiting the islands and coastal regions between the two countries. In 1597 James knighted Sir Randall's older brother, James MacDonnell, in a ceremony held with much pomp at the Scottish court. When Sir James died in 1601, Sir Randall succeeded as chief and maintained the family connection with the Scottish court, meanwhile seizing an opportune moment to defect from the rebel Tyrone's cause at the time of Kinsale.[2]

MacDonnell's shrewd transfer of political loyalty, combined with a contribution of 40 horse and 500 foot to the government's war effort, resulted in further honours. In Dublin on 13 May 1602 Lord Deputy Mountjoy on his own behalf knighted MacDonnell.[3] A year later, the government restored MacDonnell to the family's traditional territories in county Antrim. This grant of 28 May 1603 was subsequently expanded to include the castle at Dunluce, Rathlin island, and the most valuable portion of the Bann river fishery, running seven and one half miles from the salmon leap south of Coleraine out to the sea. Such was MacDonnell's skill, or perhaps fortune, that he managed during the same year to conciliate Tyrone by marrying the earl's daughter, Alice.[4]

With the government's decision in 1605 to diminish the estates of the native leadership in Ulster, however, MacDonnell's good fortune took a turn for the worse. Indeed the personal animosity of the Lord Deputy, Chichester, and the private ambitions of a small clique of adventurers in Dublin soon embroiled MacDonnell in lengthy disputes over his claim to the Bann fishery arising from conflicting interpretations placed on the letters patent conferring his estates. The resulting affray, which continued intermittently from 1604 until 1610, constitutes perhaps one of the most extraordinary cases in Irish legal history. MacDonnell, Lord Deputy Chichester, the Earl of Tyrone, the city of London and a Scottish adventurer named Sir James Hamilton all vied for possession of Sir Randall's portion of the lower Bann river.[5]

Some of the heat generated by this controversy can be accounted for by examining contemporary descriptions of the renowned bounty of the Bann river. Its waters run some 31 miles from Lough Neagh to the sea, and form the present boundary between the counties of Antrim and Derry.[6] No detailed account of the Bann fishery for the reign of James I survives, but it is known that the combined yield of the Bann and Foyle fisheries in 1609 amounted to 120 tons of salmon. Coleraine in 1635 alone produced 62 tons in a single day. The Bann was also renowned for its eels. Archbishop Laud was reported to have said that they were the 'fattest and fairest' that he had ever seen.[7] The most vivid estimate of the Bann's commercial potential is contained in the following account written in 1689 by George Phillips, grandson of the famous English adventurer, Sir Thomas Phillips.

I am loth to pass by the salmon pond (commonly called the cutt) near Colrane, because I conceive such another thing is not in the world .. a stranger would be astonished to see an innumerable company of fish riding on the backs of one another even to the top of the water, and with great ease and pleasant divertisement taken up in loops.[8]

The economic potential of the Bann fishery does much to explain the six-year feuding over rights to the river, yet motives of greed account for only part of the story. Personal animosity between Chichester and MacDonnell added further to the dispute. As commander of the royal garrison at Carrickfergus, along the government's main approach into Ulster, Chichester had experienced a number of unpleasant encounters with the MacDonnells during the Nine Years War. The most serious occurred in 1597, when Sir Randall's eldest brother, James, captured and beheaded the Lord Deputy's brother, Sir John Chichester, sending the head to Tyrone's camp where the common soldiers used it for a football.[9] Understandably, Chichester would have had little reason to approve the liberal treatment accorded to MacDonnell in 1603. What is more, the Lord Deputy was never entirely convinced of Sir Randall's loyalty, and was quick, therefore, to seize the opportunity offered by the government's offensive against the Gaelic leadership in Ulster, both to commence a campaign of personal harassment against MacDonnell, and to divest the Scot of his coveted portion of the Bann fishery. Given the Scot's influence at court, any attempts to vilify MacDonnell had to be played with skill and caution. In the event, Chichester employed a string of informers and adventurers in the north, placing his heaviest reliance on Sir Thomas Phillips, commander of the military garrison at Castle Toome, bordering MacDonnell's territories.[10] Early in August of 1604 the plot against MacDonnell began to mature. Chichester first attempted to impugn MacDonnell's loyalty to the English Privy Council by linking Sir Randall with the presence of suspicious assemblies of islanders and mercenary 'redshanks' within the Scot's territories.[11] Interpreting the presence of these professional soldiers as a threat to political stability, Chichester proposed to increase the garrison at Castle Toome, announcing that no country 'better required looking after, nor a better man for the business than Captain Phillips'.[12] Quickly adapting to his role as Chichester's sentinel in the north, Phillips reported to Salisbury that he had thwarted the desires of Sir Randall to repossess Port Rush, a beach-head notorious for mercenary 'redshanks' from the isles only a mile and a half from Castle Toome. Since Scottish mercenaries often formed the vanguard of Irish rebellion, Phillips utilized Chichester's earlier sightings of 'redshanks' in order to warn Cecil that MacDonnell aspired for the return of Port Rush, and expressed himself 'sorry to have let him have it, and would give him any reasonable thing to have it back again'.[13]

When the official campaign to limit the powers of the Gaelic leadership began in March 1605, both Chichester and Phillips renewed their attacks on MacDonnell. After proclaiming the grant of denization in Antrim during the spring of 1605, Phillips gleefully noted to Salisbury that within MacDonnell's territories the new policy 'abates the superiority of their lords to their great grief for now they fall from them and follow his Majesty's officers to crave justice against their lords'.[14] Echoing Davies' criticisms of Tyrone and Tyrconnell, Chichester faulted the liberal grants which had been bestowed on MacDonnell without care taken to establish an adequate number of freeholders who were now 'as slaves to him'.[15] As proof of MacDonnell's perfidy, Chichester went on to criticize the extent of the Scot's estate, noting that the sixteen 'tuoughes', or territories assigned in 1603, far exceeded the four 'tuoughes' held by his father, implying, in other words, that MacDonnell, like Tyrone before him, had appropriated to himself the entire property associated with his extended kin group.[16] This last criticism, which registers once again the English government's apprehension over Gaelic patterns of inheritance, was followed by further attempts to implicate MacDonnell in conspiracies in the north. Within months, Chichester reinforced his earlier suspicions about Sir Randall by capitalizing on the testimony of Neal Garve O'Donnell, kinsman to the Earl of Tyrconnell, that MacDonnell had conspired with the northern earls in some mysterious plot to restore the powers of the Gaelic leadership in Ulster. MacDonnell 'hath given out that he cares not for Sir Arthur Chichester, more than for any ordinary person, knowing the king will hear him and further his desire'.[17] In September 1606 Chichester asserted that in all the north, there was 'not a more cancered and malitious person than Sir Randall MacDonnell'.[18] In Antrim, as well as Tyrone and Tyrconnell, a deliberate campaign was afoot to strengthen English rule in the north at the expense of traditional native leadership.

MacDonnell journeyed to England during the summer of 1606 to clear himself of the libellous charges made by Chichester and Phillips. Well received at court, MacDonnell returned to Antrim to find that Phillips and a Scottish schoolmaster, Sir James Hamilton, had effected a coalition to separate him from the 'fourth part of the fishery of the Bann, being the best stay of my living'.[19] During negotiations among the contestants, Phillips physically threatened Sir Randall and his retinue with an armed company of pike and shot, heaping numerous unnamed 'provocations and injuries' on the bewildered Scot. Phillips then levied charges in the Court of Castle Chamber against sixty of MacDonnell's tenants for alleged outrages and riots committed in vindication of their landlord's title to the fishery.[20] These extraordinary events, remarkably similar to Davies' assaults on Tyrone, assume greater significance if we examine the attempts by Chichester and others to exploit the chaos of Irish conveyancing at the beginning of the seventeenth century in order to acquire Sir Randall's portion of the Bann for themselves.

II

Of the many transfers and conveyances involving the Bann fishery, the single most important instrument for passing real property took the form of a grant of fee farm or fee simple resulting from a warrant made out by the king or Lord Deputy to Chancery officials in Dublin, who in turn issued letters patent to grantees of lands rated at a specific annual value. This cumbersome procedure arose because there was no longer any ancient royal demesne to bestow in Ireland. Hence, all royal grants of real property took the form of letters patent rated, for example, at an annual value of £200 a year. In practice such grants were of the rent and reversion of leaseholds held from the crown which could, if transferred to a leaseholder, upgrade his tenure into a fee simple estate. Thus, inferior tenancies such as lands held for years or lives at a fixed rent, or land held in perpetuity for a fixed rent, could easily be transferred into a rent-free hereditary estate. Conversely an adventurer who did not possess any land could sell his grant, or 'book' as it was known to contemporaries, to someone in possession of an inferior tenancy for a market rate that varied anywhere between one and two thousand pounds for a book of land rate at £100 per annum.[21] The tenancy, accordingly, could then be recorded as a fee simple estate. Under this system, the planter class went on to acquire huge estates in Ireland. As T. O. Ranger has shown, Richard Boyle, the first Earl of Cork, owed his astounding rise to power in Jacobean Ireland to his very shrewd application of such 'books' of land to limited tenancies in Munster.[22] In the case of the Bann fishery, two such books, one to John Wakeman, a trustee of the Earl of Devonshire's will, and another to Thomas Ireland, a Scottish tavern keeper residing in London, ultimately transformed the whole of the Bann into a fee simple estate that ended in the hands of the Lord Deputy, Sir Arthur Chichester.[23]

Before discussing the series of transfers associated with the Wakeman and Ireland books, it is necessary to review several other methods of either acquiring or improving titles to land in Ireland. Apart from the passing of books in fee farm and fee simple at a rated annual value there was also the special commission for defective titles which allowed landholders to upgrade inferior tenancies, concealments and tribal tenures. As discussed in the previous chapter, this commission, established on 10 June 1606, was instrumental in breaking up the over-generous estates allocated to the Gaelic leadership in Ulster during the summer of 1606, and helped to create a network of freeholders in that province. Described by one contemporary as a 'sovereign salve to cure the breaches in men's titles and to settle their estates against all future vexation', the commission for defective titles was also rapidly exploited by the planter class to secure title to lands made unstable by years of chaotic civil strife.[24] In reality, the benefits of this commission were restricted to furthering the interests of the planter class, and complaints levelled by the Earl of Tyrone against the operation of the commission within his territories demonstrate how selective the munificence of the commission could become.[25] Sir John Davies' advice to another Irish noble, the Earl of Clanricard, in 1608, to take advantage of the commission for defective titles 'because of the danger of certain parts of his land being passed to others in books without knowledge of the king's officer', fully demonstrates that the fruits of the commission were intended for those who fought on the right side during the Nine Years War.[26]

It was also possible to convey or acquire land by conveyancing property in trust to the use of one or more third parties. With no statutory requirement to register transfers of real property, either in the Chancery or in the localities, this familiar device to avoid the feudal duties of livery and wardship and to evade the legal bar to bequeathing lands held by knight service was a frequent source of abuse at least until the passage of the Statute of Uses in the Irish parliament in 1634.[27] Since officials within the Dublin government were barred by a statute of Edward II from acquiring lands without royal licence, conveyancing to uses provided a mechanism for sharp officials in Dublin to build estates without the approval of authorities in England. In the case of the Bann, all the above methods of conveyancing played a part in the story of the disputed fishery, and the ill treatment accorded to MacDonnell by Chichester and Phillips owed not a little to the complexity of conveyances and transfers surrounding the conflicting claims.

Apart from the patent of 28 May 1603 assigning lands to MacDonnell excepting 'three parts in four of the fishery of the river Bann', the single most important conveyance to the fishery was a life estate assigned to Lord Deputy Chichester on 9 May 1604 as a perquisite arising from the governorship of Carrickfergus. According to this patent, the government granted Chichester:

the office of Admiral and commander-in-chief of Lough Sidney, otherwise Lough Neagh in the said province for disposing of all shipping, boats and vessels that shall be found there; with the fishing of the Lough, as far as the salmon leap on the Bann.[28]

As a result of this grant, Chichester acquired a life estate to three-quarters of the Bann, leaving the last quarter, running from the salmon leap to the sea, to Sir Randall MacDonnell in accordance with the terms of the patent granted in 1603. In addition, Chichester was granted Belfast Castle and a landed estate that included no less than fifty-five townlands.[29] If, however, Chichester harboured desires to improve his life estate to the Bann, either through the commission for defective titles or by other means, his ambitions were soon threatened by the arrival of a Scottish schoolmaster, Sir James Hamilton, in county Antrim. Hamilton had previously acted as an agent for the Scottish king in Dublin during the Nine Years War. He arrived in Ireland in possession of a book of Irish land, rated at an annual value of £100, made out to one Thomas Ireland, a fellow Scot and innkeeper residing in London, who had paid the sum of £1,678 6s 8d for the patent.[30] Hamilton presented himself as an assignee or agent for Thomas Ireland. In truth, he was using the innkeeper's name to separate himself from a series of dubious land transactions in Ireland. Hamilton's role in the break-up of Con O'Neill's estate in Ulster demonstrates the reasons for the Scot's desire for anonymity.[31]

Hamilton, in combination with another Scots adventurer, Hugh Montgomery from Braidstone in Ayrshire, had seized upon a chance to extort the vast portion of Con O'Neill's estate in north Down, the

Ards and upper and lower Clandeboy. The opportunity arose from Con's complicity in Tyrone's rebellion, and from a drunken affray shortly before Elizabeth's death, between several of Con's men and soldiers from Chichester's garrison at Carrickfergus. As a result of this incident, Chichester imprisoned Con in the royal prison at Carrickfergus. Montgomery and Hamilton, hearing of the Irishman's plight, held a number of meetings with Con and agreed to use their private influence at court (Montgomery's brother George was chaplain to James I) to secure him a royal pardon. In return for the pardon and a cleverly arranged escape from prison, Con agreed to divide his extensive estates in Down and Antrim with Hamilton and Montgomery.[32] On account of this extraordinary arrangement, Hamilton felt compelled to disguise any further acquisition of Irish land, and Thomas Ireland's patent provided him with the necessary cover to avoid any uncomfortable charges of peculation that might be levelled by Lord Deputy Chichester or other officials within Dublin Castle.

Lord Deputy Chichester, who had his own designs in counties Antrim and Down, looked askance at these developments and complained to Cecil during the summer of 1605 of this shameless alienation of Irish real estate. Despite Cecil's curt reply that Chichester refrain from interfering with royal largesse, the Lord Deputy attempted to thwart the two Scots by launching an investigation into Hamilton's dealings in the north.[33] To avoid a confrontation, Hamilton struck a bargain with Chichester in return for the latter's aid in sanctioning his tripartite agreement with Montgomery and Con O'Neill. As a gesture of goodwill, Hamilton conveyed a large estate to Chichester in county Antrim which included the territories of Moylinny, Ballylinny, the island of Magee, and other lands at Woodburn and Inver on the outskirts of Larne. Chichester also received the Thomas Ireland patent, which he subsequently employed to consolidate and upgrade his life estate to the Bann. In fact it is possible to deduce, from a deed registered on 3 April 1611, that Hamilton's interest in the Bann 'between Lough Neagh to the Salmon leap' passed surreptitiously through Ireland's book from Hamilton to Chichester for an undisclosed sum of money.[34] Simply stated, Chichester employed the Ireland patent to disguise his acquisition, without royal licence of a heritable fee in what had formerly been a life estate in the Bann. Since this relatively simple transaction did not appear to conflict with any alternative claims to the river, Chichester and Hamilton worked their subterfuge without so much as a stir either from the English Privy Council, or from other potential claimants in the north.

In attempting to extend their interest to include MacDonnell's portion of the Bann fishery, the unlikely combination of Hamilton and Chichester ran into trouble. Much of their difficulty arose from a second book of land for £100, dated 8 November 1603, assigned to John Wakeman, a Barbary merchant and trustee of the Earl of Devonshire's will.[35] On 2 March 1605, a grant was made to Wakeman of the entire river from the salmon leap to the sea. Then, on 21 October 1605, Wakeman granted power of attorney to Sir James Ware, Auditor of Dublin, to dispose of Wakeman's patent in satisfaction of some of Devonshire's debts in Ireland. In carrying out his duties, Ware subsequently sold to James Hamilton sometime during 1606 'all that river of the Bann in Ulster; that is from the rock called the salmon leap in the same river unto the maine sea'.[36] This book, according to the deed enrolled on 3 April 1611, was then sold to Chichester and his heirs in perpetuity on 14 May 1606, conveying a 'moyetie' of the fishery to the Lord Deputy.[37] Since there was no need to register the conveyance in the central or local archives, almost the whole of the Bann passed, for all outward appearances, to Sir James Hamilton, when in reality it resided in the hands of Lord Deputy Chichester. Once again, conveyancing through third parties avoided the statutory requirement for the Lord Deputy to acquire land through royal licence.

Apart from conflicting with MacDonnell's patent to the lower Bann, the Wakeman patent contradicted a more serious claim from the Earl of Tyrone, who objected that the former Lord Lieutenant, the Earl of Devonshire, who possessed a moiety of the Bann fishery through his assign Wakeman, had promised to convey the fishery to himself.[38] Tyrone claimed this right as repayment for £200 expended in revictualling the northern garrisons. Instead, Ware conveyed the tidal Bann to Hamilton. There is, however, an air of mystery about the projected Wakeman–Tyrone conveyance. In an undated brief concerning the Bann controversy, Davies noted that 'Sir James Hamilton agreed to pass or confer to the Earl the moyetie of the fishing for £200 to Mr James Carroll to the use of the said Sir James Hamilton which the late Earl of Tyrone satisfied to Mr Carroll accordingly.' In reporting on the complaints made by Tyrone, Chichester explained that Hamilton did indeed agree to reconvey the grant to Tyrone for the sum of £200, and while the earl seems to have lived up to his side of the bargain, neither the money nor the deed to

the Bann ever left the hands of the Vice-Treasurer, James Carroll.[39]
Tyrone was further vexed by an alternative claim lodged by the
merchant Nicholas Weston, who maintained that Tyrone, as security for a loan, had granted him the fishery of the Bann from the
'salmon leap to the sea'. Notwithstanding Sir Randall MacDonnell's
claim to the same, Weston demanded, after the flight of the earls,
either restitution of the fishery, or of the £200 at 10 per cent interest
owed to him by Tyrone.[40] This claim was later satisfied by the
government through a cash payment, indicating the Tyrone's claim
to the Bann had some substance, despite the various grants made to
Chichester, MacDonnell and others.

The truth of the matter, however, emerged in Davies' abstract of
the king's title to the escheated counties in Ulster taken after the
flight of the earls. Davies reported that it was found by office in
August 1608 that Tyrone, at the time of his treason, 'was seised of
the moyetie of the fishing in demesne'.[41] In commenting on the
alleged Hamilton–Tyrone conveyance, Davies noted that the transfer had never been formalized by government patent, even though
the earl had taken the profits from his interest in the Bann. A
subsequent incident involving the Archbishop of Armagh, Miler
MaGrath, throws further light on the affair. Following the departure
of the northern earls, MaGrath found himself under indictment
before the palatine court of Tipperary for libellously

uttering these words, or words to the same effect: That O'Neill was greatly
wronged when he was dispossessed of the fishing of the river Bann, and that
he had better right to it than any English or Scottish, yea and that he had
better right to the crown of Ireland than any Englishman or Scottishman
whatsoever.[42]

Whatever the extent of Tyrone's interest in the Bann fishery, the
incident illustrates not only the uncertainties of Irish conveyancing,
but displays the well-orchestrated campaign to reduce the size of
Tyrone's estate and livelihood. Following the earl's departure to the
continent in 1607, the incident figured prominently in Tyrone's list
of grievances sent to the king.[43] While the Dublin government
demonstrated some confusion over the validity of the Wakeman–
Hamilton–Tyrone patent before Tyrone's departure from Ireland,
the state seized upon Tyrone's flight to the continent in 1607 to
reclaim the earl's contested share of the river – thus recognizing a
claim it had previously doubted. Davies' undated brief of the Bann
controversy, examined alongside the deed enrolled on 3 April 1611,
reveals a conveyance, notwithstanding previous grants to Sir

Randall MacDonnell, of the whole fishery, less Tyrone's disputed claim, to the use of Sir Arthur Chichester and his heirs forever.[44] By 1606, one year before the departure of the northern earls, Lord Deputy Chichester had surreptitiously acquired a heritable fee simple estate to almost the whole of the Bann river running from Lough Neagh to the sea. To give a secure legal basis to this new estate, Chichester had to dispose of MacDonnell's claim to the lower quarter of the Bann.

III

These events, which go far to explain the frequent attempts by Chichester and Phillips to throw suspicion on the activities of MacDonnell, resulted in a royal directive to sequester MacDonnell's portion of the river pending a solution to the disputed claims. MacDonnell, however, attempted once again to capitalize on his connections at court and succeeded in having the sequestration removed, only to have it reimposed.[45] Royal equivocation continued, and within months, another royal order dissolved the said 'sequestration until the same shall be evicted from him by due course of our laws in some of our courts of record there'.[46] For Chichester and Phillips, who had supervised the establishment of freeholders within MacDonnell's districts, this proposition must have been unsettling. A jury of local freeholders nominated and put forward by MacDonnell during the years of 1605 and 1606 would hardly favour official attempts to purloin the lower quarter of the Bann. In spring of 1607, for example, a report from the north claimed that Sir Randall's followers had riotously asserted 'the said Sir Randall's right to a fourth part of the fishing to the Bann'.[47] As tempers flared and accusations flew back and forth across the Irish Sea, the precipitous flight of the earls in the autumn of 1607 decisively altered the delicate balance of power in Ulster. Thereafter, the Dublin government no longer felt constrained to deal cautiously with either MacDonnell or any other Gaelic leaders in the north.

In January 1608 Chichester sent a letter to the English Privy Council suggesting that the dispute over the Bann be referred to the Council in England. Enclosed with this request was a highly important brief written by Davies impugning the general validity, not only of MacDonnell's patent to the Bann, but also of the whole estate assigned to the Scot at the end of the Nine Years War. This attack, which parallels closely Davies' investigation into the patents assigned to Tyrone and Tyrconnell, anticipated a wholesale change in the previously equivocal attitude taken by the king and the English Privy Council towards MacDonnell and the contested fishery.

In outlining the metes and bounds of MacDonnell's estate, Davies testily noted that the patents assigning MacDonnell the territories traditionally occupied by his predecessors had in fact included lands wrested from the McQuillans and from Angus MacDonnell of Dunyveg. Moreover, argued Davies, neither MacDonnell nor his ancestors possessed more than four 'tuoughes', or territories of land, in Ulster before the Nine Years War. It seemed, therefore, that MacDonnell had bilked the government of over nine 'tuoughes' of land.[48] Davies also catalogued a number of defects in MacDonnell's patent of 1603, noting the failure to include Rathlin island and the existence of a significant forfeiture clause for non-payment of rent. These omissions, said Davies, had been remedied by a regrant of MacDonnell's estate on 4 July 1604.

With regard to the fishery, however, Davies discovered that the lower fourth of the Bann river had never been expressly set forth in MacDonnell's patent, yet 'three partes of the fyshery of the said river is excepted in every of the said grauntes'.[49] By drawing attention to the traditional estate assigned to the MacDonnells before and after 1603, Davies rightly argued that sequestration of the Bann fishery could hardly seem unfair. While Davies' brief also laid out Hamilton's alternative claim to the lower Bann, it warily neglected to mention the secret conveyances to Lord Deputy Chichester. As far as Davies was concerned, the dispute depended solely on the question of whether MacDonnell's patent allowed a right to 'any part of the fishing of the salmon leap or in any part of the river of the Bann'.[50]

MacDonnell's reaction to these activities reveals some confusion over precisely who was responsible for his torment. Mistaking Hamilton as his adversary, MacDonnell admitted to Salisbury during May 1608 that he was not 'so clereful in law matters as Hamilton'.[51] Recognizing the implications of Davies' brief, he further confessed that he could not take advantage of Hamilton as he 'hath done against my patent for want of one word'. As an alternative arrangement he suggested the free exercise of riparian rights to his own lands bordering the river, or failing this, a general remission of rent to 'a sum of seventy cows or seventy pounds of rent yerely'.[52] MacDonnell noted, however, that Hamilton paid no rent at all for his portion of the Bann, arguing that it could be no 'augmentation of his highness rent that my fourth part should be taken from me'. He then offered, in an attempt to retain his portion of the fishery, £100 annual rent to the crown. In view of Sir Thomas Phillips' estimate of an annual value in excess of £800, this offer reveals not only the slimness of Sir Randall's offer, but also the extreme carelessness of authorities in England to allow Hamilton/Chichester to acquire the Bann virtually free of rent.[53] These pathetic entreaties, in the end, fell on deaf ears, and the omnipresent Sir Thomas Phillips sequestered once again the disputed fishery. At every juncture, the Dublin-based conspiracy, led by Hamilton and Phillips, kept a step ahead of Sir Randall, who helplessly complained of their clever attempts to 'deprive and dispossess me of my right to the said fishery'.[54]

With the flight of the earls, MacDonnell's troubles were compounded by another more formidable claim to his fishery arising from the projected plantation in Ulster. In January of 1609 the king decided to grant the salmon and eel fisheries of the Bann and Lough Foyle to the city of London as an incentive to encourage private capital to this new enterprise in Ireland.[55] During August 1609 agents from the city of London arrived to inspect the fisheries and were reported to 'like and praise the country very much especially the Bann and the river of Loughfoyle'.[56] When the Londoners arrived in 1610 to take possession of the Bann and Loughfoyle, in accordance with an agreement already formalized in January of that year, they found to their dismay that Hamilton/Chichester had occupied the prized and coveted Bann. To solve this extraordinary dilemma, the king decided to clear the title acquired by Hamilton and Chichester by paying the costs from his own purse, which meant that eventually Lord Deputy Chichester collected £2,260 from the royal coffers.[57] This unusual transaction, which ignored Sir Randall's claim, conveyed the Bann to the Londoners through the Ireland–Wakeman patents, and it is very doubtful whether Cecil or the king understood the real story behind this remarkable subterfuge.

None the less suspicions were aroused. In a letter written on 23 January 1610, Chichester feigned ignorance of the whole affair, protesting to Salisbury that he was personally of the opinion that the 'moyetie of the fishing of that river of the Bann did revert again to the king upon Tyrone's attainder'. In explaining the need to extend a cash payment to Hamilton, Chichester noted that it was the Scottish schoolmaster, not himself, who had 'procured a declaration from some of the commissioners there appointed for Irish causes that the right of the fishery was in him'.[58] While Tyrone's portion of the river devolved to the crown by virtue of the rebel earl's attainder, the king still had to pay for the rest of the river from his own pocket. Nevertheless, before formal title could be granted to the Londoners, the government had to address itself to MacDonnell's patent.

Given the complexity of the case, and the urgency of adjudicating the various disputes over the Bann, it is not surprising that the English Privy Council decided to employ the familiar expedient of adjudicating the claims to the contested fishery by a resolution of all the Irish justices. In a letter dated 24 April 1609, the English Privy Council sent the following directive to Lord Deputy Chichester.

We direct you to call together some of the jduges and learned counsell, and to take such cause in the matter as may be most agreeable in equity and also to determine it with all convenient expedition.[59]

According to Attorney-General Davies, who argued the case on behalf of the crown during Michaelmas term 1610, 'the Lord Deputy being informed by the king's attorney that no part of the fishery passed to Sir Randall by this grant required the resolution of the chief judges being of the Privy Council in this matter'.[60] The familiar recourse to executing policy by judicial fiat assumes greater significance if we examine the substantive legal principles by which Davies attempted to lodge a superior crown right to MacDonnell's portion of the lower Bann.

Davies sought in this brief to demonstrate a royal right to the Bann by citing not only precedents drawn from the common law, but also principles drawn from continental civil law. In fact, Davies' report of the case reveals that argument from continental law served not only to elucidate the common law, but also to buttress a legal brief lacking mature principles of public law to establish a claim to the disputed fishery.[61] Davies' argument rested on a series of precedents as a basis for the claim that a fishery represented a category of freehold that excluded the banks along which it ran. This attempt to deny MacDonnell's riparian rights along the Bann seems to have troubled Davies, and some of the precedents employed in his legal paradigm were open to question. As a means of demonstrating the king's right to navigable waterways, Davies cited the royal grant to the London commission of sewers, which 'extended not only to walls and banks of the sea, but also to navigable rivers and fresh waters'.[62] More importantly, Davies contrived the argument that the city of London's right to the Thames arose only through a royal grant – establishing once again the superior prerogative right of the king in law to navigable rivers. In search for Irish precedents, Davies lifted evidence from a plea roll in Ireland, dated 40 Edward III, that maintained a royal right to the Boyne 'from the town of Drogheda up to the Trim'. Additional statute and yearbook evidence was produced to show the king's right to the rivers Barrow, Noire and Suire. Davies attempted to establish in this manner a crown right to a river in northern Ulster that had only recently been subjected to the sovereignty of English law.[63]

To fortify these common law principles, the Irish Attorney-General chose to employ elements of the civil law compatible with the common law tradition. Davies began by distinguishing between two types of rivers – navigable and non-navigable, and then laboured to validate the riparian rights of proprietors in non-navigable rivers. The common law, he argued, recognized these rights, and numerous examples from traditional common law sources including statutes, yearbooks, yearbook abridgements and contemporary law reports were cited as evidence for this point.[64] But to establish a prerogative right not only to all rivers and waterways 'so high as the sea flow and ebbs in them', but also to the high seas, Davies went on to cite from a treatise written by the French civilian Jacques Cujas that 'Regalia sunt viae publicae, flumina navigabilia, et ex quibus fiunt navigabilia, portus, vectigalia, monetae, etc.'[65] Since MacDonnell's portion of the disputed fishery included the tidal portion of the river, Davies confirmed his argument by referring to Renattus Choppinus' treatise, *De Dominia Franciae*, in which all tidal or navigable rivers flowing 'per confinium praediorum' belonged to the monarch, either by prerogative or prescriptive right.[66] Therefore, argued Davies, a prerogative right to the tidal Bann could not be impugned by the general words of MacDonnell's patent 'exceptis tribus partibus piscariae de Bann', because the king's grant 'shall not pass such special regality which belongeth to the crown by prerogative'.[67] The Irish judiciary thus stripped Sir Randall MacDonnell of his interest in the Bann fishery.

A decidedly nationalist literature had roundly criticized the litigation over the disputed fishery by asserting that the case against MacDonnell represented little more than an illegal proceeding to divest him of his rights in the Bann for the personal aggrandizement of a small group of officials in Dublin. The controversial nature of the case, in fact, imposed a historical legacy on future litigation of its kind. The famous House of Lords decision on the disposition of fishing rights to Lough Neagh in 1908 made the case of Sir Randall MacDonnell something of a *cause célèbre* within nationalist circles.[68] No less an antagonist than Tim Healy, the renowned Irish patriot, picked up the cudgel in MacDonnell's defence. The title of Healy's work, *Stolen Waters*, and its subsequent condensed version, *The Great Fraud of Ulster*, revealed a predictable theme. To Healy, the case of the Bann fishery represented 'the third case in which evidence exists that Chichester filled the role of both judge and plaintiff, while pretending that the proceeding was taken on behalf of the crown'. Moreover, Healy complained, 'in a district where the laws of England never prevailed until 1603, a tidal river was in 1610 held to be the personal perquisite of the king by ancient right'.[69] Healy's outrage has understandably influenced later scholarship; for example, Professor Perceval-Maxwell's recent study of the Scots plantation in Antrim and Down also moralizes on the fundamentally illegal nature of the proceedings against Sir Randall.[70]

Given the authority of judicial resolutions in early modern jurisprudence, it would be hard to sustain any notion of illegality in the controversial litigation over the tidal Bann. Considering MacDonnell's success in maintaining his original grant of 300,000 acres, it is also difficult to represent the seizure of the Bann as a slaughter of the innocents. While it is valid to call into question the hidden string of conveyances, and to expose the shady dealings of Chichester, Hamilton and their accomplices, the ingenuity with which the Bann was secured as an incentive to colonize the heartland of Irish revolt must still be acknowledged. Through a perfectly lawful judicial resolution confirmed by legal principles drawn from continental civil law, Davies contrived a curious twist of logic. While the dictates of natural geography suppose that rivers flow towards the sea, Sir Randall MacDonnell lost his fishery because the sea flows into rivers.[71]

Part III

JUDICIAL ENCOUNTERS: THE COLONIAL COMMUNITY

6

The mandates controversy and the case of Robert Lalor

The innovative use of judicial resolutions by Sir John Davies and the judiciary effected a sweeping alteration in the relationship between English conquerors and the native elements in Ireland. As the *Reports* demonstrate, however, judge-made law also became a tool against the Old English colonial community, the descendants of those who had settled in Ireland before the sixteenth century. This assault against a group which had been instrumental in securing the Tudor conquest may seem illogical, yet it was not without provocation.

I

Immediately after the death of Elizabeth in early April 1603, the southern towns in Ireland went on the rampage, expelling Protestants, reconsecrating Catholic churches, and defying central authority. Inspired partly by reports that James I intended to grant religious toleration to the island, the citizens of Waterford, Cork, Limerick, Kilkenny, Drogheda, Wexford, Clonmel and Cashel took the occasion to assert their solidarity against Protestant officials. In Waterford the corporation closed the city gates to Lord Deputy Mountjoy and his army of 5,000 men who had marched south from Dublin to restore order. In justification for this defiant behaviour, the unruly townsmen claimed the authority of a four-century old charter granted by King John. With Mountjoy waiting on the outskirts of the city, the corporation dispatched an ecclesiastical emissary, Father James White, Vicar-Apostolic of Waterford and Lismore, to negotiate. Leading a solemn procession from the city gates, White engaged the Lord Deputy in a theological debate over the right of Catholic subjects to take up arms against their sovereign. Mountjoy, who was known for his bookishness, bested the Catholic divine by demonstrating before an assembly of recusant townsmen that White's defence of the city rested on a deliberate misinterpretation of St Augustine, 'whereupon the doctor was confounded, the citizens ashamed and the conference ended'. When Mountjoy threatened to cut King John's charter with King James' sword, the city opened its gates.[1]

Similar events took place in Cork where municipal officials contemptuously refused to proclaim James I as lawful successor to Elizabeth. When Sir George Thornton and Sir Charles Wilmot arrived in Cork, empowered by the Munster council to hear the proclamation of the new king, the Mayor and Recorder of the city, Thomas Sarsfield and William Meade, gave them an unpleasant surprise. Meade impudently reminded Thornton and Wilmot that the recognition bestowed by the corporation on Perkin Warbeck during an earlier succession had proved unfortunate for the city. Moreover, argued Meade, the commission empowered to rule the province of Munster had no validity after the death of Elizabeth, thus depriving Wilmot and Thornton of authority to make demands upon the corporation. Passions rose and the citizens expelled the commissioners from the city. Hostilities broke out between the corporation and troops were dispatched to Cork by the Munster council.[2] On 10 May 1603, when the Lord Deputy arrived from Waterford, the corporation wisely opened its gates, and Mountjoy promptly arrested the main offenders. Mayor Sarsfield, who had reportedly paraded himself in the forefront of Catholic processions as a kind of 'Doge of Venice', wisely recanted and made full and ample submission to the Lord Deputy, in addition to acknowledging the legitimacy of the new monarch. Recorder Meade, however, adamantly refused to co-operate and was arrested and tried for high treason before the Munster Presidency Court. The account of Fynes Moryson, secretary to Lord Deputy Mountjoy, described the predictable outcome of the trial. According to Moryson, the Lord Deputy might as well have forgiven Meade, for no 'man that knew Ireland did imagine that an Irish jury would condemn him'.[3] Despite fines of £500 and government intimidation in the Court of Castle Chamber, a jury of nine Old English and three Irish freeholders refused to convict Meade. Not one to press his luck, the Recorder took the occasion of his reprieve to depart for the continent where, supported by a Spanish pension, he continued to agitate for Catholic rights in Ireland until his death.

In summarizing the events which comprised the Munster uprising to the English Privy Council, the Lord Deputy noted the absence of foreign involvement and attributed no great significance to the whole affair. Despite Mountjoy's leniency towards the towns, however, it was soon decided that for a government only just triumphant over one of the most serious rebellions in Irish history and for a monarch only recently established on the English throne, the rising of the port towns could not be ignored. The means found to force at least the outward conformity of Old English leadership in the unruly municipalities was to be consistent with the style of law reform applied to native society. The government formulated its assault against the towns in three judicial resolutions that addressed not only the issue of religion, but also the jurisdictional and economic causes of the Munster disturbances. That is, judge-made law was employed to accomplish the following ends: (1) enhance enforcement of religious conformity by validating a proclamation extending to Ireland the penal laws passed against recusants by late Elizabethan parliaments in England; (2) eliminate extensive corporate liberties that included full appropriation of the customs revenue; and (3) reform a debased national currency that had eroded local, regional and international commerce.

II

Of all the issues surrounding the Munster disturbances, the problem of recusancy most attracted the attention of contemporaries at home and abroad, and the question of religious conformity became fundamental in altering the relationship between the central government and the towns. Under the last Tudor monarch penal laws for recusancy had seldom been enforced in Ireland. The English policy of excluding Catholics from positions within the central government, the judiciary and the municipalities had never been consistently applied. As late as 1596, Robert Cecil's refusal to prosecute penal legislation against recusants in the Pale and port towns reflected the power inherent in Old English society and the government's reluctance to alienate a useful ally that had remained faithful during the endemic upheavals in the Gaelic or Gaelicized hinterland of the late sixteenth century.[4] In response to this liberal treatment, the towns provided local militia, supplies and occasional loans to aid the government's war effort. With the end of the Nine Years War, however, the equation linking the interests of the towns with the policies of the English government had lapsed, and the Tudor conquest soon forced the colonial community to recognize the unpalatable truth that its services were no longer critical to the survival of English rule in Ireland.

A preview of the government's eventual policy can be seen in Lord Deputy Mountjoy's attempt early in 1603 to revive the court of High Commission as a means to tender the Oath of Supremacy to municipal officials in Dublin. When the commissioners imprisoned several aldermen for refusing the Oath, the English Privy Council halted further proceedings as politically unseasonable.[5] After the Munster rising, however, Old English activities at court forced a change in the English Privy Council's attitude towards recusancy in Ireland. On 6 August 1603 four agents from the 'nobility and gentry of Ireland', who arrived in England to petition the king for the public use of their religion, the maintenance of Old English officials in positions of local and national government, and the reform of the coinage, were promptly arrested. Sir Roger Wilbraham, Davies' predecessor as Solicitor-General in Ireland, witnessed the event and attributed the Privy Council's action to the offensive theatrics of the recusant agents who had staged their petition in the presence of 'thirty or more persons of the nobles and gentlemen of Ireland that attended for other sorts, as though they would put his majestie in fear if he grant not their unjust desire'.[6]

Heeding the example of the English Privy Council, the Dublin government began to apply the Irish Acts of Uniformity and Supremacy as a means to purge the towns of Catholic officials, to deny the right of Catholic lawyers to plead before the Irish bar, and to eliminate Catholics from the Irish bench. The government set about substituting English for Old English lawyers in the Irish courts; proceedings were launched against civil officers in the towns, especially in the city of Dublin. Recusancy in the capital city was notorious and the complaints made by the English servitor, Barnaby Rich, that the city could 'not make a yearly choyce of a mayor and two sheriffs that will either goe to church or willingly take the oath' are confirmed in Davies' account of the election of John Skelton, a Dublin alderman, to the mayoralty of the capital city. Normal procedure required the Mayor-elect to take the Oath of Supremacy before the assembled Barons of the Exchequer.[7] Owing to the plague, however, the barons were absent from the city, and Skelton put forward the disingenuous claim that he had subscribed to the Oath before his predecessor and the assembled aldermen of the city. In the precincts of Dublin, however, the recusant clergy manufactured the fiction that Skelton had avoided taking the Oath altogether. To combat this attempt to make Skelton a popular hero for allegedly hoodwinking the state, Lord Deputy Chichester and Sir John Davies decided to convene a special commission to tender the Oath to Skelton in the proper manner.

When summoned before the commissioners, Skelton attempted to postpone the issue by asking leave to examine his conscience. The commissioners obligingly accommodated this request and arranged a conference between Skelton and a Dr Chalonner, a noted Protestant divine then resident in Dublin. Chalonner managed to convince the Mayor-elect that the Oath provided in the Irish statute of 2 Elizabeth could indeed be taken without offending Skelton's conscience. Thus satisfied, Skelton signified his willingness to indulge in the usual legal formalities at a date in the near future. But Skelton thereafter fell under the influence of an anonymous but prominent member of the recusant clergy, who 'partly with entreaty, partly with threats prevailed with him so far as he lost his resolution'.[8] A few days later, when Skelton appeared at the appointed time, he refused to acknowledge the Supremacy because the words of the statute referred to the 'Queen's Majesty' rather than that of the king. Davies informed Skelton that the word 'Queen' referred to the corporation sole, yet Skelton insisted on substituting an oath of loyalty for the Supremacy. Tiring of these tedious evasions, the commissioners angrily dismissed Skelton and ordered the alderman to elect a new mayor who would readily take the Oath. As with the incident with Sarsfield and Meade, the Skelton affair once again demonstrated the difficulty of ensuring a Protestant view among Old English officials in the towns.

Remedies for the government's problem were limited by the paucity of penal statutes at its disposal. Anti-Catholic legislation in Ireland had been in existence since the mid-sixteenth century, but the Acts of Uniformity and Supremacy were less than adequate tools with which to repair Old English recusancy.[9] As the incident with Skelton suggests, the Oath of Supremacy seems to have been only sporadically enforced, and the Act of Uniformity, which called for only a one-shilling fine for non-attendance at church, could have little effect except upon the very poor. The absence of adequate statutory authority to expel the recusant clergy and to enforce a meaningful degree of religious conformity within the colonial community prompted the novel proposal of William Saxey, Chief Justice of the Munster Presidency Court. Saxey recommended enforcement in Ireland of the English statute of 27 Elizabeth ordering the deportation of all Jesuits and seminary priests. This scheme, presented to the Irish Privy Council sometime during 1604, was challenged by an unidentified member of the Irish Privy Council who objected that 'His Majesty's dominion extended no further than England and Wales, and that English statutes without the consent of the Irish parliament, could not bind Ireland'.[10] This illuminating statement hit precisely upon the shortcomings of the Irish statute book by pointing directly at the questionable constitutional validity of extending English statutes to Ireland without the prior approval of the Irish parliament.

Caught on the point of this constitutional sword, the English and Irish Privy Councils devised a quick solution. The remedy may have originated with Adam Loftus and Thomas Jones, the bishops of Dublin and Meath. Addressing a petition to the king dated 4 June 1603, Loftus and Jones had made a plea for royal support to expel the recusant clergy and to compel the laity to attend Protestant services. This proposal, which anticipated by one month a plan submitted by the Lord Deputy and Privy Council, was subsequently endorsed by the king and the English Privy Council, resulting in a royal proclamation expelling the Catholic clergy from the realm.[11] This use of the prerogative had the advantage of avoiding the constitutional difficulties described in Saxey's dispatch to Salisbury, while the provisions enshrined in the English statute of 27 Elizabeth could also be extended to Ireland by royal fiat. The government warily decided to test the new programme in Munster under the authority of the provincial seal before extending the proclamation to the country at large.

Munster had of course been the focal point of religious and corporate discontent in 1603. As early as August 1604 the Lord President of Munster, Sir Henry Brouncker, anticipated official policy by proclaiming the removal of all 'Jesuits, Seminaries and massing priests', and offering rewards to the value of £40 for every Jesuit, £6 8s 4d for every seminary priest, and £5 for every massing priest who refused to depart the realm within thirty days.[12] Suitably impressed with Bouncker's progress, the Irish Privy Council a year later issued a royal proclamation that resembled the one employed by the Munster Presidency.[13] In addition to expelling the dissident clergy, however, the Dublin government appended to the royal edict a sweeping decree aimed at securing the outward conformity of recusant officials in the towns – particularly in the capital city. The government's procedure involved publishing the Irish Act of Uniformity under the Great Seal and thereby summoning the laity to church through letters or mandates sent to prominent citizens. Thus, by royal fiat the Dublin government extended to Ireland the tenets of the Elizabethan penal statutes, and expelled the recusant clergy from the realm. By means of the royal will, the government also demanded the attendance of prominent officials at church in the company of the Lord Deputy, or in the case of the provincial presidencies, in the presence of the Lord Presidents of Munster and Connaught.[14] Dublin became the focal point for the government's onslaught, with mandates issued to sixteen of the principal merchants and aldermen of the city, including the recalcitrant Skelton. As Davies explained to Salisbury, the government devised the new strategy to demonstrate its resolve to enforce religious conformity among the lesser sort by making examples of the principal gentlemen and householders of the capital city – men who had in effect been immune from any serious damage arising from the one-shilling fine for non-attendance at church imposed by the statute of 2 Elizabeth.[15] Davies claimed significant results by the autumn of 1605 from this novel but heavy-handed legal experiment. Despite an outbreak of the plague, the mandates formula succeeded in compelling the Mayor, seven aldermen and four hundred other persons to attend Protestant services in Dublin. There were, however, a number of prosperous merchants and aldermen who openly defied their mandates. Punishment fell upon these recalcitrants. The Court of Castle Chamber fined Skelton, four other aldermen and several of the principal merchants £50 to £100 each for contemptuous disobedience of the royal proclamation. Attorney-General Davies followed up this action by indicting four hundred Dublin householders before the Court of King's Bench.[16]

The assault continued in the provinces. In Munster, where Brouncker's earlier proclamation had served as a blueprint for subsequent policy, the Lord President proved to be an aggressive champion of Protestantism. Following Davies' lead, Brouncker issued mandates to the aldermen and burgesses of the several port towns. These townsmen, however, proved to be as obdurate as their Dublin counterparts. Brouncker retaliated by deposing the mayors of all the towns of the province, with the exception of Waterford, for refusing either to attend church or to subscribe to the Oath of Supremacy. As a further penalty, the Lord President urged the Dublin government to compel all the Munster towns to forfeit their charters for their recusancy – a policy which appears to have attracted the support of Bacon and Ellesmere on the English Privy Council.[17] Brouncker's overzealous administration of the mandates raised such a tempest, however, that officials in Munster took steps after his death in 1607 to deny rumours spread by the recusant clergy that Brouncker had perished gnawing the flesh from his hands in remorse for harsh persecution of Catholics. Even James I felt constrained to comment that Brouncker's zeal was 'more than required in a governor, however allowable in a private man'. Many of the fines imposed on the Munster towns were subsequently reduced or remitted.[18]

In Connaught, the seat of the other Presidency Court, mandates were also issued under the provincial seal but absence of records obscures the picture of developments there. Yet it is known that Sir Robert Remington, the provincial Vice-President, issued mandates to municipal officials and prominent citizens of Galway.[19] The English and Irish Privy Councils had apparently contrived a highly organized and well-co-ordinated assault against Old English privilege by working through the Presidency Courts of Munster and Connaught, as well as in the central courts of Dublin. This policy of selective repression was levelled at leading members of Old English society. But there were signs of an equally obdurate resistance to the government's attempt to impose religious conformity by executive fiat.

During early December 1605 ill feeling within leading circles of the colonial community culminated in a petition addressed to the Irish Privy Council, questioning the legality and protesting the severity of the mandate policy. Carrying the signatures of 219 members of the Pale gentry and 5 Irish peers, the petition, delivered in the aftermath of the gunpowder plot, ignored all dictates of political discretion and sparked a crisis that provoked the English and Irish judiciaries into validating the controversial mandates by means of judicial resolution.[20] Shortly after receiving the petition, Chichester ordered the ringleaders' arrest, attributing authorship of the troublesome document to a trio of Old English lawyers – Henry Burnell, Richard Netterville and Sir Patrick Barnewall. Subsequent interrogation revealed that Burnell and Netterville, who had caused Sydney so much trouble over purveyance in 1577, were the principal architects of the petition. Barnewall in particular was singled out for orchestrating the mass signatures of the Pale gentry and acting as an agent between Netterville, Burnell and certain members of the Pale nobility. On account of their extreme age, Burnell and Netterville were confined to their homes but Barnewall and two leading members of the Irish peerage, Lords Gormanston and Dillon, were thrown into prison and fined severely by the Court of Castle Chamber.[21]

The Dublin administration upon consideration decided to treat Barnewall as the principal conspirator. Since Barnewall had received funds from a national collection enabling him to act in religious and 'civil matters for the general good and benefit of the whole kingdom', this decision was not without justification. The son of Henry VIII's Solicitor-General for Ireland, Barnewall was one of the principal landowners of the Pale, and his marriage to Mary Bagenal indicated a certain Gaelic connection as well – Mary's sister, Mabel, had eloped with the Earl of Tyrone from Barnewall's house in Tarbury in 1591, and Tyrone and Barnewall became, after a fashion, brothers-in-law. There was also a cloud over Barnewall's mixed academic background. Like a good English lawyer, he derived his legal training from the English Inns of Court, but information that he was 'the first gentlemen's son of quality that was ever put out of Ireland to be brought up in learning beyond the seas' suggested something of his Catholic sympathies.[22] Indeed, Davies' complaint in early June 1605 that Barnewall refused to recall his son from a Catholic school on the continent indicated that he had no intention of giving in to the new religion at all.[23] As a Catholic lawyer and landowner with Gaelic connections, Barnewall represented everything repugnant to full extension of New English rule in Ireland.

In combination with Lord Gormanston and several other Irish peers, Barnewall had the temerity to challenge the validity of the mandates 'wherein the Court of Castle Chamber, never before used as a spiritual consistory, was used to fine, imprison and deprive men of all offices and magistracies'.[24] In correspondence with Salisbury, Barnewall truculently affirmed that 'for the drawing of men into the Castle Chamber, the learned in the laws there affirm to be contrary to the law'.[25] He cited Sir James Ley, recently appointed Chief Justice of the King's Bench, as the author of the mandates strategy, complaining that Ley 'to the great scandal of justice, denieth men the copy of their indictments'.[26] Equally intemperate charges of brutality were levelled against local Dublin magistrates for forcing entry into private homes and violently distraining the goods and chattels of numerous citizens for failure to pay recusancy fines. Barnewall summarized these complaints with an ominous warning that 'such proceedings could only lay the foundation of some future rebellion'.[27]

Such indiscretion succeeded only in forcing an indictment in the Court of Castle Chamber. But in the presence of several Dublin aldermen and merchants who were also being prosecuted for their refusal to attend church, Barnewall continued his accusatory excesses. When admonished by his adversary, Chief Justice Ley, Barnewall responded by shouting at Ley to 'leave his carping and therwith struck the cushion before the Lord Deputy in Council, and held his hand there till he was reproved for it'.[28] This exchange inspired Lord Deputy Chichester to deliver a stinging rebuke:

No sir, we have endured the miserie of the war, we have lost our blood and our friends and have indeed endured extreme miseries to suppress the late rebellion whereof your priests for whom you make petition and your wicked religon was the principal cause.[29]

This charged dialogue demonstrates the seriousness of the confrontation and helps to explain the English Privy Council's subsequent decision to support the Dublin government by roundly punishing Barnewall in England. Heeding Davies' warning that the recusant party expected Barnewall to procure a reversal of the mandates, Salisbury assured the authorities in Dublin that Barnewall would not escape 'just reproof and punishment'.[30] Upon Barnewall's arrival at court, Salisbury promptly had him arrested and committed to the Tower. For a man who had seriously expected a favourable hearing, this cavalier treatment must have dealt a serious blow to Barnewall's hopes, and the humiliation was compounded by the ease with which the English Privy Council disposed of his objections to the mandates.

The Privy Councillors began first by dealing with Barnewall's impolitic complaints against Chief Justice Ley, assuring Chichester that such criticism represented in their minds little more than 'false and forward information'. They further instructed Chichester that Sir James Ley should under no circumstances depart Ireland to answer Barnewall's charges, because the 'same will be interpreted to your disgrace'.[31] Concerning the specific point of the legal principles involved in the controversial mandates policy, the English Privy Council solicited the advice of Davies and the Irish judiciary. Even Salisbury cynically instructed Chichester to provide a list of authorities in law or precedent to which 'we would have you send us some answer rather for forms sake than that we doubt of you being easily able to give us sufficient satisfaction'.[32] Attorney-General Davies ransacked the records of Dublin Castle to comply with Salisbury's directive while Chichester expressed the Dublin government's gratitude to Cecil, noting that Barnewall's imprisonment in the Tower 'greatly comforted the state'. Chichester further advised Salisbury of his decision to 'hold on our course with the recusants of this city and are hopeful to reform the multitude generallie'.[33]

In responding to Salisbury's request for a list of precedents to legitimize the mandates, Davies and the Irish judiciary laboured to avoid the thorny constitutional dilemma mentioned by Chief Justice Saxey in 1604. Saxey had pointed out that the late Elizabethan recusant statutes in England, particularly those expelling the recusant clergy and imposing the forfeiture of £20 a month for non-attendance at church, had no force in Ireland without the approval of the Irish parliament.[34] But for a man who would argue for the legislative autonomy of Ireland in the English parliament of 1621, it is not surprising to discover Davies constructing a brief circumventing the limitations of a defective Irish statute book. Davies and the Irish judges hit upon the stratagem of legitimizing the mandates by drawing upon the legal and theological literature arising from the conflict of church and state during the middle ages.

Davies declared that a prerogative court had every right to exercise jurisdiction over ecclesiastical affairs, because the English monarchy, as illustrated by the maxim 'Rex est mixta persona cum sacerdote,' had been caesaropapist from earliest times.[35] More convincing analogues were drawn from the investiture controversy and its aftermath. Citing the famous maxim from the medieval civilian, Baldus, that the king is absolute emperor in his realm, Davies recalled the statute of *praemunire* and the power of the king over the English church. Davies, in fact, delivered an oration presenting numerous legal precepts and statutes common to both England and Ireland documenting a hierarchical relationship between the English monarchy and God that served to circumvent the authority of the papacy. This approach permitted Davies to construct a coherent body of pre-Reformation legal principles derived from 'popish judges' to establish the Court of Castle Chamber's jurisdiction over the mandates in 1605.[36]

The Irish judges supplemented this argument by delivering their own opinion that the mandates served as a legitimate tool to enforce the royal prerogative. For evidence, the Irish justices also drew heavily on medieval precedents citing, for example, the case of Anselm, who suffered loss of all his goods and chattels for departing the realm against the royal mandate. Similarly in Edward II's time, the judges noted, John of Brittany's refusal to obey a royal mandate to return from a diplomatic mission was judged a treasonous offence. That monarch had also imprisoned an Abbot Oswald for disobeying a royal mandate to attend the English parliament. Such practice, argued the judges, was evident in more recent litigation. During the reign of Elizabeth, one Bellew, an Irishman, had conspired with an unnamed printer to publish an abridgement of law reports for the reign of Richard II. Since Queen Elizabeth had granted sole licence to print law books to Tothill, with express mandate excluding all others from printing the same, Bellew was fined and imprisoned by the English Court of Star Chamber.[37]

With historical antecedents to validate the use of mandates as a means to promote religious conformity in Ireland, the Irish justices went on to refute the curiously convoluted, if not illogical, argument put forth by the recusants, that if jurisdiction enforcing punishment for non-attendance at church pertained to the prerogative, then statutory proscription of recusancy was both redundant and invalid. To this argument the Irish judges responded that the English Court of Star Chamber itself exercised jurisdiction over many statutory offences. Hence the use of mandates issued to prominent Dublin officials to amplify the insufficient penalties imposed by the Irish Statute of Uniformity was perfectly consistent with English practice. As for Barnewall's objection that the issuing of mandates was 'against men's conscience and repugnant to the law', the judges developed a line of reasoning that paralleled the hierarchical relationship between church and state perceived by Davies.

Since the laws of God and parliament compelled attendance at church services, the justices concluded, the policy of enforcing attendance at church by royal mandate rendered a favour to all Irish recusants, because they were bound 'sub poena damnationis deponere conscientam illam tanquam erroneam'. The mandates merely reflected, said the justices, the benevolent concern of the state to put Old English Catholics out of their state of damnation.[38] Nor could the exception of conscience be allowed, because the Bishop of Rome himself had yet to issue a decretal outlining the canonical and doctrinal implications of such a position. Therefore the recusant petitioners were required to submit their conscience to the 'wisdom of their magistrates and commandment of the law'.[39]

Emphasis upon domestic Irish statutes and precedents prior to the Reformation as a means to side-step the constitutional issue of extending English statutes to Ireland was in itself a clever device. But its strength was doubled when it received confirmation by way of a judicial resolution formulated by the English justices, certified by the Lord Chief Justice Popham, and returned to Ireland as formally approved by the English government. On 31 December 1606, the English Privy Council signified its assent to the controversial mandates programme by informing Chichester and the Irish Privy Council:

Concerning Sir Patrick Barnewall, the greatest judges of England being made acquainted with the reason and authority lately sent by the chief justice and the rest justifying their sending of privy seals for reducing men to outward conformity have delivered their opinion that the same is no way contrary to law nor to precedent and authority.[40]

The authority of judicial resolutions in early modern jurisprudence has been developed elsewhere in this volume. Obviously, the resolution of the English judges validating the legal principles put forward by Davies and the Irish judges helped the Dublin government to evade the constitutional problem over the validity of English penal statutes in Ireland. Having thwarted the attack of the colonial community, the English Privy Council returned Barnewall to Ireland where he was forced to yield his 'ample submission and acknowledgement in writing of his offense in Ireland to the Lord Deputy and the Irish Privy Council'.[41]

III

The humiliation of Barnewall and the validation of the prerogative mandates through pre-Reformation legal doctrine provide a context to examine other litigation before the Irish Court of King's Bench. For instance, the arrest and indictment of Robert Lalor, a recusant priest, on a charge of *praemunire* fell within the legal principles laid down by the English and Irish justices in the Barnewall affair. As a 'notable seducer of the people and alleged Vicar-General of Dublin, Kildare and Fernes', Lalor had been active in fomenting trouble in the vicinity of Dublin.[42] For eight months after the appearance of the royal proclamation expelling the Catholic clergy from the realm, Lalor succeeded in evading arrest by going to ground in the precincts of Dublin. There, under the protection of friends, he continued to carry out his clandestine activities until February 1606 when, at the height of the mandates controversy, he was betrayed by a servant and promptly arrested by Sir Oliver Lambert, the Provost Marshall of Dublin.[43]

Interrogation by his captors exposed a background that was

typical of many recusant clergymen in Ireland. According to several dispatches filed by Chichester and Davies to the English Privy Council, Lalor's career began in 1579 when Richard Brady, titular Bishop of Kilmore, ordained him a priest. Years later, Mathew de Oviedo, the titular Archbishop of Armagh, who accompanied the Spanish army to Kinsale, elevated Lalor to the archdiocese of Dublin, Kildare and Fernes.[44] Of particular interest to Davies was Lalor's close association with the Pale gentry and nobility, and further investigation revealed that Lalor was 'feofee in trust' to the greater part of the earldom of Kildare and the barony of Delvin, and that 'sundry gentlemen had also sued liveries before him.'[45] This improvident dabbling with the temporal affairs of the gentry played into the hands of Davies and Chichester, who adroitly employed Lalor's timely arrest as a counterblow to the unrest stirred up by Barnewall and the Pale gentry over the mandates.

Lalor, however, wisely decided to co-operate with the state and readily confessed the unlawful exercise of a foreign jurisdiction. When pressed with Suarez' troublesome doctrine over the Pope's power to excommunicate and depose heretic monarchs, Lalor prudently denied such authority for the simple reason that James I was not a Catholic prince.[46] This distinction failed to impress the court which convicted Lalor and sentenced him to one year's imprisonment and loss of property under the Irish statute of 2 Elizabeth for maintaining and upholding the civil and religious jurisdiction of a foreign prince or prelate. After two terms of imprisonment, Lalor petitioned the Lord Deputy for release, agreeing in the meantime to acknowledge the royal supremacy and to submit a written confession admitting his earlier transgressions. Apparently convinced by Lalor's change in religious conviction, Chichester ordered the priest's release from prison, only to find that Lalor's supporters within the precincts of Dublin had deliberately misconstrued this liberal gesture as a recusant victory for religous toleration in Ireland. Lalor himself was reported to have denied 'giving any ground in admitting royal jurisdiction over spiritual cases', maintaining instead that he had merely acknowledged the English monarch's authority in civil and temporal matters, not in spiritual affairs.[47] This repudiation of what had actually occurred during his first arrest represented, like the confrontations with Skelton and Barnewell, another attempt to test the government's will to establish outward adherence to the Protestant religion among the colonial elite.

In response, Chichester had Lalor rearrested, indicting the priest on the more serious charge of *praemunire*. An important weapon in the contest with the papacy during the late middle ages, the statute of *praemunire*, common to both England and Ireland, allowed the government to punish any persons suing actions outside the realm without royal approval.[48] In the sixteenth century the scope of the statute had been considerably broadened, and during the Elizabethan period was to provide the basis for a variety of legal actions, not only against recusants, but as a tool available to the common lawyers to prevent or defeat judgements in any one of the non-common law jurisdictions in England.[49] Assigned to the case of Lalor, Davies decided to apply the statute in its original context, and to charge Lalor with attributing ecclesiastical or temporal jurisdiction in Ireland to foreign powers. The government's pursuit of Robert Lalor, it should again be noted, conforms to the strategy of prosecuting recusancy with pre-Reformation statutes as laid down in the judicial resolution validating the mandates.

The details of the government's brief against Lalor are too lengthy to develop here, but Davies' *Reports* reveal a style of pleading consistent with previous litigation over the mandates. Beginning with a long historical disquisition demonstrating the superiority of temporal authority over ecclesiastical affairs, Davies went on to establish the existence of an independent English national church that ran from Anglo-Saxon times to his own day. The Attorney-General drew further evidence from the investiture controversy, citing numerous legal precepts, maxims and case-precedents limiting papal jurisdiction. Davies paid particular attention to appeals from the various ecclesiastical courts or controversies arising over the disposition of ecclesiastical revenue. All these laws, Davies stated, especially the statutes of provisors and *praemunire*, were passed by 'good Catholics or good subjects against the Pope', and were, by virtue of the Irish statute of 10 Henry VII c. 22, 'established and made of force in Ireland'.[50] With the legal grounds laid for the case against Lalor, Davies went on to deliver a stinging harangue against the recusant party.

So now master Lalor you have no excuse, no evasion; but your conscience must condemn you as well as the law; since the lawmakers in all ages and all religious papists and Protestants do condemn you. Unless you think yourself wiser than all the bishops that were then in England or all the judges who were learned in the civil and canon laws, as well as in the common law of England.[51]

Armed with the statutory weapons to justify Lalor's indictment, Davies produced a damning collection of evidence to procure Lalor's conviction on a charge of *praemunire*. This evidence included various letters and papers in Lalor's hand showing institution of 'popish priests to benefices', and, more significantly, Lalor's earlier confession for having violated the Irish Acts of Uniformity and Supremacy during the previous year.[52]

In his defence Lalor attempted to deny any wrongdoing, claiming that he had accepted the Catholic office of Vicar-General, 'virtute obedientiae', only to render obedience to his superior in Rome. In other words, argued Lalor, the office had been forced upon him, implying that his jurisdiction was exercised *in foro conscientiae tantum* and not *in foro judicii*.[53] Davies' rejoinder to this extraordinary defence easily rivalled and surpassed Lalor's own splitting of hairs. First, argued Davies, any office upholding a foreign jurisdiction could never be virtuous or obedient. Furthermore, Lalor's previous confession clearly superseded any plea of conscience, a point which Davies readily drove home by ordering Lalor's confession read aloud before a courtroom packed with eager recusant supporters who must have sensed that Lalor was not a 'little abashed at the publishing of this acknowledgement and confession'.[54]

Lalor attempted to deny telling friends and supporters that he had rejected the royal supremacy during his previous arrest and confinement. Rather, he declared, he refused to accept the king's supremacy in 'causes ecclesiastical but not causes spiritual'.[55] Anticipating this typical distinction, Davies demanded an explanation of the difference between causes spiritual and ecclesiastical, only to be met with a rather lame request for further time to prepare an answer. Davies, however, doggedly persisted in his attack in language consistent with his aggressive and occasionally imperious nature.

Nay we can never speake of it a better time or fitter place. And therefore, though you that beare soe reverend a title and hold the reputation of soe great a clarke, require further time, yet shall you hear that wee laymen that serve his majestie, and by the duty of our places and to maintain the jurisdiction of the crowne, are not so unprovided but that we can say somewhat ex tempore touching the matter and difference of these causes.[56]

Davies' extensively researched and well-wrought brief demonstrating the absence of any distinction between the terms spiritual and ecclesiastical belied this modest avowal. During the late Roman empire, Davies pointed out, all spiritual and ecclesiastical jurisdiction was delegated 'by the emperor and civil magistrates by rules of the imperial laws', because the canon law 'was not then dreamt of'.[57] In other words, the terms 'spiritual' and 'ecclesiastical' had been interchangeable words referring to a jurisdiction belonging to the civil power, a relationship that was resumed during the Reformation by a Protestant national church. Therefore, Davies concluded, the establishment of the king's ecclesiastical law represented little more than a resumption of original jurisdiction that had been usurped by the Bishop of Rome. Having witnessed the demolition of Lalor's defence, the jury left the courtroom and returned, within an hour, to deliver a verdict of guilty. Maximum punishment was imposed and Lalor was sentenced to forfeiture of all property and to life imprisonment.[58]

In summarizing the case to Salisbury, Davies trumpeted the state's achievement, claiming that Lalor's conviction on a charge of *praemunire* was the first ever recorded in Ireland. Davies took particular satisfaction that the verdict arose from clear evidence presented before a courtroom packed with the Vicar-General's supporters. Lalor's defeat, continued Davies, 'hath bred terror among the principal gentlemen of the Pale' who, having sued liveries and taken various dispensations from Lalor, were also subject to the penalties imposed by the same statute.[59] In other words lands held by Lalor were subject in law to forfeiture on his conviction. As said before, Lalor's conviction conformed to the general pattern of prosecuting recusancy through pre-Reformation statutes laid down by the English and Irish judiciaries in the mandates crisis. But Lalor's lands and possessions had also been voided, and his clients cut adrift. This sort of punishment also supplied the Dublin government with another tool to secure the outward conformity of Old English recusants residing in the towns and the Pale.

Orthodox historians have taken a peculiar stance in assessing the mandates controversy and the cases of Barnewall and Lalor.[60] They have denied both the validity and the success of the government's attempt to disrupt the colonial community's optimistic assumption that adherence to an outlawed religion was perfectly consistent with loyalty to the state. According to this view, the protest of the Pale orchestrated by Barnewall forced the English Privy Council to restrain the Irish administration from further punitive action against officials in the towns. In other words London had humiliated the Dublin government by forcing it to moderate its actions. It would be difficult, however, to cast doubt on the general validity of the legal principles employed to prosecute Barnewall, Lalor and other lay and ecclesiastical persons for recusancy. What has been interpreted as official displeasure with the mandates arose not from proceedings in Dublin, but from the excesses associated with Brouncker's administration of the mandates in Munster. When the English Privy Council proposed in 1607 to substitute a policy of selective repression for gradual conversion, it was Brouncker's excessive zeal in Munster that was criticized, not the Irish Privy Council's attack on Barnewall and the Pale gentry.[61] Support for the policy pursued in Dublin is easily documented in the English Privy Council's instructions to Chichester on 30 April 1606:

We do very well approve of your proceedings towards particular persons, whom you find contemptuous and seditious especially some as profess it so factiously as they make themselves procurators for multitudes, avowe harboring of priests, and in a word so publicly refused that outward obedience and respect to governors and officers of authority.[62]

The milder policy of evangelism and conversion must not be interpreted as a sign of weakness. In any future conflicts with the colonial community over religious policy, the English Privy Council advised the Dublin government and the Munster Presidency that where any 'public affront is offered, by a notorious disobedience and of pernicious example to draw others, the authority of state alloweth in discretion extraordinary punishment'.[63] Despite the appearance of equivocation, both the provincial Presidency Courts and the central courts in Dublin were to continue 'without too much strayning of the laws of the kingdom' the policy of selective repression aimed at securing the appearance of religious conformity among leading Old English officials.[64] This policy, which was designed as the necessary prelude to the mass conversion of colonial society, continued in the towns up to a year after Barnewall's release from the Tower.[65]

After the flight of the earls in September 1607, there arose an understandable desire, in unstable political circumstances, to preserve the 'good affection of the towns unto his Majestie' – a policy that was sustained, at least for a time, by improved relations with Spain.[66] And, of course, it must be conceded that the government's concerted attempt to secure the outward conformity of Old English leadership in the towns and in the Pale did not result in the mass conversion of the colonial community. But the message delivered by the resolution of the English judges certifying the extension of English penal laws through prerogative mandates based on pre-Reformation legal principles supplied by the Irish judges was very clear. The older political equation that relied upon England to continue its policy of *de facto* toleration of Catholicism in the towns and the Pale was now obsolete. The co-operation of the towns had been instrumental in ensuring the survival of English rule in Ireland, but the mandates controversy and the case of Robert Lalor should have made it strikingly evident to the colonial community that it would not share in the fruits of the victory in which it had played so vital a part.

7

The case of customs payable for merchandise

The English government's attempt to secure religious conformity among leading officials in the Pale and the port towns of Munster proved to be only one phase in its assault on the Old English community in Ireland. During the same period, Davies and the central authorities waged a systematic campaign against the cherished liberties and privileges that had allowed the port municipalities to operate independently of royal control. This jurisdictional autonomy was to be tested in Waterford's refusal to admit the Lord Deputy to the town, on the authority of a charter granted to King John.

The most valued of the municipal privileges involved the granting of a right to customs revenues, and the appointment of customs officials, normally reserved to the crown. The size of the economic stakes at issue was considerable. It is understandable, then, that the government's attempt to eliminate corporate privilege also owed something to the designs of Robert Cecil and a clique of London-based entrepreneurs who proved more than willing to manipulate state policy in furtherance of their own commercial interests.[1]

To appreciate these jurisdictional and commercial currents, it is necessary to discuss several aspects of municipal liberties. First, the towns had played a determining role in the successful outcome achieved by the aggressive Elizabethan policy of conquest and colonization in Ireland. Second, corporate liberties and franchises had long operated independently of government control. Third, the arguments propounded by Davies against Waterford were to be pivotal, since the decision in the case was to be applied subsequently to the rest of the Old English port towns.

I

The wholesale transfer of crown rights to the port towns began with Sir Henry Sydney's successful campaign (1565–75) to expand

English influence beyond the narrow boundaries of the English Pale. Sydney more than his predecessors viewed the allegiance and security of the Old English towns as vital to an aggressive policy towards the Gaelic interior. As he noted in a letter to the queen on 20 April 1567, the loss of the port towns would be tantamount to losing the whole of Ireland.[2] Sydney's political equation linking the allegiance of the towns to the security of Ireland received confirmation from one of the more succinct maxims of sixteenth-century Irish municipal history:

The corporate towns are the strength and sinews of the commonwealth in times of war and the ornaments of the commonwealth in times of peace and if these fail then the commonwealth decays.[3]

Throughout the sixteenth century urban Ireland, unlike the rest of the territory, maintained its allegiance to the crown. As citadels of English influence in the bog of civil strife and barbarism, the towns functioned as assembly areas for tactical operations against the interior, frequently providing military, logistical and financial support to a hard-pressed English government. As the most recent historian of Sydney's deputyship has shown, the perception that a successful Irish policy depended upon the loyalty of the port towns was to prove accurate.[4]

By the end of the century, however, Sir John Davies and other observers began to look askance at the favoured status granted to the towns. Municipal loyalty, they complained frequently, had not been obtained without a price. Apart from extensive jurisdictional liberties which guaranteed them almost full independence, the towns had acquired through charter, statute or prescription control of all customs appointments and of customs revenue normally due to the crown. Davies asserted that the customs revenue had been detained by the towns for over a hundred years. To illustrate the dilapidated state of the customs administration, Davies examined the Irish pipe rolls lodged in the Bermingham tower in Dublin:

Wherein the accounts of customs are contained, and found those duties answered in every port for 250 years together, but did not find that at any time they did exceed £1,000 per annum – and no marvel, for the subsidy of poundage was not then known and the greatest profit did arise from the cocket of hides, for wool and woolfels were ever of little value in that kingdom.[5]

Davies was not alone in his condemnation of the privileges the port towns had acquired. Even before the end of the Nine Years War, highly placed figures within the Irish administration had expressed

serious doubts about official policy towards the municipalities. In
1592 a royal commission had studied the nature of Irish corporate
privilege, and angrily criticized the exorbitant liberties and franchises of the Irish ports, pointing out that the cities of Ireland enjoyed
a status more favourable than that granted to any English muni-
cipality.[6] Even so, Sir Anthony St Leger, a Munster servitor,
informed the English Privy Council in 1599 that the loyalty of the
towns could not be taken for granted. As a protective measure, St
Leger advised the construction of Fort Haulbowline, which was
subsequently demolished by the irate citizenry in the Munster
disturbances of 1603.[7] St Leger's observation, in combination with
events in Cork during the Munster rising, records an increasingly
uneasy relationship between the central government and the corporation.

Following the defeat of the Spaniards at Kinsale, criticism of the
towns became more frequent. Sir George Carew, Lord President of
Munster, informed Robert Cecil and the English Privy Council in
January 1602 that the structure of corporate privilege in Ireland was
detrimental to the queen's service.[8] By March 1602, Carew refused a
petition by the freemen of Cork to enlarge their existing liberties, a
decision later endorsed by the queen. Petitioned by the citizens of
Kinsale to renew their charter, the English Privy Council, in general
references to all the port towns, irately informed Sir George Carew
that the liberties and franchises bestowed on the towns were both
'immoderate and inconvenient' for the proper administration of
efficient government.[9] This obvious displeasure undoubtedly
rippled through official circles in Dublin. Fynes Moryson, secretary
to Lord Deputy Mountjoy, remarked that Mountjoy, despite his
moderate dealings with the towns in 1603, intended to 'procure the
cutting off of many exorbitant privileges in the renewing of their
charters'.[10] Mountjoy's subsequent removal from the Irish scene and
premature death did not diminish the threatened assault upon municipal privilege. The colossal Irish war debt incurred by Tyrone's
rebellion soon prompted an impecunious English government to
cast a covetous eye on the long-neglected customs administration
appropriated by the various towns. Although the towns had provided the necessary counterweight to subdue the restive natives, the
fiscal imperatives of the English government made it doubtful that
the extensive municipal privileges would survive the Tudor
conquest.

The government's assault on the privileged status of the Irish towns must be viewed in conjunction with the commercial interests that first suggested the move to reorganize the Irish customs. This projected reform paralleled changes in English customs administration during the same period. English officials concluded in 1604 that direct government administration of the customs had been less rewarding than farming the customs out to private individuals. As a result, the English customs were leased to a circle of London merchants headed by Francis Jones, Nicholas Salter and William Garway for a rent of £112,000, a sum increased in 1607 to £120,000.[11] This consolidation of the English customs undoubtedly provided a model for a similar scheme for Ireland, and on Christmas Day of 1604 Arthur Ingram, the controller of the customs for the port of London, began negotiations for a farm of the Irish customs based on the English pattern. Ingram, who had been actively involved in negotiations for the farm of the English customs, enjoyed a close association with Lionel Cranfield. Both had earlier dealings with maritime traffic in the port of London, and both men had a personal interest in the Irish project. This interest received strong support from Robert Cecil, who then emerged as a central figure in the plan to divest the Irish towns of their extensive privileges.[12] Cecil's role was confirmed by John Bingley, Chief Remembrancer of the Irish Exchequer. Writing thirty-four years after the event, Bingley recalled to Ingram how Cecil had laboured to effect a new administration that would add vigour to the moribund system of customs collection in Ireland. As Bingley remembered it, he had informed

the late noble Earl of Salisbury of the little custom that Ireland paid to the crown, they were exceeding glad and strove how to improve them and had many conferences with you about it.[13]

Bingley's letter makes it clear that Cecil, as in the religious mandates policy, played a significant role in determining policy towards the towns.

In 1604, therefore, it was clear that an official enquiry into the long-neglected status of the Irish customs was in the offing. This investigation was hastened by a bid to farm the Irish customs by a clique of London speculators that included Arthur Ingram, Lionel Cranfield and Ingram's patron, the Earl of Nottingham.[14] In the autumn of 1606, a study carried out on behalf of Cecil and the English Privy Council by Sir Thomas Ridgeway, Irish Treasurer at War, revealed that the net customs revenue did not exceed £200 per annum. Ridgeway attributed this dismal return partly to the vicissitudes of war which had severely restricted international trade with England and Spain, and partly to inefficient administration of the Irish Exchequer. In Ridgeway's estimation, however, the most serious difficulty arose over the extensive privileges and liberties of the port towns. This last problem, he felt, could only be overcome by parliamentary statute. In fact, it was extremely unlikely that an Irish parliament would ever provide the necessary consensus to legislate against the liberties of the port towns.[15]

II

Inspired by a prediction from Ridgeway that the collection of Irish customs could be increased to over £10,000 per annum, the English Privy Council informed Lord Deputy Chichester that the king intended to establish a consolidated farm of the Irish customs, and that two agents, Robert Cogan and Thomas Waad, had been authorized to carry out an enquiry of all corporations claiming exemptions from customs duties.[16] Cogan was connected with the clothworkers' syndicate in London and was a kinsman to Ingram, while Waad, an associate of Ingram, had been involved in business dealings with Cranfield in the farm of the English tobacco duties. Both Cogan and Waad later became shareholders in the farm of the Irish customs, and Cogan himself served as the first Surveyor-General of the Irish customs at a fee of £100 per annum, a reward no doubt for the thorough investigation carried out in 1607.[17]

On the job for only a short time between March and June 1607, Cogan and Waad quickly discovered an appalling alienation of crown rights in the various Irish ports. In the southern towns the investigators noted that the ports of New Ross, Wexford, Waterford, Cork, Dungannon, Kinsale, Dingle, Youghal and Limerick all claimed exemption from customs duties through charter or prescription and that none had paid any revenue since the reign of Henry V. In smaller ports scattered throughout Ireland, such as Strangford, Ardglass, Sligo, Baltimore, Crookhaven, Wicklow, Arklow and the Skerries, none had paid any revenue for years and all claimed exemption by either charter or prescription. In still other ports, the administration of the customs revenue had been granted to a handful of servitors and local officials at extraordinarily low rents. In Dublin, the farm of the Irish customs, by the end of Elizabeth's reign, had fallen into the hands of the Grimsditch family for a rent of £173 6s 8d

Irish. In Drogheda, the customs were leased by John Bingley at a rent of £104 2s Irish. In the north, the customs of Carrickfergus were taken up by Roger Longford at a rent of £10 sterling. The ports of Derry and Ballyshannon, newly created in 1604, were leased to another servitor, Richard Bingley, at £1 6s 6d Irish. In Dundalk, the customs were leased to a former military man, Rice Ap-Hugh, for £5 Irish. The port of Carlingford, long considered part of the Bagenal inheritance, was held by that family in fee simple, and in the west the port of Galway was leased to the Mayor and commonalty for a rent of £36 12s 6d sterling.[18]

In summarizing the results of their investigation, Cogan and Waad concluded that customs revenue for the four years since the accession of James had yielded a total gross revenue of only £554 which, after deducting salaries and expenses, left a residual net income of only £238.[19] What little revenue the crown derived from the Irish ports came only from poundage paid on prohibited goods traded under licence, the petty custom levied on merchant strangers, and the custom of a few native commodities such as timber, hides and furs that were unregulated by the Trade Acts of 1569–71. Thomas Ridgeway, who collated the findings of Cogan and Waad's researches, drew attention once again to the hindrance of existing corporate privilege, commenting in particular on the exemption from poundage granted to the freemen of Dublin, Waterford and Drogheda by the Poundage Act of 1500. Ridgeway also declared that the benefit of the customs revenue and the control of the officers appointed to collect such customs had, in the majority of cases, been appropriated by the towns, frequently by the authority of royal charter.[20]

Of all the towns, however, Waterford, with its profitable deep-water port and strong chartered privileges, stood out as the worst offender. Situated on the south-east coast, Waterford was second only to Dublin in the volume of trade in its port. Throughout its history, Waterford had remained steadfast to the crown, and when the Anglo-Norman colony threw its support behind the Yorkist pretenders, Simnel and Warbeck, in the late fifteenth century, the city refused to join the conspiracy. A grateful crown in return rewarded the city with the title *urbs intacta*.[21] But the devotion of Waterford, as Mountjoy discovered in 1603, had proved inconsistent with the title granted by the first Tudor king. As a renegade city, moreover, Waterford had a great deal to lose, for over the years the corporation had acquired the right to collect the great custom, the small custom, the subsidy of poundage and the right to appoint a customer or collector of the customs, a controller of the customs, and a searcher/gauger.[22]

The government began its assault in May 1607 by instructing Davies to set up *quo warranto* proceedings against the corporations of Waterford and Drogheda. From a collection of crown briefs currently lodged in the British Library and a fragmentary transcript of a King's Bench plea roll in Dublin, we know that Davies also initiated proceedings against the corporations of Dublin, Limerick, Kinsale, Youghal and Dungarvan.[23] The opening blow, however, was aimed at Waterford. Before exploring this litigation it will prove useful to review the kinds of duties levied upon Irish trade during the sixteenth and early seventeenth centuries.

Apart from Dr V. R. Treadwell's thesis on the administration of Irish customs in the early seventeenth century, the best account is still to be found in Davies' *Reports*. Indeed Davies' research into the Irish pipe rolls and other records then extant in the Bermingham tower in Dublin was so thorough that medieval historians have yet to alter his basic conclusions. In his report of the case against Waterford, Davies enumerated the several types of customs and subsidies levied on merchandise in Ireland. The most important of these imposts were the great custom, the petty custom and the subsidy of poundage.[24]

The great custom, introduced into Ireland by a writ of Edward I, represented a standard levy on the principal exports of wool, wool-fells and hides. This levy consisted of 6s 8d for each sack of wool of 364 lb. and for every 300 wool-fells, and 3s 4d for a last of hides, counting 200 to the last, on all exports shipped abroad by English subjects, with an added duty of one-third of the above rates to be paid by aliens.[25] The petty custom, established in Ireland during the early fourteenth century, imposed an additional duty of 3d in the pound on the imports and exports of all aliens.

By far the most valuable source of customs revenue was the subsidy of poundage, a 5 per cent *ad valorem* duty placed on all imports and exports. The original purpose of Irish poundage differed considerably from its English counterpart. English poundage was appropriated by the crown, while Irish poundage, established by statute in 1474, had been devised to support a special paramilitary group known as the fraternity of St George.[26] This corporate body, consisting of thirteen landowners of the Pale, was to protect the ever-shrinking boundaries of English influence from incursions by the Gaelic Irish. Exemptions from payment had been granted, however. In 1474 Waterford and Drogheda were freed from paying poundage on hides and other commodities, an exemption extended the following year to all residents of the Pale who made other contributions to the defence of the colony.[27] Poynings' parliament dissolved the fraternity in 1495, but the levy of poundage, formerly collected by the fraternity, was appropriated by the government with exemptions from payment granted to the freemen of Dublin, Waterford and Drogheda.[28] In 1500 the crown had secured an Act for the grant of poundage in perpetuity, but due to unsettled conditions it confirmed the privileged exemption formerly granted to the freemen of Dublin, Waterford and Drogheda.[29] Wine escaped effective taxation until 1569, as Treadwell has shown. Prisage, consisting of a levy of 1 tun of wine in every cargo of 9 to 19 tuns, was collected by the earls of Ormonde and yielded only a very small sum to the state. Tunnage, a duty granted out of every tun of wine imported, remained unknown in Ireland until 1608.[30]

The piecemeal alienation of customs revenue was aggravated by the loss of government control over the appointment of patentee officers in the various ports. These administrators, whose presence gave a port official status, included: the customer/collector who had the authority to receive revenue, keep accounts and to certify the loading or unloading of all shipping under warrant of the port coquet seal; the controller who kept a parallel account as a check on the customer; a searcher/packer/gauger who examined cargoes and certified goods liable to duty to the customer; tide waiters who were required to keep watch on ships awaiting permission to break bulk, and land waiters who attended onshore cargo.[31]

In England, the authority to appoint these officials rested with the Lord Treasurer whose warrant served as lawful authority. In Ireland, the situation was somewhat different. The Irish Lord Treasurer theoretically possesed the same power as his English counterpart, but the realities of Irish practice meant that the Lord Deputy appointed customs officials under authority of the Great Seal. Twice during the sixteenth century, in 1589 and 1594, the Irish Lord Treasurer, the Earl of Ormonde, attempted to resurrect his latent powers of appointment, but this questionable endeavour was confined solely to the ports of Dublin and Drogheda.[32] The rest of the towns had, during the course of the sixteenth century, acquired effective control of all customs appointments.[33]

These then were the most significant customs revenues and

appointment powers appropriated by Waterford and other major ports during the course of the late middle ages and during the reign of the Tudors. Waterford, which possessed the strongest privileges, was selected as a test case. By 1 July 1607 Davies was to refer contemptuously to the feeble defences offered by the towns, and he predicted a quick victory for the crown.[34] Taking Davies' estimate to heart, the English Privy Council on 6 August 1607 informed Chichester that no corporations were to have their charters renewed until Davies determined the full extent of crown rights by *quo warranto* against Waterford.[35] Thomas Ridgeway, the Treasurer at War, was less sanguine and stated to Dorset on 3 June 1607 that some of the towns were building a defence on charters antecedent to the Poundage Act of 1500, and that Waterford had presented a case so strong that the crown would be fortunate to gain more than the petty custom on strangers.[36]

III

The *quo warranto* proceedings against Waterford were opened before the Irish Court of King's Bench during Michaelmas term 1607. The enquiry sought to determine the validity of the city's claim to the great and small custom and the subsidy of poundage, and of their claim to appoint a customer, collector, controller and searcher/gauger within the port. In its rejoinder, the city pleaded its several charters, the first of which dated from the reign of King John.[37] This charter, which caused so much trouble for Mountjoy in 1603, had granted extensive jurisdictional autonomy, as well as the custom of murage and of all commodities bought and sold 'sicut Burgesses villae suae de Bristol habebant'. By a second charter, dated 6 May 1 Henry V, the city had expanded its privileges through a royal grant of the coquet customs.[38] By virtue of a third charter, dated 12 May 3 Henry VII, the citizens had received a further grant exempting them from the custom of poundage.[39] These claims had been strengthened by a fourth charter, dated 8 February 11 Elizabeth, which granted to the corporation the authority to appoint a searcher/gauger and other 'usual necessary officials' to attend the administration of the customs. Thus the corporation chose to sanction the appointment of a customer and controller, being necessary officers to administer the coquet custom granted by the charter of 1 Henry V.[40] Against this formidable accretion of rights and privileges, Attorney-General Davies demurred, attempting to demonstrate that the exemptions claimed by the corporation on the basis of its four charters represented a gross misinterpretation of the powers actually conferred upon the city.

As with other cases in the *Reports*, Davies buttressed his argument with citations from Roman law sources. The crown's prerogative right to the customs revenue, for example, was based upon principles found in the *Corpus Iuris Civilis* of Justinian. In the apparent absence of common law principles, Davies' proof developed along lines consistent with the arguments he had used to justify a prerogative right to impositions set fourth in an earlier treatise on government finance in England.[41] The authority to regulate trade, said Davies in the case against Waterford, sprang from the *ius gentium* and the Law Merchant which, separate from the common law, developed to the crown by prerogative right. To illustrate this claim, Davies drew attention to the legal history of Rome, citing the following passage which he ascribed to Justinian's *corpus*: 'Vectigal origina jus caesarum & regum patrimoniale est.'[42] On the basis of this text of the Roman law, Davies sustained a prerogative right to collect the customs revenue because 'the rules of our law are agreeable to those of the imperial law'. He further declared that the Roman law foundation of this English 'jus caesarum' could not be faulted, for the simple reason that the levy of English customs lacked the severity of customs duties imposed by the monarchs of Turkey, France, Tuscany and Spain.[43]

In dealing with the more specific powers granted to the city of Waterford by each of the four charters, Davies adopted a rather different tactic that attempted to invalidate the charters on more narrow legal grounds. Pleading against the first charter granted by King John awarding murage to the English city of Bristol, Davies convinced the court that murage amounted to nothing more than a toll payment for the repair of city walls taken from retail sales in the city market, not from the import and export trade conducted in the harbour. Moreover, murage could not be conferred by grant, he asserted, but only by prescription. As for the clause referring to Bristol, Davies noted that it was necessary for the corporation to aver a certain toll or custom at the time of the grant – a certainty conspicuously absent in the mention of Bristol in Waterford's charter. Davies also pointed out that the corporation of Bristol, lying outside the kingdom of Ireland, could not serve as a valid plea for corporate rights in Ireland, because Ireland was a kingdom distinct from England.[44]

Against the charter of 6 Henry V granting the coquet custom – a levy collected for validating payment of customs duties – Davies found himself on weaker ground. In presenting the crown's case, Davies objected that the coquet represented only a bill validating the payment of customs duties 'so the merchant is de custuma quietus'.[45] The general words implied in the city's charter, Davies argued, could never alienate the great custom, it 'being a special inheritance of the crown'.[46] It appears that agents of the corporation then made the rejoinder that the express words of the charter conferring 'custumam vocatum the coquet' sustained the corporation's plea for the great custom. In the end, the judges upheld the city's claim, understanding coquet to imply the great custom on wool, wool-fells and leather, but they ruled that the petty custom of 3d in the pound on the merchandise of aliens, as an ancient heritage of the crown, did not pass to the city by the express words of the charter.[47]

Conceding that the express words of the charter exempted the city from payment of poundage, the judges proceeded to declare that the grant of exemption did not allow the corporation to collect for their own use the poundage of all merchant denizens and aliens. They further noted that the Act of Resumption of 10 Henry VII subjected all merchants, denizens and aliens to payment of poundage, saving those specifically exempted by the Act.[48]

The defects found in the charters of Henry V and Henry VII enabled the judges to question the appointment of customs officials allegedly conveyed by the charter of 8 February 11 Elizabeth. Since the pleading over the charter of Henry V and Henry VII maintained a crown right both to the petty custom and to poundage, the charter of 11 Elizabeth could not be interpreted to imply the right of municipal officials to collect the revenue of the crown. Accordingly, the judges resolved that the charter allowing the appointment of a 'searcher/gauger and other officers and ministers whatsoever' could not be allowed.[49] This privilege, they argued, in the absence of a lawful claim to collect the petty custom and the levy of poundage, rendered municipal appointments unnecessary.

Such were the arguments offered by the state to impose a prerogative right to the Irish customs revenue, and it is clear from the *Reports* that the court was on the verge of agreeing with the pleas outlined by Davies. A final verdict from the Irish Court of King's Bench, however, was never obtained. Official impatience in Westminster with the time-consuming litigation, in combination with pressure from private commercial interests, led to a most extra-ordinary step. The *quo warranto* proceedings were taken out of the hands of the Irish courts and assigned to a special deliberating body at Serjeants' Inn in London.[50]

The impetus of this action came in part from the same group of speculators who had been angling for a share of the reformed Irish customs all along. During November 1607, at the height of the *quo warranto* proceedings against Waterford and the other towns, Lord Nottingham and his son had received a grant of £3,000 for seven years out of the Irish customs.[51] This eleemosynary largesse, drawn on account from an inchoate customs administration, undoubtedly reflected official optimism over Davies' prediction of a quick victory before the Irish courts. Events in Dublin, however, must have moved too slowly, despite the fact that Henry Hobart, the English Attorney-General, and John Foster, learned Serjeant-at-Law, had been dispatched by the English Privy Council to aid the preparation in the legal assault on the port municipalities.[52] Advised by Davies, the English Privy Council had pressed home its attack. On 14 November 1607, Chichester and the Irish Privy Council were informed that the pleas at Waterford and the rest of the towns were 'utterly insufficient in law and that their grants also are of no validity to give unto them the subsidy of tonnage and poundage which they claim by the same'.[53] The Privy Council had further instructed Chichester to inform the towns that unless they yielded their claims to the various customs duties, the municipalities would be charged with arrearages that would 'lye very heavy and burdensome upon them'.[54] These threats had undoubtedly owed something to the intrigues of the private sector. Despite all of these pressures, the pleadings in Dublin dragged slowly on. Out of personal anxiety for his pension of £3,000 per annum from the Irish customs, Nottingham testily complained to Salisbury on 4 June 1608 about the corrupt officials in Dublin who prevented an end to the litigious proceedings before the Irish courts.[55]

The cumulative impact of official displeasure at the recalcitrance of the port towns and the pressures of private interests finally compelled the English Privy Council to the extraordinary recourse of assembling elements of both the English and Irish judiciaries at Serjeants' Inn in London in order to issue an authoritative collective decision on the matter. Noting the great 'offence and distaste taken by the various port towns of Ireland taken against them by quo warranto', the English Privy Council referred the case to London for a 'further trial by the judgement of the chief judges of this land'.[56]

The strategy of effecting change by judicial resolution, now familiar from the earlier discussion of cases in Davies' *Reports*, conforms in tone and style to those procedures outlined in Professor W. J. Jones' comments on the Exchequer Chamber for Debate in England. In the case of Waterford, however, both the place of meeting and the personnel comprising the deliberating body of judges differ slightly from that described by Jones. Instead of referring the case to the Exchequer Chamber for debate at Westminster Hall, the judges adjourned to Serjeants' Inn on Chancery Lane. And rather than assembling all the English justices, the Privy Council ordered a tribunal to be constituted from both sides of the Irish Sea. Those present were: Sir Lawrence Tanfield and Sir James Heron, Chief and Second Barons of the English Court of Exchequer; Sir John Dodderidge, King's Serjeant and future Justice of the English King's Bench; Sir Henry Hobart, English Attorney-General; Sir James Ley, Irish Chief Justice; Sir Anthony St Leger, Irish Master of the Rolls; and Sir John Davies, Irish Attorney-General.[57]

From the text of Davies' *Reports*, as well as some other stray information, it appears that this unprecedented body upheld the earlier pleas reported by Davies in the *quo warranto* proceedings begun before the Irish Court of King's Bench in July of 1607.[58] At Serjeants' Inn, however, the litigation involved not only Waterford, but also ten other municipalities which had sent their representatives to London to plead their various charters. The judges decided to affirm Davies' arguments against Waterford, but strangely enough only Dublin appears to have seriously challenged the principles laid down in Davies' earlier report of the proceedings against that city. Represented by Sir Richard Bolton, the Recorder of Dublin, the capital city built a defence around an ancient charter granted to the corporation by Henry II. This charter, which had granted the right to appropriate *theolonea* and *consuetudines*, was construed by the town to imply a right to the great and petty customs.[59] To advance this argument, Bolton rather lamely defined *theoloneum* according to the text in St Matthews's gospel in which a sort of custom or toll was supposedly implied. Annoyed by these quibbles, Davies replied that it was not the Gospel that served as the font of English law, but the 'interpreters of our law'.[60] Davies then cited Fitzherbert to show that the word *theoloneum* referred to a petty duty levied on retail sales in markets and fairs, not to a levy on overseas trade. On this point he was sustained by the court.

As for *consuetudines* in Dublin's charter, Davies conceded that one of its several meanings did indeed imply a right to collect customs payable for merchandise. But the justices resolved that *consuetudines* signified far too many meanings, and that such a general term could never denote a special royal duty like the customs revenue. Other data on the case of Dublin may be gleaned from Bolton's letter to the city's Mayor on 24 December 1608. Accepting defeat over the charter of Henry II, Bolton attempted to cut his losses by pleading an alternative claim to the petty custom. Bolton claimed that 'private intelligence' had reported that Davies would base the crown's claim to the petty custom on the Act of Resumption of 20 Henry VII. Forewarned, Bolton, in the absence of documentary evidence, craftily averred that the city's collection of 3d in the pound on the merchandise of aliens represented a municipal, not a national, levy for the maintenance of the city walls.[61] The judges in this instance allowed this municipal levy by prescriptive right, but took back the petty custom for the crown. Bolton later crowed to the Mayor of Dublin that 'we shall hold what we receive, and the strangers shall be double charged'.[62] As for the levy of poundage, Davies was once again frustrated by the Poundage Act of 1500 which had exempted the freemen of the city from the 5 per cent *ad valorem* duty on all merchandise imported and exported.

The paucity of manuscript materials on the pleas of the other port towns obscures the rest of the litigation at Serjeants' Inn. But it seems fairly certain that the ruling against Waterford served as a paradigm for defeating the claims of the other towns. After a second hearing at Serjeants' Inn, the judges returned a certificate of their decision to the English Privy Council on 16 December 1608.[63] This document shows that the judges resolved that the customs revenue had in fact been unlawfully detained by eleven port towns. Three types of customs duties due to the government were identified. First, the judges resolved that the custom of poundage, the 5 per cent *ad valorem* tax on imports and exports, belonged to the crown by virtue of the Irish statute 15 Henry VII. The great custom was held to be an ancient right of the crown by inheritance, while the Irish statute 22 Edward III vested the petty custom in the possession of the crown.[64]

With respect to collection of these customs duties, the judges ruled that the freemen of Dublin, Waterford and Drogheda were exempt from paying poundage by virtue of the Poundage Act of 1500. Merchant aliens and all others were, however, subject to payment of poundage within the precincts of the three privileged ports.[65]

Further exemption was granted the town of Galway, where freemen and merchant strangers were, on the basis of two charters, 36 Henry VIII and 20 Elizabeth, freed from paying poundage.[66] The judges also declared that the city of Cork and the towns of Limerick, Wexford, Ross, Youghal, Kinsale and Carrickfergus were, without exception, to yield up the levy of poundage.[67]

For the collection of the great and small customs, the judges ruled that all the charters purportedly granting such rights from the last year of Edward II to the first year of Henry VII's reign were void by the Act of Resumption dated 1 Henry VII.[68] Some equity was shown, however, in the execution of this decision. In Cork, the great and petty customs were found for the king, but the justices exempted the citizens and freemen from paying the great custom.[69] In Limerick, the justices allowed the corporation to collect the petty custom but maintained a royal right to levy the great custom.[70] In the cities of Drogheda, Wexford and New Ross, both the great and petty customs were resolved to lie with the king.[71] In the port of Kinsale, the great and petty customs were found once again for the king, but the justices mitigated this loss by sustaining the corporation's right to collect the coquet custom conferred in a charter by Elizabeth for 31 years.[72] Similarly in Youghal, the justices allowed the town to collect the coquet of hides for the repair of the city walls.[73] In Galway, freemen, commons and merchant strangers were released from both the great and petty customs excepting the coquet of hides which was leased from the crown.[74] In Carrickfergus all customs were subject to the strangely worded charter of 20 Elizabeth which divided customs duties 'within the bounds of breare homes and the fair furlong' between the crown and freemen of the town. Two-thirds of the proceeds of the duties were assigned to the queen and her successors, while one-third went to the town.[75]

The certificate of the judges, which detailed the application of the principles laid down by Davies against the city of Waterford to the rest of the port towns, demonstrates once again the extent to which the novel use of judge-made law emerged as the preferred instrument of major political innovation in early Jacobean Ireland. Despite the decision, however, the major towns continued through the first half of 1609 to swamp the English Privy Council with petitions for exemption from the effects of the judicial resolution. Some towns even alleged at one point that the absence of an adequately printed and collated book of Irish statutes had prevented them from preparing a proper defence.[76] In January 1609 the English Privy

Council, by order of the king, admonished Chichester and the Irish Privy Council to transfer troublesome suits to England. The Council further informed the Irish government that the king, by virtue of the resolution against the towns, wished to inform the municipalities that their former liberties amounted to little more than a temporary arrangement which, in view of the Tudor conquest, could no longer be tolerated.[77]

This rigid backing of the judges' decision was tempered by remission to the towns of all arrearages due from uncollected customs revenue. As we have seen, the government also renewed many of the lesser privileges. In Munster almost all the towns were allowed to maintain existing leases of the coquet of hides for the maintenance of city walls and other public works; Youghal and Galway even succeeded in enlarging their privileges.[78] The port of Kinsale, in recompense for the desolation incurred by the Spanish invasion in 1601, was even freed from the stringent fines for recusancy imposed by the overzealous Lord President Sir Henry Brouncker.[79]

Other developments served to hasten the application of the judges' decision against the towns. With the appearance of an official book of rates and the termination of all temporary farming arrangements that followed the resolution of December 1608, the path lay clear for a centralized administration of the Irish customs on the English model.[80] By May 1610 Davies could boast of his achievement to Salisbury, remarking that it was his own labour and experience that resulted in the successful case against the towns, and that the customs revenue was now ready to be farmed.[81] On 18 March 1611 the king issued a directive to the Lord Deputy that the 'resolution as to the customs' should be enforced and that collection should begin at once.[82]

Unfortunately, obstacles remained. During the summer of 1611 the Ingram group dispatched Robert Cogan, who was now Surveyor-General of the Irish customs, and William Massam, a bankrupt associate of Ingram and Cranfield, to Ireland. Ingram, however, was forced to stay behind on account of business affairs in England and the government sent Lord Carew, former Lord President of Munster, in his place.[83] On 28 July 1611, Chichester wrote to Salisbury that all the towns were beginning to have second thoughts about the judicial decision of December 1608 and were deliberately obstructing the appointment of customs officials in the various ports.[84] Several months later, Cogan toured the major Irish ports, reporting that the towns of Dublin, Waterford, Drogheda and Galway still insisted on their privileges, particularly the exemption of freemen from poundage allowed by the judges in 1608.[85] Despite municipal uneasiness, Cogan estimated a potential customs revenue of £211,000 of which about half would come from the port of Dublin. Of the three towns, Dublin, Waterford and Drogheda, enjoying exemptions of freemen from the collection of poundage, Cogan estimated a combined commercial traffic yielding a potential value of £170,000 per annum. On the basis of these figures, Cogan predicted that the collection of poundage had the potential of yielding a total revenue of £10,500 per annum which, on account of the exemptions granted to the freemen of the three privileged towns, reduced the overall figure to about £2,000 per annum.[86] Since the judicial resolution had allowed this exemption, the English government, taking its cue from Davies, made up for its loss by levying an imposition of 12d in the pound on the freemen of the privileged ports for all merchandise imported and exported. This imposition, which caused howls of protest from the towns of Dublin, Waterford and Drogheda, is only one illustration of the growing confidence exhibited by the central government in Dublin.[87] During the month of July 1611, the government renewed its attacks on recusancy, issuing a proclamation similar to that of 1605 banning Jesuits and massing priests from the realm and reviving the Oath of Supremacy to purge recusants from municipal office and from the legal profession.[88]

By 1612, the central government had succeeded in placing a corps of state customs officials in nine of the port towns.[89] This firm extension of royal control yielded within the year an annual customs revenue of £1,500 which in the estimation of the Earl of Northampton, Nottingham's cousin, could be raised to a sum of £6,000 per annum.[90] As rumour of this potential windfall spread, two groups began to contend for the lease of the Irish customs farm. One was led by Ingram and the other by John Swinnerton, the farmer of French and Rhenish wines in England, who had unsuccessfully bid for the farm of the English customs in 1604.

In the end, the contending parties reached an agreement in which a number of familiar names reappear. While the original lease bore the names of Arthur Ingram, Richard Calthorpe, Martin Freeman and George Law, it is known that the active partnership included almost all those who laboured to bring about a successful conclusion to the farm of the Irish customs. These persons included Lionel Cranfield, John Bingley, Robert Cogan, William Massam and Thomas Waad.

The terms of the new arrangement called for a lease of 9½ years with an annual rent of £12,000 to be paid in six-month instalments of £6,000 to the English Exchequer.[91]

This firm installation of a consolidated administration of the Irish customs, based on the judicial resolution reported by Davies in 1608, eventually succeeded in transforming the almost non-existent customs revenue into one of the main pillars of state income. Dr Treadwell, who has thoroughly examined the reform of the Irish customs administration during the reign of James I, provides some interesting statistics to show the contribution made by the customs to government finance. In 1606 and 1607, at the time of Treasurer-at-War Ridgeway's initial enquiry into the Irish customs revenue, the income derived from the Irish customs amounted to only £574 per annum. During the period 1623–4, the same revenue rose to the unprecedented net income of £9,000 per annum.[92] When examined against the whole of Irish revenue, these figures assume even greater significance. During the period 1607–8, annual crown revenue stood at £21,648, of which only £700 or approximately 1/30th was derived from the customs. In 1623 the customs amounted to £10,783, or 30 per cent of a total annual revenue of £37,000.[93] With the general reduction of the military establishment, the consolidation of the Irish customs administration helped to limit the massive inflow of English money to finance the high cost of Irish administration. By the end of the reign of James I, the customs revenue, in combination with income derived from a revitalized administration of Irish wardship, became one of the two pillars of government finance that lasted until the outbreak of the civil war.[94]

Davies' role in shaping this achievement has never been entirely recognized. In general agreement with earlier historians who dismissed the judicial proceedings against the towns as so much legal casuistry, Dr Treadwell has gone so far as to deny the authority of the resolution against the towns.[95] In a recent article, Treadwell stated that the resolution reported by Davies against Waterford and the towns was not binding, and that it was only the fortuitous acquiescence of the towns that prevented the re-opening of time-consuming *quo warranto* proceedings against the towns before the Irish Court of King's Bench.[96]

We now know, however, that the government's application of this decision fell in line with the attitudes of contemporary jurists outlined in the third chapter of this book. This is particularly evident in official correspondence between the king, the English Privy

Council and the Irish Privy Council during the spring and summer of 1611 when the ports of Dublin, Drogheda, Waterford and Galway began to drag their feet, seeking further concessions to enhance their claims to the customs revenue and to maintain their exemption of freemen from poundage. In a royal directive dated 15 March 1611, the king wrote to Chichester ordering that the 'resolution of the customs of Ireland' be put in force.[97] In further correspondence with the Irish executive during July 1611, the English Privy Council reaffirmed the resolution of the 'Lord Chief Baron, the barons of the Excheqer of England, the King's learned counsel of England and his Attorney-General of Ireland'.[98] A third directive written during September 1611 again referred to the resolution of 1608 as the authority upon which the crown justified its claims to the long-dormant customs revenue.[99] This preference to execute a major change in the relationship between the towns and the central government by judicial fiat can be understood, once again, as a response to fears of opposition within the Irish parliament. This anxiety, in view of the mandates controversy and the *quo warranto* proceedings against the towns, was confirmed in the parliament of 1613–15, when the government attempted to terminate the various exemptions granted to the freemen of Dublin, Waterford and Drogheda from the levy of poundage and, in select cases, from the great and petty customs.[100]

The bill, however, met with a strong and determined resistance which successfully countered the government's attack. Existing but fragmentary evidence indicates that the upper house introduced the bill on 14 October 1614.[101] Four days later the bill was engrossed and transmitted to the lower house by John Blennerhasset and Robert Oglethorpe, Lord Barons of the Exchequer.[102] On 19 October the bill received its first reading and was trenchantly opposed by Richard Bolton, the former Recorder of Dublin, who had so staunchly advocated that city's cause in the litigation before Serjeants' Inn during December 1608. Sir Oliver St John, former Master of the Ordnance, attempted to deflect Bolton's speech on procedural grounds, claiming that 'none could speak to a bill at first reading'.[103] At this juncture it appears that foes of the bill succeeded in quashing further deliberation and the bill never emerged for a second reading.

This determined resistance meant in the end that the judicial resolution reported by Davies provided the sole legal basis for a reformed customs administration that demolished the old political equation linking crown policy to the interests of the towns. The firm installation of a state bureaucracy to collect the long-neglected customs revenue secured a fundamental shift in the relationship between the central government and the towns. In the wake of the Tudor conquest, the dismantling of the medieval lumber of corporate privilege which resulted in an extension of a national customs administration in the port towns was accomplished not by statute law, but by the extraordinary conclave of English and Irish justices at Serjeants' Inn in London.

8

The case of mixed money

Traditional accounts of events in the Munster towns during the spring of 1603 have understandably drawn attention to the obvious religious and jurisdictional undercurrents involved in the civil disturbances in these major corporations. Davies' *Reports*, however, point to equally significant economic aspects of this unrest brought about by government insolvency that precipitated attempts to tamper with the coinage. With disastrous results, the government sought to finance the cost of Tyrone's rebellion by debasing the Irish coin in 1601 from 9 oz. fine to 3 oz. fine of silver.[1] Failure to withdraw the old sterling money from circulation, combined with the government's inability to gain acceptance of the base coin at face rather than intrinsic value, rapidly inflated the price of grain and other foodstuffs. Increased prices were further aggravated by the refusal of merchants to accept the base coin in commercial transactions, which led to disruption of the vital subsistence links connecting England with the port towns. The unrest launched by the appearance of the base coin was the subject of frequent complaint, and the role of the bogus shilling in feeding the fires of anarchy in the corporations has not received the study it deserves.[2]

I

This oversight is particularly striking when balanced against remarks by contemporaries. The comments by Lord Deputy Mountjoy and Solicitor-General Davies clearly registered the difficulties caused by the new coin. In his march south to subdue the unruly towns, Mountjoy blamed the base money for aggravating municipal discontent, and he confided to Cecil that:

The discontentment of the coin is infinite and more insupportable to us all for it is generally refused. I know of no way to make it current where I go but by the cannon.[3]

Six months later Sir John Davies, newly arrived in Ireland, observed the continuing corporate unrest over the base coin, and he remarked that riots in Galway had caused the Lord Deputy to commit 'divers tradesmen for refusing to accept the base coin'.[4] Davies' reference to the Galway disturbances and Mountjoy's comments on the deteriorated coin serve to underscore the seriousness of the problems created by Elizabeth's billon coin. In view of this testimony, it is surprising to find that the history of Elizabeth's Irish debasement has neither been fully told nor placed within its proper political context.

If the constitutional changes inaugurated by the judicial resolutions against the native tenurial system and those enforcing religious conformity in the Pale and port towns were to be taken seriously, a means had to be devised to restore public confidence in a national monetary system that reflected the extension of English rule to the whole of Ireland. This public law context to the problem of the base coin is best revealed in Davies' comment on the utility of a national monetary system:

In every commonwealth, it is necessary to have a certain standard of money. For no commonwealth can subsist without contracts, and no contracts without equality, and no equality without money.[5]

A viable coinage possessed important economic and juridical symbolism. In order to give strength to this new coinage, the Irish government utilized the method it had employed to other complicated issues of public law. Thus reform of the Irish coinage was executed by judicial fiat based upon a collective resolution of the Irish judiciary. As in adjudication of the case of the Bann fishery, the judicial resolution concerning the validity of the debased coinage also made significant use of legal principles drawn from continental civil law.

The 1601 debasement must be examined in light of the rising cost of the Irish wars and, more particularly, the heavy loss resulting from the Earl of Essex's failure to score any success against Tyrone. The story of Essex's return to England and subsequent fall from grace has been well told, and there is nothing more to add to that sad narrative. None the less, a quick review of the cost incurred by the Essex fiasco serves to justify the queen's displeasure with her former favourite.

According to Professor Dietz, Essex's leisurely progress through Leinster and Munster in the summer of 1599 ran up a cost of £280,000, an expenditure that inaugurated a vicious spiral in military

spending that did not end until spring of 1603. With Essex's departure from Ireland, Tyrone pillaged the borders of the Pale and
conspired to bring in troops from Spain. As military tension
increased, the English government, between March 1600 and March
1601, invested a further £206,673 in the Irish morass. Still the war
continued. From March 1601 until April 1602, Spanish intervention
resulted in a further outlay of £415,401, and an English victory at
Kinsale did not prevent a return to the small-unit savagery of earlier
campaigns in Ulster. From 1 April 1602 until 30 September 1603,
Tyrone's rebellion consumed another £125,795.[6] At war's end in
April 1603, the total cost of the Nine Years War came to the
staggering sum of £1,845,696.[7] If this figure is compared to the
£1,419,496 spent on military subvention in the Low Countries
during the period 1585–1603, the rising of Hugh O'Neill clearly
emerges as the most expensive of Elizabeth's wars.[8] It is not surprising, therefore, that the soaring Irish war debt inspired the
English Privy Council to pay off a substantial portion of Tyrone's
rebellion in bad coin.

It should be noted, however, that the debasement of the Irish coin
which began in 1601 had a number of antecedents, and a review of
the history of the Irish coinage is necessary in order to place the
Elizabethan debasement in historical context. Until recently, Irish
numismatics has been a relatively neglected field, broken only by
occasional antiquarian research. During the last decade, however,
Michael Dolley and C. E. Challis have remedied this absence of
scholarship with several preliminary studies on the history of the
Irish monetary system.[9] A brief review of their research indicates
that alteration of the Irish coin in 1601 had several medieval and early
modern precedents. From the thirteenth to the mid-fifteenth
century, all coins minted in Ireland corresponded in intrinsic value to
English coins of the same weight and denomination. This monetary
union between England and Ireland existed for obvious economic
and political reasons. Among other benefits, it permitted massive
withdrawals of Irish sterling to finance the ambitions of Plantagenet
kings. The wholesale removal by 1460 of Ireland's silver reserves,
however, inspired the Irish parliament to initiate protective legislation to prevent further removal of Irish specie. In what amounts to
the first debasement in Irish history, the Drogheda parliament
reduced the intrinisic value of the Irish coin by over 20 per cent,
lowering the bullion content of the Irish shilling from 11 oz. fine to 9
oz. fine of silver.[10] This action represented an attempt at an official

standardization of intrinsic values between English and Irish coins at the ratio of 3:4 – a measure which lasted, with a few exceptions, for the next 150 years. At a practical level, the demise of the monetary union between the two kingdoms meant that an Irish groat or fourpenny piece contained only threepence worth of silver or, conversely, an English shilling circulated in Ireland brought a premium of 16 Irish pence. It needs to be stressed, however, that unlike subsequent alterations of the Irish coin, the statutory debasement of 1460 was self-imposed by the colonial community and represented a debasement by weight rather than alloy. As Dolley has shown, the initiative taken by the 1460 parliament succeeded in cutting off the outflow of Irish silver by tariffing the Irish coin at a value less than English coins of the same denomination.

Sixteenth-century alterations of the Irish coin, imposed by the metropolitan rather than the colonial government, differed considerably from the protective measures set down by the parliament of 1460. That is, the debasement policies pursued by Tudor monarchs, which were exploitative and opportunistic in nature, were dictated by the debilitating cost of military ventures engendered by frequent revolt. This pattern emerged first in the reign of Henry VIII. To balance the £40,000 spent in subduing the Geraldine revolt, the Henrician government between 1534 and 1546 gradually lowered the intrinsic value of the Irish coin from the nine-ounce standard set by the Drogheda parliament to an alloy or billon coin composed of only 3 oz. fine of silver.[11] This base issue was notable for its novel appearance. Struck in shillings and groats, the new coin bore on the obverse a crowned shield with the arms of England and France, and on the reverse, for reasons which are still not understood, a crowned harp. The new 'coin of the harp', as it was called by contemporaries, was also distinctive for its epigraphy. Beginning with the issue of 1541, the legend on the coin propagated the new constitutional relationship between England and Ireland by substituting *Rex* for *Dominus* on the coin's reverse. This 3 oz. base coin continued to be struck during the reigns of Edward and Mary, and Elizabeth's first coins, struck in shillings and groats in 1559, were as disreputable as those struck by her three predecessors. Not until 1591 was the base coin of 3 oz. fine of silver to be replaced by a sterling issue approximating the ratio of 3:4 set down by the Drogheda parliament in 1460. As Dolley again has shown, the new coin, struck in shillings and groats, consisted of an alloy of 90 per cent silver.[12] The 1561 issue was also distinctive for its impression on the reverse that featured three small harps in place of the single harp struck by Henry VIII, Edward and Mary. The intrinsic value of the new coin, when juxtaposed to the base money issued by Elizabeth's predecessors, must have led to extensive hoarding, because circulation of the revalued coin seems to have been limited.

II

The outbreak of the Nine Years War in 1594 tempted the English government once again to revalue the Irish coin along the lines set down by Henry VIII, Edward and Mary. As previously mentioned, the prohibitive cost of O'Neill's rebellion led to massive expenditure of English silver. In 1600 George Carey, the Irish Treasurer, complained to Cecil that the Irish wars:

exhaust the treasure of England, that the state of England doth ever groan under the burden thereof, and that we expend faster here than you can gather it in England.[13]

In response, Elizabeth returned to the three-ounce standard set by her three predecessors, and the new coin, which appeared on 24 May 1601, was struck in shillings, sixpences and threepenny pieces. This currency bore on the reverse a crowned harp, and on the obverse the arms of England, replacing the royal portrait featured on the sterling issue of 1561 and on coins struck during the reigns of Edward and Mary.[14] In addition to the altered silver coin, the English government also sent to Ireland for the first time a large quantity of copper pennies and halfpennies to serve as a medium of exchange for petty consumer transactions and payment of wages. Despite the unpopularity of the copper money, it gained grudging acceptance and undoubtedly helped enterpreneurs to save on wages while expanding a money economy.

Few clues survive to trace the exact origins of the decision to alter the Irish coin in 1601. As previously shown, Sir Roger Wilbraham, who served as Solicitor-General for Ireland from 1586 to 1603, claimed on the day of Salisbury's death in 1612 that Robert Cecil alone was instrumental in determining Irish policy.[15] This comprehensive statement, in so far as it relates to the 1601 debasement, is confirmed by a letter written to Cecil by Thomas Hayes, the man responsible for coining the new money, sometime during 1602. According to Hayes, it was Cecil who convinced the Lord Treasurer and the queen of the plan's utility.[16] There appears to have been little disagreement within the English Privy Council itself over the decision to alter the Irish coin. Wilbraham's diary account of the English Privy Council's deliberations demonstrates, however, an awareness of the evils traditionally associated with debasement. Recognizing that their decision would probably condemn the army and civil populace to rapid inflation, the Privy Council defended its position on grounds of military policy. The debasement would, they argued, cut off the flow of specie to Tyrone who was known to employ English sterling to purchase arms and munitions from Spain.[17]

Whether the Privy Councillors actually believed that a wholesale debasement of the Irish coinage would cut Tyrone off from continental support is not clear. Contemporary observers in Ireland, however, were not convinced of this argument, and it was faulted on a number of grounds. In the first place, tantalizing references in the Irish state papers indicated that it was Spanish rather than English coin that served as the primary means of monetary exchange within O'Neill's autonomous Gaelic lordship.[18] Whether this Spanish coinage originated from the Armada wrecks is doubtful, but a proclamation issued by Tyrone on 23 January 1601 directed that Spanish coin, on penalty of death, would pass as current money within his territories.[19] But even if we admit that alteration of the coin would result in the withdrawal of specie from rebel hands, there is evidence to show that the illicit supply of arms ran unabated. Allegations of a clandestine arms trade between unscrupulous merchants in the port towns and the northern rebels are too emphatic to ignore.[20] Yet apart from the seedy transactions of renegade gunrunners, an anonymous discourse written in 1602 has greater plausibility. The absence of specie, the writer argued, could have little permanent impact on a semi-nomadic society whose basic commodities of tallow, sheepskin and wool served as ample exchange to purchase the sinews of war.[21] Despite official claims to the contrary, the debasement of 1601 can more arguably be seen as an attempt to dump a large part of the colossal Elizabethan war debt on the army and civil population in Ireland.

Providing, of course, that the government could circulate the base money at face rather than intrinsic value, this last attempt to alter the coin promised to yield enormous profit to an impecunious crown. The government's potential return is best illustrated by Dr Challis' figures on the intrinsic values of the silver and copper metal employed in manufacturing the new coin. One pound of silver valued at 16s 1¼d would yield, when coined into base money, a face value of 62 shillings. Similarly one pound of copper worth 6¾d would circulate at a face value of 16 shillings. Stated more clearly, the total face value of the base money, amounting to £307,281, cost the English government only £84,526 to produce.[22] It should be stressed, however, that full realization of the expected profit depended on the government's ability to ensure confidence in the new coin, which in turn depended on the successful withdrawal of the nine ounce sterling money from the Irish economy. To facilitate this withdrawal, the proclamation establishing the base coin forbade the circulation of all sterling and foreign money by decrying it as bullion. The edict also established a second control measure by erecting exchange banks in the cities of Chester, London, Dublin, Cork, Galway and Carrickfergus, where sterling was to be exchanged for the new base coin.[23]

The obvious aims of this procedure were to collect the old sterling money and to monitor more closely the movement of trade into Ireland. But an examination of the mechanics of the exchange serves to elucidate the other intentions of the government. According to the proclamation, all persons, including soldiers and servitors returning to England, were required to turn in their base Irish money for bills of exchange drawn in English sterling at the rate of 21 shillings Irish for every English pound. Conversely English merchants trading in Ireland were to receive 21 shillings Irish for each pound sterling turned into the exchange. Since the wages of most soldiers and servitors were consumed in Ireland, the success of the scheme depended on the willingness of merchants to comply with the exchange regulations and to refrain from raising prices for commodities traded in base money. Within a year, complaints by the Irish Privy Council dimmed expectations of merchant co-operation and seriously reduced official optimism of realizing a profit from the base money.

In the spring of 1602 Robert Morgan, the master of the Cork exchange, reported that he had not taken in any of the old sterling harps.[24] The old sterling coin continued to circulate, despite the provisions of the proclamation, and from 2 May 1601 to 31 March 1602 the Irish Lord Treasurer Carey's accounts show that only £19,093 17s 3d of the old sterling money passed into the net of the Irish exchange.[25] Indeed, for the two-year period encompassing the debasement, only £40,680 3s 8d of the old sterling harps were collected. When balanced against the £297,070 3s 4¼d paid out by the English Exchequer in sterling money for Irish bills of exchange, it appears that the control measures set down to regulate the transfer of currency leaked like a sieve.[26]

The coexistence of two standards of money allowed unscrupulous merchants to exploit the different intrinsic values of old and new money by deliberately inflating the price of commodities paid in base coins to double or triple their former value. The persistence of the decried money can best be explained by the rather low premium of 5 per cent given for its redemption in the exchange. This led to hoarding and to clandestine trafficking in the old coin by businessmen at a premium of 50 to 100 per cent more than the government rate. As Robert Morgan, the master of the Cork exchange, wryly commented, 'Her Majesty's exchange must needs fail where she is outbidden.'[27] In rural areas, sharp traders dealing in whiskey, wine and cloth were known to insist on payment in the decried harp shilling without informing their clients of the difference between the two coins. Morgan also declared: 'when required to forego the old money, merchants would quickly learn them the difference'.[28] The failure to withdraw the old money was further complicated by an extensive net of counterfeiting. Richard Hadsor, an Irish servitor, complained on 4 July 1602 to Cecil that a Breton goldsmith counterfeited coins of the new standard, selling his bogus money at the rate of £100 sterling for every £1,000 of counterfeit base money.[29] Six months earlier Carew, the Lord President of Munster, had stated that the exchange would be jeopardized by counterfeiters, and that Tyrone himself had set up a counterfeit mint at Dungannon to exploit the chaos inflicted by the debasement.[30] These and other abuses compelled issuance of the second proclamation designed to establish more stringent controls on the exchange.

This second proclamation attempted to accelerate the removal of the old sterling harps by stipulating that 25 per cent of the total exchange had to be submitted in the old sterling money. To prevent unlawful transactions in sterling money, merchants exchanging base money were required to submit a customs certificate to the exchange master accounting for the value of merchandise sold in Ireland. This certificate, when compared to the amount of base money exchanged for sterling, would supposedly reveal unreasonable profits and expose clandestine commerce in the old sterling money. As a concession to the military and civil establishment, the proclamation exempted soldiers and servitors from the requirement to submit 25 per cent of their exchange in sterling. To discourage speculation among soldiers and servitors, however, any exchange in excess of an individual's salary was subject to the same restriction imposed on the merchant class. The proclamation also established punitive measures to discourage unlawful circulation of the decried coin. All persons apprehended for either hoarding or trafficking in the nine-ounce sterling coin were subject to fines and/or imprisonment with rewards of up to one-half of all confiscated coin to be paid to informers.[31]

Despite these restrictions, the second proclamation succeeded no further than the first in withdrawing sterling from Ireland – a fact that is confirmed by frequent illustrations of merchant fraud in the Irish state papers. In order to understand the collapse of the exchange, it will be useful to examine some of the devices used to circumvent the regulations. One anonymous compendium of entrepreneurial abuse, dated November 1602, serves to demonstrate the extent of commercial misconduct performed by merchants against the exchange. In particular, this document accuses the merchants of Cork, Galway, Kilmallock and Youghal of trafficking in sterling money, buying up £200 Irish for £100 English money and turning the base money into the exchange at a handsome profit.[32] Another favourite trick seems to have involved processing bills of exchange under other men's names. This subterfuge was practised by Richard Martin, an English goldsmith, who attempted to conceal clandestine sales of plate by transferring his profit of £100 in to a bill of exchange submitted by a London haberdasher named Arnold. Arnold willingly subscribed to this scheme, but, under interrogation by suspicious exchange officials, later confessed his complicity in furthering Martin's fraud.[33] Such dealings were difficult to detect, and frequent references to this particular abuse in the state papers seem to demonstrate its popularity among dishonest businessmen. There is, however, one more example worthy of consideration.

This last illustration of commercial misconduct involved a clandestine liquor trade between English merchants and rebel forces in Ulster. This illicit commerce served not only to defraud the exchange, but also demonstrated the impossibility of drawing commerce and money away from the rebel forces. Actual operation of this business can be illustrated from official records. Two London merchants, Gunter and Bowling, were discovered, for example, buying up many tuns of white *aqua vitae* on the London market at 2s 8d per gallon. Gunter and Bowling shipped their cargo from London to Carrickfergus where an agent offloaded the liquor and adulterated it with a 'yellowish stain'. Following this metamorphosis, a middleman, one 'Moses Hill of the isle of Magee', marketed the concoction to rebel forces, selling it as genuine Irish whiskey at a price of ten shillings a gallon – a mark-up of 500 per cent.[34] Since Tyrone maintained a counterfeit mint at Dungannon to imitate the base shilling, it is possible to infer that our English bootleggers may have been paid in bogus coin which was then converted to sterling in bills of exchange. English officials experienced particular annoyance with this clandestine liquor trade, because alcohol was seriously esteemed as one of the principal provisions of the rebel army. One English official, complaining of the great strength and comfort alcohol gave to the rebels, confessed that 'our English nation cannot devour such quantities for it is known they do not much accustom to drink thereof'.[35] Even in the sixteenth century, the Irish were renowned for a prodigious capacity for strong drink.

Given these illustrations of continued commercial misconduct, it appears that the restrictions laid down by the second proclamation succeeded no further than the first in withdrawing the old sterling money from the economy. The inability to prevent business fraud forced the government to issue a third proclamation on 24 January 1603 that established more severe exchange regulations. To speed the withdrawal of sterling from the economy, the third proclamation increased the sterling requirement for merchants changing base money to sterling from £25 to £40 sterling for every £100 turned into the exchange. As a further measure to supervise such exchange, the proclamation reduced the number of exchange banks from six to two, leaving only London and Dublin to satisfy the demand for bills.[36]

The effects of this third proclamation upon Anglo-Irish trade and the vital supply of foodstuffs to the port towns were disastrous. Impatient with the extreme distance involved in travelling to London to negotiate these bills of exchange, English merchants from Chester, Lancashire and Wales expressed their contempt over slack payment of bills by withdrawing completely from Irish commerce.[37] The stoppage of trade is reflected in numerous references to food shortages in the municipalities. In January 1603, for example, John Tirrell, the Mayor of Dublin, complained to Cecil of acute grain shortages in the city. He further advised the secretary that only an emergency grain shipment from England paid for in English sterling could prevent starvation conditions.[38] Further comment on the shortage of provisions in the port towns came from the Irish Privy Council, which blamed the merchants who 'refused to import things from abroad alleging their slack payment of their bills whereby they are not able to hold traffic'.[39] By the end of February, only slightly more than one month before the Munster disturbances, Lord Deputy Mountjoy advised Cecil that due to the bad coin prices had risen fourfold and not even his own salary was sufficient to provide a living commensurate with his high office.[40] Given the testimony of contemporaries, it seems a plausible inference that the English government had unwittingly jeopardized the subsistence trade links between England and Ireland by reducing the number of exchange banks to only Dublin and London. Bread has served as the traditional rallying cry of many revolts, and Ireland at the end of the Nine Years War was no exception. The base money had disrupted trade and helped to inflate commodity prices beyond the reach of the civil populace. A scarcity of food and bad coinage had certainly helped to fuel the municipal revolt in 1603. Mountjoy's comment on the base coin, made during his hurried march south to subdue the Munster insurrection, that he knew no way of making the base money current, except by the cannon, provides a fitting epitaph for the last Tudor debasement in Ireland.[41]

Recognizing the vital role of English commerce in victualling the Irish towns, James took it upon himself to revive Anglo-Irish trade by issuing a proclamation setting the base coin at a value consistent with its silver content.[42] Thereafter, base shillings were tariffed as groats, with other coins decried proportionately according to their denomination. It was deemed necessary, however, to encourage retail transactions by continuing the circulation of the copper money at its face value. This reduction of the base money to its intrinsic value was followed by the appearance in 1603 of a new Irish coin bearing, on the reverse, a crowned harp and, on the obverse, a portrait of the new king. Issued in denominations of shillings and half-shillings, the Jacobean coin contained 9 oz. fine silver and was therefore consistent with the standard laid down by the parliament of 1460. English money was thus allowed after 1607 to circulate freely within Ireland, with a premium of 25 per cent over Irish coins of the same denomination. In 1607, the government also removed the base coin from circulation. The disappearance of the base money and free circulation of English sterling represent, in effect, a return to the two-tier currency system set out by the parliament of 1460; after 1607, an Irish coinage ceased to be struck altogether.[43]

III

Although the proclamation restoring the harp shilling to the nine-ounce standard revived the crucial subsistence trade between England and the Irish towns, the edict failed to put an end to further disagreement, frauds and controversies over the mixed money. The Irish state papers continued to vent government invective against commercial intrigues, singling out merchants for profiteering on the base coin by purchasing it at a price less than its silver content. This subterfuge was encouraged by dishonest brokers who convinced the local populace that the silver content of the base money consisted of less than 3 oz. fine.[44] Another problem arose over the term 'sterling', which unscrupulous merchants and landlords misrepresented to imply an obligation to pay sixteen pence Irish, the intrinsic or silver value of English shillings circulating in Ireland.[45] This second difficulty continued unabated in Ireland until 1637 when a royal proclamation ordered that all 'accomptes, receipts, payments and issue of his majesties moneys in Ireland' would be rendered and accounted in English rather than Irish money.[46]

Particular confusion arose, however, over a third issue involving payment in base money for debts incurred prior to the debasement. This last difficulty seems to have arisen largely with contracts negotiated for Irish trade in England payable in English rather than Irish money. Following the debasement, such commercial contracts commonly attempted to guarantee payment in English sterling, thereby avoiding the Irish exchange requirements.[47] But by the summer of 1604, controversies concerning payment in base coin for obligations antecedent to the debasement precipitated a major constitutional crisis by questioning the validity of the base coin to pass as legal tender for payment of public and private obligations.

The incident that provoked the juridical crisis over the base coin arose from litigation between an Irish merchant, one Brett of Drogheda, and an English merchant from London named Gilbert.[48] Brett had purchased wares from Gilbert to the value of £100, making out a conditional bond for £200 of which he was quit, providing that the obligation to pay for the wares was tendered at some mutually agreed date at the tomb of Strongbow in Christ Church, Dublin. Following the proclamation decrying the Irish coin from 9 oz. fine to 3 oz. fine of silver, Brett tendered his debt in base Irish money which led Gilbert to bring suit to recover Brett's debt in English sterling.

The significance of this case was not lost on contemporary Irish jurists and Solicitor-General Davies reported that:

Inasmuch as this case related to the kingdom in general, and was also of great importance in consideration of reason of state, Sir George Carey, then Lord Deputy and also Treasurer, required the Chief Judges (being of the Privy Council) to confer on and consider this case, and to return their resolution on it.[49]

Brett of Drogheda refused to tender his obligation to Gilbert in English sterling rather than base Irish money. In their deliberations, the Irish justices resolved the case on three general principles dealing with (1) the prerogative, (2) the nature of sterling money and (3) the time of payment. As in the case of the Bann fishery, the arguments reported by Davies to support the resolution validating payment made in the base money rested heavily on legal principles drawn from continental civil law. The crown's argument that all proclamations concerning the minting of money possessed the power of statute relied heavily on some of the more authoritarian doctrines of sixteenth- and seventeenth-century civil lawyers. The use of continental sources by the Irish justices demonstrates a striking awareness of foreign jurisprudence dealing with the minting of money. Indeed on the basis of Davies' citations, it appears that the majority of the civil law references used in the crown's brief were culled from a compendium of civil law treatises entitled *De Monetis et Re Nummaria*, edited by René Budelius in 1591.[50] A civil lawyer responsible for supervising the Bavarian mint, Budelius enjoyed a reputation among contemporaries as one of the most learned jurists on the public law concerning money. Davies specifically cited Budelius as one of the principal authorities to establish a prerogative right for English monarchs to alter the intrinsic value of money. According to Budelius, alteration of a national currency could be accomplished by royal or imperial edict without the consent of a national assembly. Davies found further support for the English prerogative by citing from a tract written by the Spanish canonist, Leyva Covarruvius. Bishop of Segovia (1563) and president of the Castilian senate, Covarruvius also authored an influential treatise concerning the public law of coining money. The Spanish bishop proved particularly useful for the Irish justices, because he denied the need to consult national assemblies to alter money in time of war.[51] With the English monarch's right to alter the coin thus established, Davies justified the use of civil law principles in common law litigation by saying simply that the 'common law of England agrees well with the rules of the civil law'. He failed, however, to cite many congruent statements in the common law.[52]

The next issue resolved by the Irish justices dealt with whether the base money tendered by Brett of Drogheda could lawfully be taken as sterling money. To resolve this difficulty, the Irish justices sought to establish a one-to-one ratio between the base Irish and English sterling money by setting forth the etymology and historical development of sterling money in England and Ireland.[53] In an impressive display of learning, Davies' report of the case sketched out the common origins of sterling money in the two kingdoms by citing, once again, a number of continental jurists. The method employed differed, however, in tone and style from the civil law citations used to uphold the English monarch's prerogative of minting money. In this instance, continental jurists were in disagreement with the state's argument. To obtain an acceptable etymology of sterling, the crown felt constrained to correct the errors of Covarruvius and Renattus Choppinus, a sixteenth-century French civilian. Misinformed by Polydor Vergil, Choppinus held that sterling evolved as a diminutive form of the Latin verb *stare*, which was then stamped on English coins.[54] Equally mistaken, according to Davies, was Camden's historical argument that sterling derived from the coining of money in Stirling Castle, Scotland. To correct these misstatements, the justices cited Mathew Paris' *Chronica Majora* in which sterling is clearly shown to derive from the word Esterling, a name applied to the Ostmanni or Vikings who 'were the first to coin money not only in England, but also in Ireland'.[55] The Vikings, then, had established sterling as current money common to both England and Ireland; positing this, Davies then upheld a one-to-one ratio between the sterling base coin of Ireland and the sterling money of England. Davies achieved this point by resorting to some truly extraordinary mental gymnastics derived from Budelius' distinction between *bonitas extrinsica* and *bonitas intrinsica*. The legal question revolved upon the difference between the face (*bonitas extrinsica*) as opposed to the metallic (*bonitas intrinsica*) value of coin in normal commercial transactions. The crown argued that, of the two values, the *bonitas extrinsica* was the more important, because it was the stamp of the monarch or emperor, not the metallic content, that makes a coin pass as money.[56] Davies concluded that, as the king by his prerogative can exalt a lowly person through a title of honour, so he is able to give value to base money by setting his impression on the coin. The civil law distinction between *bonitas extrinsica* and *bonitas intrinsica* served to validate Brett of Drogheda's tender in base money, which the Irish justices resolved to be identically valuable as sterling English money of the same denomination.

Having determined the base Irish sterling to be equivalent in law to English sterling, the Irish justices proceeded to deliberate what was probably the key issue in the case of mixed money. Did Brett of Drogheda's tender in mixed money amount to full and valid payment for an obligation contracted before the debasement? The justices confined their discussions on this question of defining the words 'current money' as employed in the contract between Brett and Gilbert. According to the terms of the contract:

Brett shall pay or cause to be paid £100 sterling current money etc. and therefore such money shall be paid as shall be current at such future time.[57]

In analysing this passage, the justices emphasized the meaning of 'current money' rather than the date of the contract negotiated between Brett and Gilbert. Their legal argument once again relied heavily on principles drawn from the civil law. Davies succinctly summarized the contents of Budelius' compendium: 'All the doctors who write De Re Nummaria agree in this rule verbum currentis monetae tempus solutionis designant'.[58] In other words, the judges validated Brett's payment by simply agreeing that 'current money' pertained to the time of payment, not to the money current at the time of contract. Additional support for the argument came from a gloss by the English canonist Lyndwood, who stated that wills which 'non excedit centum solidorum sterlingorum' were to be determined in 'monetae currentis et non respectu antiquae'.[59]

The Irish justices therefore found that current money in Brett of Drogheda's contract meant an obligation in the debased currency circulating at the time payment came due, not in circulation at the time the contract was made. Moreover, they argued, since the proclamation voiding the nine-ounce harp shilling made it unlawful to traffic in the decried coin, Brett had no choice but to tender payment in the debased money.[60] To buttress this last point, the Irish justices referred to a maxim cited by Budelius that all contracts negotiated by merchants were determined by:

Consuetudo et statuta loci, in quem est destinato solutio, respicienda sunt.[61]

In this manner, the Irish justices upheld not only Brett's payment to Gilbert in mixed money, but also the validity of the government's tender of public obligations in the base coin.

The precise impact of the judicial resolution legitimizing the 1601 debasement is, in the absence of records, difficult to determine. From references in the state papers, however, it is clear that the Irish government had, in the absence of statutory authority, enough confidence in the judicial resolution on the case of mixed money to use it as a mechanism to halt further controversies over the mixed coin. As Davies testified:

According to this resolution other cases of the same point were afterwards ruled and adjudged in the several courts of record in Dublin.[62]

The resolution supporting Brett of Drogheda's refusal to tender an obligation in sterling money of the nine-ounce standard also served to validate all payments made in the base coin. No less a figure than Lord Deputy Carey felt the impact of the provisions in the resolution. Following his dismissal from office, the English Privy Council demanded restitution of money paid by Carey to 'the captains and officers of the army' in the nine-ounce standard. The government disallowed Carey's payment in the old standard because the 3 oz. base coin was still the current money of the realm and not due for recall for several days.[63] One other instance furnishes significant example of the influence of the case of mixed money on future litigation. Despite John Dodderidge's assertion that Davies' *Reports* 'fuerent faits pour le meridian de Ireland seulement', the case of mixed money, with its heavy reliance on civil law principles, served as future precedent to guide litigation in the highest tribunal in the United States.[64] Against the backdrop of the American civil war, the Supreme Court validated an obligation tendered in paper money for a debt contracted before the appearance of the Yankee 'greenback dollar'. To decide the case, the Supreme Court employed Davies' civil law interpretation of 'currentis monetae' to justify payment in paper currency. Some 250 years after the resolution on the base coin in Ireland, Davies' report of the case of mixed money, with its heavy emphasis on civil law, served as an authoritative guideline in determining the outcome of common law litigation in the United States.

Part IV

CONCLUSION

9

Sir John Davies, the ancient constitution and civil law

The chapters dealing with the case of the Bann fishery and the case of mixed money have demonstrated how Sir John Davies, as Irish Attorney-General, supported both private and public interests in Irish litigation through argument from Roman law. In these and other cases in the *Reports*, Davies' use of continental law was so extensive as to cast doubt upon the conventional notions of an insular common law mentality put forward by Professor J. G. A. Pocock. In his well-known study, *The Ancient Constitution and the Feudal Law*, Pocock asserted:

There was no reason why a common lawyer should compare his law with that of Europe except an intellectual curiosity arising and operating outside the everyday needs of his profession.[1]

This assumption that English lawyers practised their trade in a professional climate devoid of all practical contact with European law, is, however, extremely narrow and fails to take into consideration the extent to which common lawyers were exposed to the civil law tradition in the seventeenth century. The major points of contact with foreign legal sources were: the law practised in the numerous non-common law jurisdictions; the legal training at the universities and Inns of Court; the early Stuart political controversies concerning public law; and finally the movement for law reform that began at the end of the sixteenth century. All these influences gave common lawyers considerable exposure to the principles and procedures of the civil law, and as Davies' work in Ireland demonstrates, this familiarity often had concrete effects in the decisions rendered by common law judges in litigation pending before the central courts.

   Even a cursory glance at the English legal system as it existed in the early seventeenth century reveals the plethora of non-common law jurisdictions that operated alongside the common law courts.

These included the hundreds of church courts that adjudicated English ecclesiastical law, the High Court of Admiralty and twenty Vice-Admiralty courts that exercised their authority according to the rules of an emergent system of international maritime law, and the small and infrequently convened Court of Chivalry that determined cases according to the law of arms. Professor Brian Levack has shown that all these minor non-common law jurisdictions were readily accommodated, even by Coke, within the larger framework of the common law; for English jurists held that these lesser jurisdictions and their substantive law had been used time out of mind, and had acquired the full status of customary law.[2] In his study of English law reporting, Dr Lewis Abbot argued that common law judges and advocates frequently consulted civilians on difficult points of law outside the purview of the common law.[3] Coke himself admitted that the common lawyers 'in matters of difficulty do use to confer with the learned in that art or science, whose resolution is requisite to the true deciding of the case in question'.[4]

The English universities and Inns of Court provided additional opportunity for acquaintance with the civil law tradition. As university education became less clerical in the sixteenth century, and as admissions to Oxford and Cambridge increased between 1540 and 1640, many future practitioners of the common law spent at least some time at universities where training in the classics, in rhetoric and in the civil law itself was not unusual.[5] One recent study has shown that this exposure to classics and to continental law was sustained through private study at the Inns of Court. Lord Chancellor Ellesmere himself acquired the basics of Roman law through study at Lincoln's Inn.[6] William Fulbecke, a member of Gray's Inn trained in both the civil and common laws, wrote a treatise in which he openly encouraged students of the common law to learn the fundamentals of Justinian's *Corpus Iuris Civilis*.[7] The judge James Whitelocke was a student of Gentili, and John Dodderidge, Justice of the Court of King's Bench, was reputed to have been trained, not only in the civil law, but in the canon law as well.[8]

If the existence of the non-common law tribunals and of the civil law training at universities and Inns of Court shows the avenues by which continental law could penetrate English legal thinking, the political debates of the Jacobean period provide dramatic examples of the uses to which such knowledge could be put, particularly in controversies surrounding public law and the nature of the royal prerogative. Perhaps because the common law evolved as an accretion of rights, duties and obligations over real property, legal controversialists found its vocabulary deficient for enunciating principles of public law. Searching for additional and more fruitful concepts, Jacobean lawyers were understandably attracted by the Roman law of Justinian. There they could find, as Maitland pointed out in his introduction to *Bracton and Azo*, a highly organized and flexible system of public law to buttress the less adequate formulations of their own legal tradition.[9]

A striking example occurs in the debates over impositions which featured certain borrowings from the more universalist second-century Roman concepts enshrined in the *ius gentium* or natural law.[10] It will be recalled that in 1610 the House of Commons aired a number of secular and ecclesiastaical grievances which led into a debate on the ability of the king to levy impositions without parliamentary approval. Dissenting voices argued that the royal prerogative itself did not constitute sufficient authority either to make or alter a law. As Justice Whitelock asserted, in Acts of parliament the 'act and power is the King's but with the assent of the Lords and Commons which maketh it the most sovereign and supreme power above all and controllable by none'.[11] While some opposed this view by defining sovereignty as vested in the king's person rather than in the corporation of the king-in-parliament, more innovative royalists like Sir John Davies got around Whitelock's theory by recourse to the laws of nature or of nations. In his treatise on impositions, Davies argued that the king's right to levy impositions had no relationship to parliamentary authority at all. On the contrary, parliament had no jurisdiction in such matters, because impositions had their origins in the 'ius gentium, the law of nature and the law merchant, which pertained to the crown alone'.[12]

Appeals to the *ius gentium* of ancient Roman law could also be employed against the interests of the crown. In 1604, the law of nature served to justify a proposal by Nicholas Fuller, a puritan lawyer, to abolish the Court of Wards.[13] In 1628, Serjeant Ashley explained confidently to the House of Lords that it was 'the ius gentium whichever serves for a supply in defect of the common law when ordinary proceedings cannot be had'.[14] This pragmatic view was corroborated by John Dodderidge, Chief Justice of the Court of King's Bench, whose manuscript treatise on the king's prerogative cited over 38 civilians and canonists. Dodderidge confessed that:

We do, as the Sorbonnists and civilians, resort to the law of nature, which is the ground of all law, and then drawing that which is more comfortable for the commonwealth, do adjudge it for law.[15]

Thus even senior members of the English bar acknowledged the usefulness of Roman doctrine in formulating principles of public law.

The pragmatic approach to use of Roman doctrine was not limited to issues of constitutional law. In 1604, Sir Thomas Craig, a Scottish Bartolist, wryly commented that the common lawyers, while never admitting the use of Roman law, could still readily 'salute it from the threshold'.[16] He then went on to show how Roman private law, particularly the laws of female succession and heritable property, featured in the reports of Plowden and Dyer. The traditional interpretation of the Germanic origins of seisin has also been called into question, and Professor Charles Donahue has cautiously put forth a notion suggesting a parallel between the Roman law of acquisitive prescription and the law of possession arising from the Limitation Act of 1624.[17] Even in the realm of property law, the common law was influenced by foreign legal doctrine.

At this point an important qualification is necessary. Outlining the attractions which made some common lawyers abandon their Littleton for Justinian is not equal to supporting those historians who argue that the common law was severely threatened by a 'reception' of Roman law either in 1534 or in the first decades of the seventeenth century. Such was the thesis put forward by Maitland for the 1530s in his famous Rede Lecture, a theory which was subsequently revived and applied by C. H. MacIlwain to the early Jacobean period.[18] If, however, by reception of Roman law we mean the assimilation of an expeditious Roman procedure to overcome the shortcoming of the more dilatory common law, or a conspiracy to build a more centralized and perhaps despotic government – then nothing of the sort took place in either period. As Professors Thorne, Elton and others have shown, the humanist Thomas Starkey's suggestion in the 1530s that England receive the law of the Romans amounted to little more than one man's modest programme for law reform.[19] We know also that neither Henry VIII nor Thomas Cromwell had any intention of erecting a despotic government inspired by the principles of the *Lex Regia* found in Justinian's *Corpus*, and that the new prerogative courts cannot be described as forums of strict civil law procedure. As Elton has shown, the purpose of the prerogative courts was to supplement and correct the common law in those areas where its enforcement or authority was deficient.[20] There is slightly more basis for a 'reception' in the early seventeenth century when tracts by two civilians, John Cowell,

Regius Professor of Civil Law at Cambridge, and Alberico Gentili, Regius Professor of Civil Law at Oxford, appeared to uphold an expanded royal prerogative on the basis of maxims drawn from the *Lex Regia* of Justinian's *Corpus*.[21] But such was the public outcry that James himself was compelled to repudiate the powers urged on his behalf.

Enough has been said to indicate the ways in which English common lawyers could exploit the civil law, but it is important to note also the growing support for law reform within the legal profession during the early seventeenth century. The common law itself did possess the means to execute change – by statute, by equity as illustrated by the use of trust, and by constructive fiction as in the replacement of real actions by ejectment. None the less pressures to reform the statute law in the 1590s, the proposed union between England and Scotland in 1604, and the English expansion into Ireland compelled English jurists such as Dodderidge, Bacon, Hobart and the civilians Cowell and Hayward to compare the deficiencies of the common law with the codified and more systematic civil law.[22] Once more, the picture of common law insularity and antagonism to foreign innovation gives way before the common lawyers' pragmatic appreciation of the civil law tradition.

To this point we have found that both legal training and the existence of numerous non-common law tribunals would have acquainted Jacobean lawyers with the precepts and practice of continental law, at the same time that the political and administrative problems of the period encouraged selective use of the civil law tradition for rhetorical purposes and to supply deficiencies in the common law itself. Given these facts, we must conclude that Pocock's argument for a common law 'frame of mind' is, if not illusory, at least very much overstated. This impression becomes even stronger if we examine more closely the specific evidence upon which Pocock based his conclusions.

Like so much of the literature on Jacobean law, Pocock's theory of a common law *Zeitgeist* bears the indelible stamp of Sir Edward Coke. For Coke the common law embodied the 'highest perfection and reason', and his voluminous *Reports* are riddled with rhetorical bombast praising the certainty, immutability and perfection of the common law whose origins stretched unbroken into some distant and idealized Anglo-Saxon past.[23] For Coke a continuum of English law ran from Anglo-Saxon time to the early seventeenth century, a truly Teutonic vision made possible by interpreting the Norman incursion of 1066 as the vindication of a valid claim to the English throne through trial by combat. By denying the Norman conquest, Coke maintained that the ancient laws survived intact, unsullied by the corrupting influences of Norman feudal law, or of the Roman and canon laws practised in continental tribunals. Coke's antipathy to the civil law tradition was notorious and is best summarized in the famous passage in his *Institutes* where he claimed:

Upon the text of the civil law there be so many glosses and interpretations and again upon these so many commentaries and all these written by doctors of equal degree and authority and therein so many diversities of opinion that they do rather increase the doubts and uncertainties and the professors of that noble science say that it is like a sea full of waves.[24]

This invective against the civil law seems to support Pocock's assertion that Coke was insular as insular could be, but there are strong reasons to suspect that neither the *Institutes* nor the *Reports* represents an adequate measuring stick to gauge Coke's attitude towards the civil law. An examination of Coke's library, for example, shows that the Chief Justice maintained a complete collection not only of the *Corpus Iuris Civilis* and the canon law, but also of the glossators as well as selected works of the humanist jurists.[25] In commenting on Coke's awareness of continental law and jurisprudence, T. E. Scrutton, in his study of Roman law influence in early modern England, uncovered quite a number of references to the civil law in Coke's *Reports*.[26] More recent scholarship has reinforced Scrutton's findings, and Professor Peter Stein has discovered that some of Coke's maxims were derived from Justinian's *Digest*.[27]

If Coke's aversion to using civil law principles when expedient is itself in doubt, it is equally unclear to what extent he typified the English legal profession in the early Stuart period. Among contemporaries, Coke's place as a jurist seems to have been less influential than many modern historians assume. Sir Francis Bacon, for example, spoke slightingly of Coke's *Reports* and cautioned readers that there were 'many peremptory and extra judicial resolutions more than are warranted'.[28] In 1615, Lord Chancellor Ellesmere, in his *Observations upon the Lord Coke's Reports*, provided a more devastating critique of the corpus of Coke's work and summarized the *Reports* as 'sunt mala, sunt quaedam mediocria, sunt bona plura'.[29] He then went on to warn that Coke, 'in order to serve his own conceits', deliberately misrepresented judgement to establish his own views touching the decision of the court. It seems, therefore, that even among contemporaries Coke did not possess the inviolable authority depicted by many modern historians. In the eighteenth century, Justice William Mansfield described Coke as an 'uncouth crabbed author who has disappointed and disheartened many a Tyro'.[30] In the nineteenth century, one English jurist wryly observed that Coke rarely had any authority for what he wrote, and James Stephen, in his history of English criminal law, written in 1883, attributed Coke's prominence not to any technical legal expertise, but to the fact that his voluminous *Reports* dominated English legal literature – a monopoly 'behind whose work it was not necessary to go'.[31]

If Sir Edward Coke cannot be seen as wholly representative of English legal thought in the seventeenth century, it is necessary to examine the remaining evidence that supports Pocock's 'common law frame of mind'. Aside from Coke, the balance of Pocock's argument rests on Sir John Davies' introduction to the *Irish Law Reports*.[32] No other English lawyer of the seventeenth century, with the exception of Coke, praised the certainty of the common law more than Davies; no other English jurist compared the common law more favourably to the civil law. A brief illustration of Davies' rhetorical style provides a flavour of his invective against civilian critics of the common law. Against aspersions cast at the dilatory nature of English litigation, Davies cited Bodin's reference to a case that lay pending in the French courts for over a hundred years.[33] He then launched a rejoinder to the civilians and canonists by comparing, as Coke compared, the decisions of the doctors to a sea full of waves. To elaborate his point, Davies borrowed a rather extraordinary metaphor from the sixteenth-century Spanish canonist Loudovico Gomez who compared the work of the civilians and canonists to:

Calices in capite elephantis, qua vident priora et posteriora.[34]

On the basis of such evidence, it was not unnatural for Pocock to conclude that Davies conformed to all the attitudes ascribed to Coke. This interpretation, however, can only be sustained by isolating the introduction from the text of Davies' *Reports*. If we peer beyond the introduction and examine the substance of the legal arguments reported by Davies in the Irish courts, a rather different pattern emerges. Indeed the *Reports* show that the Irish Attorney-General cited the civil and canon laws as frequently as statute law in active

Irish litigation.[35] On the basis of the *Reports* themselves, we must conclude that Davies does not fit the pattern of a common law orthodoxy.

Davies' familiarity with the Roman and canon laws probably originated in his educational training at Oxford and the Middle Temple. If it is true that Davies studied at New College, Oxford, we can infer some exposure to the civil law tradition there. The New College statutes, issued by William of Wykeham in 1379, established a strong legist tradition by stipulating that ten fellows were to study canon law and ten civil law.[36] Such an emphasis on legal training and the college's collection of civil and canon law manuscripts, second only to that of All Souls, provided ample study material, and we know from the text of the *Reports* that Davies consulted some of the college's canon law manuscripts.[37] A more important source of contact with civil law practice may have been Davies' friendship with the Dutch civilian, Paul Merula. During the autumn of 1592, while still a student at the Middle Temple, Davies journeyed with two friends to the Low Countries to visit Merula at the University of Leyden. Professor of civil law and jurisprudence and mentor of Grotius, Merula was one of the premier jurists of his day.[38] Two letters written by Davies to Merula reveal a close professional friendship, and we cannot discount the possibility that Davies' mysterious absence from the Middle Temple records between 16 October 1595 and 9 February 1598 may have been due to an extended period of study on the continent.[39] This sojourn in the Low Countries, where the civil law was accepted in commerce and in other areas where it did not conflict with Dutch customary law, provides an analogy to the situation in England and Ireland, and Davies' subsequent use of the civil and canon laws to consolidate the Tudor conquest may reflect his observations on the relationship between the civil and customary law in the Netherlands.

Of course, residual civil law influences existed in Ireland as they did in England at the beginning of the seventeenth century. There were the same ecclesiastical and Admiralty jurisdictions, Trinity College Dublin was empowered to confer degrees in civil law, and certain categories of Roman law may have supplied the organizational framework to administer the brehon law.[40] However the use of the civil law in Ireland was significantly expanded by Davies and other English jurists as they attempted to justify and consolidate English sovereignty over the island.

The most important and most drastic use of civil law principles is found in the assertion by Davies and other contemporary jurists of an English title to Ireland by right of conquest. According to established civil law doctrine, conquest eliminated all prior and current rights to property and rule on the part of the conquered. Professor Donald Sutherland has shown that the patterns of proprietary exclusiveness laid down in Justinian's *Corpus* to describe the status of real and moveable property taken by conquest were elaborated and extended by medieval and early modern jurists to imply a sovereign title to all conquered territory.[41] The classical antecedents to this latter doctrine are particularly evident in Grotius, Gentili and Zouche, and the same principles appear to have coloured discussions on Irish sovereignty even before Davies used similar arguments in the *Reports* and the *Brief Discovery*.[42] As early as 1534 Patrick Finglas, Henry VIII's Chief Baron of the Exchequer, claimed that the true restoration of English sovereignty in Ireland lay in a military conquest.[43] This proposition may have influenced Thomas Cromwell's draft bill of the same year to establish a public law title to Ireland by right of conquest.[44] The purpose of Cromwell's plan was to exploit the radical powers conferred by conquest to secure a resumption of all spiritual and temporal land by the crown. At the time, the state lacked the financial and military assets to make this claim a reality, but in 1558 a proposal was again made to initiate a military conquest based on the model of the Roman law, anticipating by 45 years the solution applied by Davies and other English jurists at the end of Tyrone's rebellion in 1603.[45]

In the wake of Tyrone's rebellion, the legal theory of conquest as propounded by Davies had two purposes. First, Ireland, including the Gaelic dynasts, would have to accept the English common law as its own, without competition from the brehon law, especially such customary procedures of Gaelic landholding and descent as gavelkind and tanistry. Second, conquest would justify the eradication of the domestic Irish laws and the elimination of all derivative claims, foreign and Gaelic, that were contingent upon the papal donation of Ireland in 1154.

The papal donation, a legacy from the middle ages, cropped up on several occasions during the sixteenth century and compelled English lawyers and polemicists like Davies, Ellesmere and Coke to deny papal temporal jurisdiction in Ireland by invoking the powers of conquest.[46] Thus despite Pocock's claim that 'conquest was not admitted in the age of Blackstone any more than in the age of Coke', Davies and other legal theorists held that the military victory of 1603 superseded the limited sovereignty left by an incomplete medieval conquest.[47] This use of the conquest doctrine imposed a legacy on future discussions of Irish sovereignty. As Dr A. G. Donaldson has shown in his study of English statutes in Ireland, the maxims of the Roman law doctrine of conquest continued to serve as a justification for English sovereignty through to the end of the nineteenth century.[48]

The text of Davies' *Reports* shows that the civil and canon laws also played a significant role in litigation argued before the central common law courts in Dublin. This projection of continental law on to the forum of active litigation represents an elaboration of the tendency of the common lawyers to identify the law practised in the various civil law jurisdictions as the common law of the land.[49] Davies endorsed this tendency to ascribe a customary status to foreign law in his application of the medieval canon law to several common law cases argued before the central courts in Dublin.

Davies' obvious familiarity with the medieval canon law can only be explained by the fact that, despite the split with Rome, the canon law continued to be used in the various ecclesiastical jurisdictions within England. There had been, it is true, a number of attempts to adapt the old 'Popish canons' to the radically altered political situation launched by the supremacy. In 1534, the English parliament provided that the king might appoint a commission of thirty-two jurists to prepare a new code of the 'King's ecclesiastical laws of the church of England', but the king failed to act on the statute.[50] A further enabling statute passed in 1536 extended the provision of the Act of 1534, but Henry once again failed to act. In 1544, a new statute authorized another commission which apparently did receive the royal assent, but the appearance of a new book of ecclesiastical law in 1546 failed to obtain royal approval. A similar effort authorized in 1550 to carry on the task of Henry's earlier commission was discontinued during the Marian reaction. Further attempts to reform the old canon law under Elizabeth were no more successful, and the appearance of John Foxe's *Reformatio Legum Ecclesiasticarum*, which represented a synthesis of the work of earlier reformers, never received the approval of the queen, parliament or convocation.[51] This meant that the pre-Reformation *Corpus Iuris Canonici*, excised of those provisions repugnant to the royal supremacy, continued to be practised in the various ecclesiastical courts in England. In his use of this canon law, Davies like other English civilians and common lawyers took the position that the canon law of Rome was received through the medium of provincial and diocesan legislation – a view which attained the status of orthodoxy and was espoused by Stubbs and the Anglican hierarchy at the end of the nineteenth century.[52] In other words, Davies subscribed to a constitutional theory which held that the *Decretum* of Gratian, the *Decretales* of Gregory IX, the *Liber Sextus* of Boniface VIII, the *Clementines* or rescripts of Clement V and the *Extravagantes* or uncodified edicts of succeeding popes all represented a body of law that had acquired the status of English customary law.

Such was the rationale Davies used in arguing the Irish case of commendams, where he defined the evolution of the legal doctrine authorizing clerics to hold plural benefices *in commendam* by citing no less than a dozen authorities from the standard text of the *Corpus Iuris Canonici*.[53] Davies explained his lavish display of canonical learning by claiming that the canon law of papist Europe was accepted as a customary law of the English church.[54] The argument is further developed in Davies' presentation of the case of proxies and the case of the dean and chapter of Fernes.

In the case of proxies, argued on a demurrer before the assembled Barons of the Irish Exchequer Court in 1605, Davies secured a crown right to procurations, a kind of tax levied by the bishops to support ecclesiastical visitation, which before the dissolution had belonged to the hospital of St John of Jerusalem and to the Victorine Abbey of Thomas Court in Dublin.[55] Following the dissolution, the rectories to which these procurations had been appendant were leased in fee farm by the crown to reward faithful service by government officials and select members of the Pale gentry. Thereafter the crown never attempted to collect the proxies that had appertained to lands so leased. When, during the early seventeenth century, the Dublin government identified ecclesiastical procurations as a potentially lucrative source of revenue, litigation resulted, often involving prominent local officials who denied any liability to make either retroactive or future payment of proxies. In a test case that was endorsed by a judicial resolution, Davies succeeded in securing a resumption of the coveted proxies by supplementing his common law brief with numerous citations from the medieval canon law.[56]

In this instance, however, Davies took a slightly different approach from that pursued in the case of commendams. Rather than define the nature of proxies through the standard text of the *Corpus Iuris Canonici*, he referred instead to two well-known sixteenth-century secondary handbooks on the medieval canon law. From the text of the *Reports*, it is possible to identify these secondary works as the *Institutiones Iuris Canonici*, written by the sixteenth-century Italian jurist, Giovanni Paolo Lancelloti, who organized the canon law according to the categories set down in Justinian's *Corpus Iuris Civilis*, and the *Catalogus Gloriae Mundi*, a compendium of legal and antiquarian knowledge assembled by the sixteenth-century French jurist Barthélemy de Chassaneux.[57] Unlike the standard corpus of the canon law, these secondary works proved particularly useful to persons lacking formal training in the canon law for the simple reason that they were indexed. Not only were these sources instrumental in recovering the procurations to the crown, but they were also subsequently endorsed, through Davies' *Reports*, as an authoritative exposition of Anglican canon law in John Godolphin's *Repertorium Canonicum* in 1678.[58]

This reliance on secondary texts is further illustrated by the case of the dean and chapter of Fernes where the canon law of corporate consent was defined once again through Lancelloti and supplemented by the fifteenth-century Italian jurist, Nicolo de Tudeschi, whose authority in canonical studies earned him the title 'lucerna iuris', or 'lamp of the law'.[59] In this instance the Roman canon law facilitated the recovery of the manor of Fedart which had been unlawfully alienated by the dean and chapter. Like the case of proxies, the case of the dean and chapter of Fernes also served to define precisely, through the vehicle of the Roman canon law, the canon law of Protestant England concerning valid alienation of ecclesiastical property. Gibson's eighteenth-century edition of the Anglican canon law used this case as an authoritative exposition of the ecclesiastical law of corporate consent.[60]

In his interpretation of the medieval canon law, Davies was in line with the view taken up by Phillimore, Stubbs and the Anglican hierarchy in the late nineteenth century. This orthodox position, which was almost universally upheld by English theologians and ecclesiastical historians from the time of the Reformation, maintained that the canon law of England, before and after the Reformation, was binding in the English ecclesiastical courts, not by reason of papal *auctoritas*, but through the discriminating authority of English provincial synods. This official interpretation of the medieval canon law remained unchallenged until the appearance of Maitland's devastating study of Lyndwood's *Provinciale*.[61] Contrary to accepted theory, Maitland discovered that medieval English canonists and theologians readily accepted the canon law on the basis of papal *auctoritas*, and that English provincial synods had no authority either to receive or to reject decretals from Rome.

The practice of ascribing customary status to continental law was also followed in some of the secular litigation in the central Irish courts. In the case of the county palatine of Wexford, Davies discussed the origins and the jurisdictional powers assigned to a palatinate by citing the well-known maxim attributed to Baldus, the famous medieval Italian jurist that 'solus princeps qui est monarch et emperator in regno suo, ex plenitudine potestatis potest creare comitem palatinum'. He then went on to say that according 'to this rule, the king of England may well create an earl palatine, as he is monarch and emperor in his reign'.[62] The importance of the case lies in its definitive statement of the nature and authority of palatine jurisdictions in Ireland, and it is significant to note that the case was cited as justification for restoring the Ormonde palatinate in 1660.[63] A further illustration of Davies' pragmatic approach to the civil law may be seen in his arguments reported in the case of the Bann fishery. In the absence of fully adequate common law precedents, Davies fortified his brief to secure the seizure of the richest fishery in Ulster by citing 'divers rules of the civil law and the customary law of France agreeable to our law in this point'.[64] Once again the corpus of civil law, as defined by the sixteenth-century French humanist legal scholars, Jacques Cujas and Renattus Choppinus, made up for the shortcomings of Davies' own legal brief. Although the dictates of natural geography tell us that rivers flow towards the sea, Davies' application of the civil law led to the government's seizure of the Bann fishery because the sea flows into rivers.[65]

The case of mixed money reveals Davies once again exploiting the civil law on a difficult question of public law. The case arose from the refusal of Irish merchants to accept base money for debts antecedent to the appearance of the debased coin in 1601. In the absence of common law principles, Davies justified a prerogative right to alter the coinage by referring to a compendium of civil law tracts entitled *De Monetis et Re Nummaria*, edited by René Budelius, a sixteenth-century French civilian responsible for the operation of the Bavarian mint.[66] Through Budelius, Davies adopted some of the more authoritarian legal principles developed by Bodin, Dumoulin and other French humanist lawyers to establish a prerogative right to alter the intrinsic value of money without the consent of estates or parliaments.[67] As Davies smugly noted, 'in this point the common law of England agrees well with the rules of the civil law'.[68] The results of the case were to saddle the merchant class and the army with the Irish war debt. In 1609, four years after the case of mixed money, Davies demonstrated his esteem for Budelius' work by sending a copy to Cecil as a gift to guide him in legal matters associated with his newly acquired post of Lord Treasurer.[69]

Davies' legal pragmatism could be illustrated by further litigation from the *Reports*, but the examples already discussed are more than sufficient to show that Davies' alleged common law orthodoxy arises solely from Pocock's uncritical acceptance of the introduction divorced from the text of the *Reports*. As we have discovered, a more critical examination of that text shows Davies to have been a thoroughly cosmopolitan and innovative legal thinker fully acquainted with the sources of continental law and jurisprudence. Indeed, Davies' familiarity with the civil law tradition justifies not only a revision of the notion that common lawyers in the Jacobean period rejected foreign doctrine in framing principles of common law, but also a revision of Pocock's central thesis – that the common lawyers' sense of history stemmed from their ignorance of continental legal scholarship.

Such is the reputation of Pocock's thesis that it has reappeared in a more recent historical controversy. In an exchange in *Past and Present*, Mr Christopher Brooks and Mr Kevin Sharpe took issue with Dr D. R. Kelley over the alleged insularity of the common lawyers.[70] Like Pocock before him, Kelley contended that in the political controversies of Jacobean England, English lawyers, untouched by the scholarly tradition of the French historical school of jurisprudence, interpreted their history through the ahistorical context of some mythical Anglo-Saxon past. By contrast, French lawyer-polemicists served the political controversies of the French wars of religion in a different way. They exploited the counterpoint of written civil law and unwritten customary law to unravel their historical past through the feudal origins of their laws and institutions. In other words, the historical arguments put forth by the common lawyers in the political controversies of early seventeenth-century England, as evidenced by writers like Sir Edward Coke and Sir John Davies, were possible only because English jurists remained ignorant of the civil law tradition, and of the impact of humanist scholarship on the development of law and jurisprudence on the continent. Since it has been argued here that Coke himself was not wholly ignorant of the civil law tradition, and that Davies was thoroughly familiar not only with the Roman and canon laws, but also with the literature of French legal humanism, it is no longer possible to accept the view, as presented in *The Ancient Constitution and the Feudal Law*, that the common lawyers' sense of history stemmed from their congenital ignorance of continental law and jurisprudence. In other words, the creation of a common law 'frame of mind' to explain the use of a mythical Anglo-Saxon past in structuring the course of English history needs to be thoroughly revised, because it implies that lawyers like Davies did not understand what they read. Such a revision lies beyond the scope of this study, but future research might very well focus on simpler and more obvious reasons of utility.

Given the convoluted nature of hermeneutics and philology developed by continental legal scholars, the myth of an Anglo-Saxon heritage, which appeared as early as the reign of Edward I in *The Mirror Justices*, provided a ready-made and far more straightforward instrument to structure a national past.[71] Although Kelley recently altered his description of early modern common lawyers from 'insular' to 'peninsular', a more fitting adjective would be 'eclectic'.[72]

Notes

1 Law as an instrument of colonization

1 N. P. Canny, *The Elizabethan Conquest of Ireland: A Pattern Established 1565–1576* (Hassocks, 1976).

2 Sir John Davies, *Le Primer Report des Cases in les Courts del Roy* (Dublin, 1615). There is an excellent English translation: *A Report of Cases and Matters in Law Resolved and Abridged in the King's Courts in Ireland* (Dublin, 1762); hereafter cited as *Reports*.

3 J. C. Becket, *The Making of Modern Ireland, 1603–1923* (London, 1961), p. 36.

4 T. W. Moody, F. X. Martin and F. J. Byrne, *A New History of Ireland* (Oxford, 1976), p. 196; F. W. Harris, 'The Rebellion of Sir Cahir O'Doherty and its Legal Aftermath', *Irish Jurist*, 15 (1980), pp. 298–325.

5 D. B. Quinn, 'Ireland and Sixteenth-Century European Expansion', *Historical Studies*, 1 (1958), pp. 20–32; also useful is Karl Bottigheimer, 'Kingdom and Colony in the Westward Enterprise, 1536–1660', in K. R. Andrews, N. P. Canny and P. E. Hair (eds.), *The Westward Enterprise: English Activities in Ireland, the Atlantic and America, 1480–1650* (Liverpool, 1978), pp. 45–64.

6 R. Reynolds, *Europe Emerges* (Madison, 1961), pp. 434, 495–500; M. Jenson and R. Reynolds, 'European Colonial Experience: A Plea for Comparative Studies', *Studi in Onore di Gino Luzzatto*, 4 (1950), p. 77; C. Verlinden, *The Beginnings of Modern Colonization* (Ithaca, 1970), pp. 7–8. For a social scientist's perspective see M. Hechter, *Internal Colonialism* (London, 1975), pp. 84–7, 102–4; also useful is R. R. Davies, 'Colonial Wales', *P & P*, 65 (1974), pp. 3–23.

7 B. Bradshaw, *The Irish Constitutional Revolution of the Sixteenth Century* (Cambridge, 1979), pp. 193–257; A. Clarke, 'Ireland, 1534–1660', in J. Lee (ed.), *Irish Historiography 1970–79* (Cork, 1981), p. 38.

8 B. Bradshaw, 'Sword, Word and Strategy in the Reformation in Ireland', *HJ*, 21 (1978), pp. 475–502; also 'The Elizabethans and the Irish', *Studies*, 66 (1977), pp. 38–50.

9 Canny, *Elizabethan Conquest*, pp. 117–36; *The Formation of the Old English Elite in Ireland* (O'Donnell Lecture, University College Dublin, 1974), p. 17.

10 Canny, *Elizabethan Conquest*, pp. 122, 133–4.

11 For the origins and development of conquest right in Western legal thought see D. Sutherland, 'Conquest and Law', *Studia Gratiana*, 15 (1972), pp. 35–51.

12 Henricus de Segusio, *In Quinque Decretalium Libri Commentaria et in Sextem Decretalium Librum*, 4 vols. (Venice, 1581), vol. 3, p. 128b: 'Mihi tamen videtur, quod in aduentu Christi omnis honor, et omnis principatus, et omne dominium, et iurisdictio de iure et ex causa iusta . . . omni infideli subtracta fuerit et ad fideles translata.' For Innocent IV see *Commentaria Super Libros Quinque Decretalium Gregory IX* (Frankfurt, 1570), p. 430b: 'Imo si male tractarent Christianos, posset eos priuare per sententiam iurisdictione et dominio, quod super eos habet, tamen magna causa debet esse, quod ad hoc veniat, debet enim Papa eos quantum potest sustinere, dummodo periculum non sit Christianis, nec grave scandulum generetur.'

13 K. Pennington, 'Bartolomeo de Las Casas and the Tradition of Medieval Law', *Church History*, 39 (1970), p. 152; J. H. Parry, *The Spanish Theory of Empire in the Sixteenth Century* (Cambridge, 1940), p. 13; see also his *Age of the Reconnaissance* (London, 1963), pp. 373–4; L. Hanke, *The Spanish Struggle for Justice in the Conquest of America* (Philadelphia, 1949), p. 28; J. Muldoon, 'The Contribution of the Medieval Canon Lawyers to the Formation of International Law', *Traditio*, 28 (1972), p. 492.

14 J. Muldoon, 'The Remonstrance of the Irish Princes and the Canon Law Tradition of Just War', *AJLH*, 22 (1978), p. 310.

15 For the application of conquest right to Ireland see my recent article: 'Sir John Davies, the Ancient Constitution and Civil Law', *HJ*, 23 (1980), pp. 689–702.

16 Davies, *Reports*, p. 111.

17 SP/63/219/fos. 109b–110a; *CSPI, 1603–6*, p. 575.

18 Davies, *Reports*, p. 112.

19 *Ibid.*, pp. 101, 109, 112; K. Zweigert (ed.), *Legal Aspects of Economic Development, Surveys Made at the Request of UNESCO* (Paris, 1966), pp. 75–9.

20 A. MacFarlane, *The Origins of English Individualism* (Cambridge, 1978), pp. 80–130.

21 K. W. Nicholls, *Gaelic and Gaelicized Ireland in the Middle Ages* (Dublin, 1972), pp. 8–10, 25–30, 57–65; Davies, *Reports*, p. 134; SP/63/219/fos. 109b–110a; *CSPI, 1603–6*, p. 575.

22 Davies, *Reports*, p. 134. This view was shared by other English jurists in Ireland at that time. See Huntingdon Library, MS 7042; I wish to thank Professor Nial Osborough of the Law Department at Trinity College, Dublin, for providing me with a typescript of this manuscript.

23 Nicholls, *Gaelicized Ireland*, pp. 59–60; Davies, *Reports*, p. 136.

24 K. W. Nicholls, *Land, Law and Society in Sixteenth-Century Ireland* (O'Donnell Lecture, University College Cork, 1976), p. 20.

25 Davies, *Reports*, pp. 134–8; SP/63/219/fos. 109b–110a; *CSPI, 1603–6*, p. 575.

26 *The English Reports, King's Bench Division* (London, 1909), vol. 91, pp. 356–7.

27 *The English Reports, Chancery* (London, 1903), vol. 24, p. 646.

28 W. Blackstone, *Commentaries on the Laws of England*, 4 vols. (Oxford, 1773), vol. 1, p. 107; see also J. H. Merivale's report in the case of *Attorney-General* v. *Stewart* in 1817 in *The English Reports, Chancery* (London, 1904), vol. 35, pp. 899–900. Also useful is the case of *Cooper* v. *Stewart* concerning New South Wales. *The Law Reports, Appeal Cases before the House of Lords and the Judicial Committee of the Privy Council* (London, 1889), vol. 14, p. 293. Particularly helpful from a jurisprudential view is A. C. Castles, *An Introduction to Australian Legal History* (Melbourne, 1971), pp. 1–11.

29 Sir Frederick Pollock, *The Expansion of the Common Law* (London, 1924), pp. 16–17, 134–5.

30 Zweigert, *Legal Aspects of Economic Development*, p. 77.

31 O. Adewoye, *The Judicial System in Southern Nigeria 1854–1954* (London, 1977), p. 14; also useful is A. G. Hopkins, 'Property Rights and Empire Building: Britain's Annexation of Lagos, 1861', *Journal of Economic History*, 40 (1980), pp. 777–97.

32 Morley, p. 259.

2 Sir John Davies: a biographical sketch

1 With the exception of a few details, this biographical sketch follows closely upon a path laid down by others. None the less, as a synthesis of more recent studies, this chapter differs considerably in emphasis from any previous work. There is a mammoth literature on Davies, particularly with respect to his literary career. For a complete bibliography see James L. Sanderson, 'Recent Studies in Sir John Davies', *English Literary Renaissance*, 4 (1974), pp. 411–17. The present account owes much to R. Krueger (ed.), *The Poems of Sir John Davies* (Oxford, 1975), pp. xxiii–xlvii; J. R. Brink, 'Sir John Davies: His Life and Major Works' (University of Wisconsin, unpublished Ph.D. thesis, 1972), pp. 8–82; T. J. Childs, 'An Edition of "Nosce Teipsum" by Sir John Davies with an Introductory Account of his Work' (University of Oxford, unpublished M. Litt. thesis, 1939), pp. 1–109; Margaret Seeman, *Sir John Davies, Sein Leben und Seine Werke* (Vienna and Leipzig, 1913); C. Litton Falkiner, 'Sir John Davies', in *Essays Relating to Ireland* (London, 1909), pp. 32–55; G. J. Hand, 'Sir John Davies, 1569–1626', *Gazette of the Incorporated Law Society of Ireland*, 64 (1971), pp. 174–7; Mary Von Roemer, 'Notes on the Descendants of Edward Combe of Bridsor in Tisbury', *Wiltshire Notes and Queries*, 8 (1914–16), pp. 63–73.

2 A. B. Grosart (ed.), *The Works in Verse and Prose Including Hitherto Unpublished Manuscripts of Sir John Davies*, 3 vols. (Blackburn, 1869–76), vol. 2, pp. xxix–xxx.

3 These poems, with the rest of Davies' poetic works, are featured in Krueger, *Poems*, pp. 1–126.

4 HMC, *Hastings MSS*, vol. 4, p. 352.

5 T. F. Kirby, *Winchester Scholars* (London, 1888), pp. 147–8; Krueger, *Poems*, p. xxvi.

6 A. Clarke (ed.), *Register of the University of Oxford*, 2 vols. (Oxford, 1887), vol. 2, pt. 2, p. 147. The matriculation registers show a John Davies who

took his degree from Magdalen College in 1590, but this was probably a man of the same name from Monmouth who entered Magdalen in 1585. *Ibid.*, vol. 2, pt. 3, p. 160; J. Foster (ed.), *Alumni Oxoniensis*, 4 vols. (Oxford, 1891), vol. 1, p. 380.

7 *MTR*, vol. 1, p. 296.

8 The fee for former residents of New Inn was set at 20 shillings.

9 *MTR*, vol. 1, p. 354.

10 *Ibid.*, pp. 293, 419.

11 *Ibid.*, p. 318.

12 *Ibid.*, pp. 327–8; for other disciplinary action see pp. 311, 318, 320 and 332. For student disorders at the Inns see W. R. Prest, *The Inns of Court under Elizabeth and the Early Stuarts, 1590–1640* (London, 1972), pp. 94–100.

13 For Merula's letter to Camden see BL Cotton MS Julius C.v, fo. 49a; for Davies' letters see Bodl. D'Orville MS 52, fos. 49a–50a.

14 *Ibid.*, fo. 49a.

15 *Ibid.*, fo. 50a.

16 SP/63/218/fo. 152a; *CSPI, 1603–6*, p. 463; 'For myself I have lost so noble a patron of my poor fortune as the Earl of Devonshire, who first transplanted me here.' Mountjoy became the Earl of Devonshire in 1603.

17 *MTR*, vol. 1, p. 228.

18 Bodl. Carte MS 62, fo. 590a.

19 Krueger, *Poems*, p. 89.

20 John Aubrey, *Brief Lives*, 2 vols. (Oxford, 1898), vol. 2, p. 48.

21 BL Harl. MS 1576, fos. 562–3.

22 SP/63/222/fo. 319a.

23 BL Harl. MS 5353, fo. 127b.

24 J. L. Sanderson, 'Epigrames per Benjamin Rudyerd and Some Stolen Feathers', *Review of English Studies*, 17 (1966), pp. 251–3.

25 BL Harl. MS 1576, fo. 556.

26 *Ibid.*, fos. 561–2.

27 *Ibid.*, fo. 559.

28 P. J. Finklepearl, 'Sir John Davies and the Prince d'Amour', *Notes and Queries*, 208 (1963), pp. 300–2.

29 BL Harl. MS 1576, fo. 559; J. R. Brink, 'The Composition Date of Sir John Davies' *Nosce Teipsum*', HLQ, 37 (1973), pp. 24–7.

30 *MTR*, vol. 1, pp. 379–80.

31 BL Harl. MS 5353, fo. 12b.

32 W. P. Baildon (ed.), *The Black Books of Lincoln's Inn*, 4 vols. (London, 1899–1902), vol. 2, p. 55; Brink, 'Davies' Life and Works', pp. 23–4.

33 Baildon, *Black Books*, vol. 2, p. 55; between 1590 and 1599 there were a total of eight personal assaults at the Inns, five of which were committed with a weapon. Prest, *Inns of Court*, p. 99.

34 H. H. Hudson (ed.), *John Hoskins, Directions for Speech and Style* (Princeton, 1935), p. 22.

35 Bodl. Carte MS 62, fo. 590a.

36 A. Wood, *Athenae Oxoniensis*, 2 vols. (London, 1722), vol. 1, p. 506; Grosart, *The Works in Verse and Prose of Sir John Davies*, vol. 2, pp. xxix–xxx.

37 A. L. Rowse, *The England of Elizabeth: The Structure of Society* (London, 1973), p. 564.
38 Krueger, *Poems*, p. xxv.
39 Bodl. Autog. MS d. 21, fo. 147a.
40 N. E. McClure (ed.), *The Letters of John Chamberlain*, 2 vols. (Philadelphia, 1939), vol. 1, p. 189; hereafter cited as *Chamberlain's Letters*.
41 BL Harl. MS 5353, fo. 127b.
42 Bodl. Carte MS 62, fo. 590a.
43 J. P. Collier, *A Bibliographical and Critical Account of the Rarest Books in the English Language*, 2 vols. (New York, 1865), vol. 1, p. 237.
44 BL Lansdowne MS 88, fo. 4a.
45 *Chamberlain's Letters*, vol. 1, pp. 177–8.
46 Perhaps Davies' association with Robert Cotton and the Society of Antiquaries brought him into influential circles. Cotton and Davies were admitted to the Middle Temple within one week of each other, and they were also chambermates. *MTR*, vol. 1, p. 322. Cotton must have discontinued his stay at the Middle Temple because on 2 June 1595 Davies was assigned a new chambermate. *Ibid.*, p. 353; while in Ireland, Davies maintained his contact with Cotton. In 1607 Davies sent Cotton several maps of Irish towns. BL Cotton MS Julius C.iii, fo. 134a; Grosart, *The Works in Verse and Prose of Sir John Davies*, vol. 2, pp. cxiv–cxv; Davies delivered several discourses on legal history to the Society of Antiquaries entitled *Antiquity, Use and Ceremonies of Lawful Combats in England* (given 22 May 1601); *The Antiquity and Office of the Earl Marshal of England* (12 Feb. 1603); *The Antiquity, Authority and Succession of the High Steward of England* (4 June 1603). These may be found in print in Thomas Hearne (ed.), *A Collection of Curious Discourses*, 2 vols. (Oxford, 1771), vol. 1, pp. 238–45; vol. 2, pp. 108–11; vol. 2, pp. 35–7; also in Grosart, *The Works in Verse and Prose of Sir John Davies*, vol. 3, pp. 285–306.
47 BL Lansdowne MS 88, fo. 34a; see also BL Cecil MS 90, fo. 68a; HMC, *Salisbury MSS*, vol. 11, p. 544.
48 Huntington MS 2522; I wish to thank Miss Kate Howells for sending me a transcription of this manuscript.
49 Lord Stowell, 'Observation on with a Copy of, the Proceedings Had in the Parliament of the Middle Temple Respecting a Petition of Sir John Davies to be Restored to the Degree of Barrister, AD 1601', *Archaelogia*, 21 (1827), p. 112; *Chamberlain's Letters*, vol. 1, p. 126. During the period 1580–99, there were a total number of 25 expulsions from the Inns of Court of which only four, from Lincoln's Inn, were not readmitted. Thus Davies' return to grace fits within a general pattern of discipline at the Inns. See Prest, *Inns of Court*, p. 96.
50 *MTR*, vol. 1, p. 429; vol. 2, pp. 482, 511 and 524; for his nephew's admission see *ibid.*, vol. 2, p. 578.
51 Davies also made speeches concerning the transportation of English money overseas and in support of the trade of painter stainers. Heywood Townshend, *Historical Collections, or an Exact Account of the proceedings of the Four Last Parliaments of Queen Elizabeth* (London, 1680), pp. 227, 270; John Hutchins, *The History and Antiquities of the County of Dorset* (Westminster, 1861), p. 472.

52 Townshend, *Historical Collections*, p. 244.
53 *Ibid.*, p. 242; See also S. D'Ewes, *The Journal of All the Parliaments during the Reign of Queen Elizabeth* (London, 1682), p. 555.
54 Townshend, *Historical Collections*, p. 244.
55 *Ibid.*, p. 244; D'Ewes, *Journal of All the Parliaments*, p. 656.
56 Townshend, *Historical Collections*, p. 258.
57 D'Ewes, *Journal of All the Parliaments*, p. 656.
58 John Hutchinson, *A Catalogue of Notable Middle Templars* (London, 1902), p. 244; Vicary Gibbs (ed.), *The Complete Peerage of England, Scotland, Ireland, Great Britain and the United Kingdom*, 13 vols. (London, 1910), vol. 1, p. 343.
59 SP/63/227/fo. 173a; *CSPI, 1608–10*, p. 244; SP/63/227/fo. 135b; *CSPI, 1608–10*, p. 297.
60 *A Complete Collection of State Trials and Proceedings for the High Treason and other Crimes and Misdemeanors from the Reign of Richard II to the End of the Reign of George I*, 6 vols. (London, 1730), vol. 1, pp. 366–73; see also Caroline Bingham, 'Seventeenth-Century Attitudes towards Deviant Sex', *Journal of Interdisciplinary History*, 1 (1971), pp. 447–72; *MTR*, vol. 2, p. 531.
61 HMC, *Hastings MSS*, vol. 4, p. 17.
62 SP/14/139/135; *CSPD, 1619–23*, p. 400.
63 *Chamberlain's Letters*, vol. 2, p. 444.
64 George Ballard, *Memoirs of Several Ladies of Great Britain* (Oxford, 1752), p. 274; for Lady Eleanor's printed works see C. J. Hindle, 'A Bibliography of the Printed Pamphlets and Broadsides of Lady Eleanor Douglas the Seventeenth-Century Prophetess', *Edinburgh Bibliographical Society Transactions*, vol. 1, pt. 1 (1935–6), pp. 65–98.
65 Ballard, *Memoirs of Several Ladies*, p. 278; M. W. Greenslade, *A History of the County of Stafford*, 3 vols. (Oxford, 1970), vol. 3, p. 59.
66 SP/16/255/19 and 20; *CSPD, 1633–4*, p. 261; SP/16/255/21; *CSPD, 1633–4*, p. 274.
67 The letter is reprinted in Brink, 'Davies' Life and Works', p. 62.
68 *Ibid.*, p. 63.
69 Ballard, *Memoirs of Several Ladies*, p. 278.
70 Philip Hardacre, 'Gerrard Winstanley in 1650', *HLQ*, 22 (1958), pp. 345–9.
71 Davies was appointed Solicitor-General on 25 November 1603, and subsequently advanced on 9 May 1606 to replace Charles Calthorpe as Attorney-General. Rowley Lascelles, *Liber Munerum Publicorum Hiberniae*, 2 vols. (Dublin, 1810) vol. 1, pt. 2, pp. 573 and 575; Erck, pp. 15, 29 and 280.
72 Bodl. Carte MS 62, fo. 568a.
73 SP/63/216/fo. 34a; *CSPI, 1603–6*, p. 155.
74 SP/63/229/fos. 34a and b; *CSPI, 1608–10*, pp. 451–2.
75 Dublin Castle – Genealogical Office: Herald's Visitation MS 45, pp. 56–7; *Cal. Car., 1603–24*, p. 383; W. A. Shaw, *The Knights of England*, 2 vols. (London, 1906), vol. 2, p. 129. Davies also became one of the more prominent members of the King's Inns, the Irish Inn of Court. Dublin, King's Inns Library, Black Book, fo. 3.
76 PRO/31/8/200/fo. 245; *CSPI, 1611–14*, p. 285; Brink, 'Davies' Life and

Works', p. 56; Davies acquired enormous tracts of land in Ireland. For his holdings there see Griffith, pp. 164, 189, 202, 206, 213, 216, 250, 257, 258, 259, 268, 293, 294, 315, 343, 389 and 426. See also Davies' will: PCC 145 Hele F.2826.

77 Sir John Davies, *A Discovery of the True Causes Why Ireland Was Never Subdued Nor Brought under Obedience of the Crown of England* (London, 1612). The work is reprinted in Morley, pp. 213–342.

78 Davies, *Reports*.

79 Bodl. Carte MS 62, fo. 590b; HMC, *Hastings MSS*, vol. 4, p. 5.

80 The best summary description of the 1613–15 parliament may be found in the commissioners' report over the disputed election: SP/63/232/fo. 131a; *CSPI, 1611–14*, pp. 426–8.

81 Bodl. Fortescue MS 2, Fo. 160a; Lascelles, *Liber Munerum*, vol. 1, pt. 2, p. 73.

82 Sir John Davies, *A Perfect Abridgement of the Eleven Books of Reports by Sir Edward Coke* (London, 1651).

83 Sir John Davies, *Nosce Teipsum, Hymns of Astrea in Acrosticke Verse, Orchestra or, a Poeme of Dauncing* (London, 1622).

84 Anon., *Proceedings and Debates of the House of Commons in 1620 and 1621*, 2 vols. (Oxford, 1766), vol. 1, p. 327; Wallace Notestein, *Commons Debates 1621*, 7 vols. (New Haven, 1935), vol. 2, p. 323; vol. 3, p. 90; vol. 5, pp. 101, 350; vol. 6, p. 108; T. Pape, *Newcastle-under-Lyme in Tudor and Early Stuart Times* (Manchester, 1938), pp. 137–8, 259; William Page, *A History of the County of Stafford*, 4 vols. (London, 1908), vol. 1, p. 254.

85 BL Harl. MS 758, fos. 61a–62b; J. S. Cockburn, *English Assizes* (Cambridge, 1972), pp. 270–1, 308–11; J. Bruce (ed.), *Liber Familicus of Sir James Whitelock* (New York, 1968), p. 102.

86 To Davies, impositions had their origins in the 'ius gentium the law of nature and the law merchant which pertained to the crown alone'. BL Harl. MS 278, fos. 411a–412b, 418b–422b; Sir John Davies, *The Question Concerning Impositions* (London, 1656), pp. 1–9.

87 HMC, *Hastings MSS*, vol. 2, p. 67.

88 Bodl. Wood MS F.39, fo. 375a; Bruce, *Liber Familicus*, p. 105.

89 Carte MS 62, fo. 590b.

3 Ireland and the origins of 'stare decisis'

1 Davies, *Reports*, pp. 31–2; anon., 'The History of Law Reporting in Ireland', *Irish Law Times and Solicitor's Journal*, 3 (1869), p. 659.

2 G. R. Elton, *Reform and Renewal* (Cambridge, 1973), p. 67.

3 There is an extensive historiography on Poynings' Law. See in particular D. B. Quinn, 'The Early Interpretation of Poynings' Law: Part 1, 1494–1534', *IHS*, 2 (1941), pp. 241–54; R. D. Edwards and T. W. Moody, 'The History of Poynings' Law: Part 1, 1494–1615', *IHS*, 2 (1941), pp. 415–25; A. Clarke, 'The History of Poynings' Law, 1615–41', *IHS*, 18 (1973), pp. 207–22.

4 These figures are based largely on those supplied by C. Litton Falkiner, 'The Parliament of Ireland under the Tudor Sovereigns', *RIA Proc.*, Section C, 25 (1904–5), pp. 508–41; the most recent review of the Irish

Tudor parliaments is B. Bradshaw, 'The Beginnings of Modern Ireland', in B. Farrell (ed.), *The Irish Parliamentary Tradition* (Dublin, 1973), pp. 68–87.

5 Bradshaw, 'Beginnings of Modern Ireland', pp. 76–8. This point is elaborated much further in Dr Bradshaw's thesis: 'The Irish Constitutional Revolution, 1515–1557' (University of Cambridge, unpublished Ph.D. thesis, 1975), pp. 217–66.

6 Bradshaw, 'Irish Constitutional Revolution', p. 248.

7 The best study of the radical programme is Canny, *Elizabethan Conquest*.

8 B. Bradshaw, 'The Opposition to the Ecclesiastical Legislation in the Irish Reformation Parliament', *IHS*, 16 (1969), pp. 285–303; 'The Edwardian Reformation in Ireland, 1547–53', *Arch. Hib.*, 24 (1976–7), pp. 83–99; V. Treadwell, 'The Irish Parliament of 1569–71', *RIA Proc.*, Section C, 55 (1967), pp. 55–89. On the failure of the Reformation in Ireland see B. Bradshaw, 'Sword, Word and Strategy in the Reformation in Ireland', *H J*, 21 (1978), pp. 475–502; also N. P. Canny, 'Why the Reformation Failed in Ireland: Une Question Mal Posée', *Journal of Ecclesiastical History*, 30 (1979), pp. 423–50.

9 A. G. Donaldson, *Some Comparative Aspects of Irish Law* (Durham, NC, 1957), pp. 8–9, 13–17; T. C. Barnard, *Cromwellian Ireland* (Oxford, 1975), pp. 249–51.

10 G. J. Hand and V. W. Treadwell, 'His Majesty's Directions for Ordering and Settling the Courts within His Kingdom of Ireland, 1622', *An. Hib.*, 26 (1970), pp. 183–4; K. W. Nicholls, 'Some Documents on Irish Law and Custom', *An Hib.*, 26 (1970), pp. 105–10, and 'A Calendar of Salved Chancery Pleadings Concerning County Louth', *County Louth Archaeological Journal*, 17 (1972), p. 250.

11 H. Wood, 'The Court of Castle Chamber or Star Chamber of Ireland', *RIA Proc.*, Section C, 32 (1913–16), pp. 152–69; Erck, p. 39; J. G. Crawford, 'The Origins of the Court of Castle Chamber; A Star Chamber Jurisdiction in Ireland', *AJLH*, 24 (1980), pp. 22–55. The decree book for the Court of Castle Chamber survives: see BL Add. MS 47,172; HMC, *Egmont MSS*, vol. 1, pt. 1, pp. 1–60.

12 For the Munster Presidency Court see D. J. Kennedy, 'The Presidency of Munster under Elizabeth and James I' (University College Cork, unpublished MA thesis, 1973); the Munster Council Book survives in BL Harl. MS 697.

13 Nat. Lib. Dublin, MS 11,044; see also V. T. H. Delaney, 'The Palatine Court of Tipperary', *AJLH*, 5 (1961), pp. 95–117; *Fifth Report of the Deputy Keeper of the Public Records in Ireland* (Dublin, 1874), pp. 32–41; E. S. Bade, 'A Princely Judgement', *Minnesota Law Review*, 23 (1939), pp. 925–40.

14 The distinction between this group and the rest of Irish society was stated by Richard II in his threefold division of Irish society: 'les irrois savage, nos enmis' (Irish enemies), 'les irrois rebelz' (degenerate English gone native) and 'les englois obeissant' (obedient vassals); R. D. Edwards, 'Ireland, Elizabeth I and the Counter-Reformation', in S. T. Bindoff, J. Hurstfield and C.H. Williams (eds.), *Elizabethan Government and Society* (London, 1961), pp. 315–39; R. Bagwell, *Ireland under the Tudors*, 3 vols.

(London, 1963), vol. 3, pp. 17–20; A. Clarke, *The Old English in Ireland, 1625–42* (Ithaca, 1966) and 'The Policies of the Old English in Parliament, 1640–41', *Historical Studies*, 5 (1965), p. 86, Canny, 'Formation of the Old English Elite'.

15 Liam Cosgrave, 'The King's Inns', *Dublin Historical Record*, 21 (1967), p. 45; G. T. O'Brien, 'The Old Irish Inns of Court', *Studies*, 3 (1914), p. 594; Mary J. Neylson, 'King's Inns Library, Dublin' (mimeo., King's Inn, 1982), pp. 3–4.

16 V. T. H. Delaney, 'A note on the History of Legal Education in Ireland', *NILQ*, 21 (1955), pp. 216–18; helpful but less satisfactory are: B. T. Duhigg, *A History of the King's Inns* (Dublin, 1806); G. E. Hamilton, *An Account of the Honorable Society of King's Inns, Dublin* (Dublin, 1915); W. J. Johnston, 'Ireland and the Medieval Law Courts', *Studies*, 12 (1928), pp. 553–7.

17 Farrell, *Irish Parliamentary Tradition*, pp. 81–7.

18 SP/63/215/fos. 143a–145b; *CSPI, 1603–6*, pp. 50–3; SP/63/215/fo. 151a; *CSPI, 1603–6*, pp. 55–6; SP/63/215/fos. 177a, 181a; *CSPI, 1603–6*, pp. 65–6; SP/63/215/fo. 271a; *CSPI, 1603–6*, p. 68.

19 SP/63/215/fo. 127a; *CSPI, 1603–6*, pp. 65–8; SP/63/215/fo. 209b; *CSPI, 1603–6*, p. 78; Bodl. Tanner MS 458, fo. 33b; SP/63/216/fos. 163a and b. *CSPI, 1603–6*, pp. 219–20; PROI, Ferguson MS 11, fos. 41, 185 and 241. See also C. Hughes (ed.), *Unpublished Chapters of Fynes Moryson's Itinerary, Shakespere's Europe* (London, 1903), p. 229.

20 SP/63/224/fos. 19b–20a; *CSPI, 1606–8*, pp. 507–8; Everard's brother was a notorious Jesuit living in the vicinity of Cashel. In early 1608, complaints indicated that he had gone so far as to forbid the children of Cashel to pray for the king. PRO/31/8/201/fo. 132; *CSPI, 1603–6*, p. 299.

21 Bodl. Carte MS 1, fo. 42a; Dublin, RIA, MS 12.G.1, fo. 12; F. E. Ball, *The Judges in Ireland, 1221–1921*, 2 vols. (New York, 1927), vol. 1, p. 231.

22 SP/63/221/fo. 65a; *CSPI, 1606–8*, pp. 117–19; Bodl. Carte MS 30, fo. 53a; *CSPI, 1606–8*, p. 116; SP/63/219/fo. 90a; *CSPI, 1603–6*, p. 575. To enhance the appeal of a career on the Irish bench, Irish justices were to be dignified with the title of Lord and promoted to Serjeant-at-Law. SP/63/218/fo. 186a; *CSPI, 1603–6*, p. 484; as a further incentive, the fees of all justices were substantially increased. SP/63/218/fos. 195a–b; *CSPI, 1603–6*, p. 489.

23 D. F. Cregan, 'Irish Recusant Lawyers in Politics in the Reign of James I', *Irish Jurist*, 5 (1970), p. 308.

24 SP/63/228/fo. 207a; *CSPI, 1608–10*, pp. 420–4; Fynes Moryson was also consistent in his criticism of the native legal profession. See his 'Commonwealth of Ireland' in C. Litton Falkiner (ed.), *Illustrations of Irish History* (London, 1904), pp. 278–9.

25 For a discussion of the origins of *stare decisis* see J. P. Dawson, *Oracles of the Law* (Ann Arbor, 1968), pp. 70–1; C. K. Allen, *Law in the Making* (Oxford, 1961), pp. 203–8; F. G. Kempin, 'Precedent and Stare Decisis', *AJLH*, 3 (1959), pp. 28–33.

26 W. S. Holdsworth, 'Case Law', *LQR*, 50 (1934), p. 187.

27 W. J. Jones, *Politics and the Bench* (New York, 1971), p. 49.

28 The statute of 31 Ed. III c. 12 for example established the Court of

Exchequer to determine cases upon writs of error from the common law side of the Exchequer. The statute of 27 Eliz. c. 5 authorized the justices of the Common Pleas and the Barons of the Exchequer to reverse judgement on writs of error brought from the Court of King's Bench. There was also another tribunal which functioned as a court of equity solely for the Exchequer. The Exchequer Chamber for debate had no statutory foundation and was so called because it served as a convenient meeting place. See Sir Edward Coke, *The Institutes of the Laws of England*, 4 vols. (London, 1671), *Fourth Institute*, p. 119; Blackstone, *Commentaries on the Laws of England*, vol. 3, pp. 55–6; W. H. Bryson, *The Equity Side of the Exchequer* (Cambridge, 1975).

29 L. W. Abbot, *Law Reporting in England, 1485–1585* (London, 1973), pp. 189–90; Dawson, *Oracles*, pp. 70–1; T. F. T. Plucknett, *Concise History of the Common Law* (London, 1956), p. 347; for a case illustration see A. W. B. Simpson, 'The Place of Slade's Case in the History of Contract', *LQR*, 74 (1958), pp. 381–91; for the fifteenth-century origins of this process see M. Hemmant, *Select Cases in the Exchequer Chamber, 1461–1509* (Selden Society, 51, London, 1933), p. xxxvi; YB 1 Rich. III, Mich. No. 2 in *Les Reports des Cases in Les Ans des Roys Edward V, Richard III, Henrie VII and Henrie VIII* (London, 1679). See also Hovel's case in C. O. Pike (ed.), *Yearbooks of the Reign of 19 Edward III* (Rolls Series, London, 1906), pp. 138–41.

30 Jones, *Politics and the Bench*, pp. 51–2.

31 *The Reports of Sir Edward Coke*, 7 vols. (London, 1826), 1 *Coke Rep.*, p. 51b.

32 4 *Coke Rep.*, pp. 92b and 93a.

33 Coke, *Second Institute*, p. 618.

34 James Spedding (ed.) *The Works of Francis Bacon*, 7 vols. (London, 1905), vol. 7, p. 642.

35 Henry Yelverton, *Les Reports* (London, 1674), p. 20.

36 T. B. Howell (ed.), *A Complete Collection of State Trials*, 21 vols. (London, 1816–98). For the trial of Sir Edward Hales see vol. 11, pp. 1254–5.

37 Morley, p. 18; for the problem of Gaelic tenures see chapter four of this study.

38 Papal *dominium* of Ireland was based on the notion that the donation of Constantine also granted ownership over all islands. For Ireland see L. Weckman, *Las Bulas Alejandrinas de 1493 y la Teoría Política del Papado Medieval; Estudio de la Supremacía Papal Sobre Islas 1091–1493* (Mexico City, 1949), pp. 45–68; M. Sheehy (ed.), *Pontifica Hibernica: Medieval Papal Chancery Documents Concerning Ireland, 640–1261*, 2 vols. (Dublin, 1962), vol. 1, pp. 19–23. See also J. Muldoon, 'The Remonstrance of the Irish Princess and the Canon Law Tradition of the Just War', *AJLH*, 22 (1978), pp. 309–25; R. Holinshed, *Chronicles*, 3 vols. (London, 1587), vol. 2, p. 420.

39 BL Add. MS 4793, fos. 45b, 53b–54a.

40 Davies, *Reports*, pp. 78–115, 134–8; HMC, *9th Rep. MSS of the Marquess of Drogheda*, p. 311; HMC, *Hastings MSS*, vol. 4, pp. 153–4.

41 BL Cott. MS Titus B.x, fos. 202a–205b; SP/634/229/fos. 128a–130a;

CSPI, *1608–10*, pp. 499–501; Morley, p. 384; SP/63/228/fo. 153a; *CSPI,
1608–10*, pp. 409–11; SP/63/228/fos. 138a–146b; *CSPI, 1608–10*, pp.
403–4.

42 Davies, *Reports*, pp. 150–8; see chapter five of this study.
43 PRO/31/8/199/fos. 197–8; for Chief Justice Popham's certification see
   SP/14/24/fo. 51b; *CSPD, 1603–10*, p. 339; TCD MS 843 (F.3.17), fo.
   401; *CSPI, 1603–6*, pp. 584–9. See chapter six of this study.
44 *Reports*, pp. 41–2. See chapter seven of this study.
45 *Reports*, p. 77. See chapter eight of this study.
46 *Cal. Car., 1603–24*, p. 167.
47 See 'traverse' in G. Jacob, *A New Law Dictionary* (London, 1772) and
   Blackstone, *Commentaries on the Laws of England*, vol. 3, p. 260.
48 SP/63/223/fo. 113a; *CSPI, 1606–8*, pp. 432–3; SP/63/234/fo. 140a.
49 SP/63/234/fo. 141a; *CSPI, 1615–25*, p. 181. Traversing of inquisitions in
   cases not affecting the crown continued.
50 SP/63/234/fo. 140a.
51 The difficulty with procurations seems to have troubled Davies for some
   time. See his letter to Salisbury concerning Beeston's case in 1608:
   SP/63/223/fo. 122a; *CSPI, 1606–8*, p. 436; *CSPI, 1608–10* (Philadelphia
   Papers), p. 247; *Cal. Pat. Rolls James I*, p. 105; G. O'Brien (ed.),
   Advertisements for Ireland (Royal Society of Antiquaries of Ireland,
   Dublin, 1923), p. 17; PROI, Chancery Decrees Al; Ferguson MS 11, fos.
   42, 49, 65; 27, fo. 16.
52 O'Brien, *Advertisements for Ireland*, p. 17; further details of proxies
   assigned to the Bishop of Meath can be found in the visitation of Meath
   of 1622 printed in C.R. Elrington (ed.) *Usher's Works*, 17 vols. (Dublin,
   1847), vol. 1, appendix v, pp. lvii–lviii; on proxies granted to the
   Archbishop of Dublin see SP/63/242/fos. 229a and 241a; *CSPI, 1625–32*,
   pp. 111, 115. The case of proxies represents one illustration of a general
   attempt to restore the patrimony of the church. See W. A. Phillips, *The
   History of the Church of Ireland from the Earliest Times to the Present Day*, 3
   vols. (Oxford, 1933), vol. 2, pp. 498–500.
53 H. F. Kearney, 'The Court of Wards and Liveries in Ireland, 1622–24',
   RIA Proc., Section C, 57 (1956), p. 36.
54 SP/63/239/fo.98a; *CSPI, 1615–25*, p. 576; SP/63/239/fos. 98a and 100a;
   CSPI, 1615–25, p. 577.
55 SP/63/227/fo. 98b; PRO/31/8/201/fo. 534; *CSPI, 1611–14*, p. 106;
   SP/63/234/fo. 26a; *CSPI, 1615–25*, p. 173; SP/63/232/fo. 86a; *CSPI,
   1611–14*, p. 304. It is interesting to note that in 1613, the recusant party of
   the Irish parliament formally complained about cases between 'party and
   party which are properly determined by the ordinary cause of law, are
   directed at the council table, and the cause of common law, and
   execution of judgement sometimes stayed by warrant from them, which
   is contrary to express laws and statutes made in that kingdom'. In his
   reply, Lord Deputy Chichester pointed out the 'cause of the common
   law is very seldom seized by order from the table, but when some stay is
   made, it is done either in case of great equity, or upon some reason of
   state, which in question of law doth arise at the table, the judges, who are
   of the Privy Council do always give rule in such causes'. J. Lodge,

Desiderata Curiosa Hibernica, 2 vols. (Dublin, 1772), vol. 1, pp. 243, 260–1; SP/63/232/fo. 102a; *CSPI, 1611–14*, p. 373.

56 Ball, *Judges in Ireland*, pp. 238–41, 312–24; Sir John Davies himself, it will be recalled, was appointed Chief Justice of the Court of King's Bench in 1626; Sir James Ley, Chief Justice of King's Bench in Ireland, became Chief Justice of King's Bench in England in 1622; Sir Humphrey Winch, Chief Baron of the Irish Exchequer, became a justice of the English Common Pleas in 1612; Sir John Denham, Chief Baron of the Irish Exchequer, became a Baron of the English Exchequer Court in 1617.

4 The cases of gavelkind and tanistry

1 Morley, p. 18.
2 Spedding, *Works of Francis Bacon*, vol. 7, p. 660; see also Bradshaw, *Irish Constitutional Revolution*, pp. 11–13.
3 Robin Frame, 'Power and Society in the Lordship of Ireland, 1272–1377' *P & P*, 76 (1977), pp. 3–33.
4 Ir. St. 40 Ed. III; see also E. Curtis and R. B. McDowell (eds.), *Irish Historical Documents* (London, 1943), pp. 52–9; G. J. Hand, 'The Forgotten Statutes of Kilkenny: A Brief Survey', *Irish Jurist*, 1 (1966), pp. 299–312.
5 Ir. St. 10 Hen. VII, c.8; 28 Hen. VIII, c. 15.
6 J. Morrin (ed.), *Calendar of Patent and Close Rolls of Chancery in Ireland of the Reigns of Henry VIII, Edward VI, Mary and Elizabeth* (Dublin, 1861), p. 7.
7 *Ancient Laws of Ireland*, 6 vols. (London, 1865).
8 D. A. Binchy, 'The Linguistic and Historical Value of the Irish Law Tracts', *Proceedings of the British Academy*, 29 (1943), pp. 195–224; 'Ancient Irish Law', *Irish Jurist*, 2 (1967), pp. 84–90.
9 Binchy, 'Ancient Irish Law', p. 89; also G. MacNiocaill, 'Notes on Litigation in Late Irish Law', *Irish Jurist*, 2 (1967), p. 304.
10 Nicholls, *Land, Law and Society*, pp. 3–5.
11 G. A. Hayes McCoy, 'Gaelic Society in Ireland in the Late Sixteenth Century', *Historical Studies*, 4 (1963), pp. 49–50.
12 Nicholls, *Land, Law and Society*, pp. 3–26.
13 Hayes McCoy, 'Gaelic Society', p. 49; Binchy, 'Historical Value', pp. 222–3; Nicholls, *Gaelicized Ireland*, p. 26.
14 Nicholls, *Gaelicized Ireland*, p. 24.
15 *Ibid.*, pp. 31–7, and *Land, Law and Society*, pp. 12–20; see also collection of Tyrone's rents in Bodl. Carte MS 61, fos. 30a–31a, and Dublin, RIA MS 12.S.3, fo. 129. For exactions levied in Munster see K. Caulfield and J. F. Ferguson, 'Exactions Incident to Tenures in Ireland', *Topographer and Genealogist*, 3 (1858), pp. 137–41; Lam. Pal. MS 617, fos. 212b and 213a; *Cal. Car., 1589–1600*, p. 71.
16 Nicholls, *Gaelicized Ireland*, pp. 79–91; in Fermanagh, Davies described their tenure as a form of free land. 'Namely such land as is possessed by the Irish officers of their countrey; viz. chroniclers, Galloglass and divers others'. BL Add. MS 4793, fo. 50b; see also the list of tribal exactions of the hereditary military castes in *Cal. Car., 1601–3*, pp. 454–9; J. P.

Prendergast, 'The Ulster Creaghts', *Kilkenny Archaeological Society Journal*, 3 (1855), pp. 420–30.

17 SP/63/217/fos. 43a–44a; R. Steele (ed.), *A Bibliography of Royal Proclamations of the Tudor and Stuart Sovereigns and of Others Published under their Royal Authority, 1485–1714*, 2 vols. (Oxford, 1910), vol. 2, no. 167a, p. 15, vol. 2, nu. 180, p. 17; the proclamation is printed in M. J. Bonn, *Die Englische Kolonisation in Irland* (Stuttgart and Berlin, 1906), p. 394; see also W. F. T. Butler, *Confiscation in Irish History* (Dublin, 1917), p. 37; the most recent exposition on the status of landless undertenants is Nicholls, *Land, Law and Society*, pp. 1–26.

18 For a general discussion on alienage see W. Holdsworth, *A History of English Law*, 16 vols. (London, 1922–66), vol. 9, pp. 72–104; F. W. Maitland and F. Pollock, *The History of English Law before the Time of Edward I*, 2 vols. (Cambridge, 1973), vol. 1, pp. 458–67; still useful is F. Plowden, *A Disquisition Concerning the Law of Alienage* (Paris, 1818); see also 'denizen', 'alien' and 'naturalization' in Jacob, *A New Law Dictionary* (London, 1772); Davies' views on alienage have aroused controversy among medieval historians. See G. J. Hand, 'Aspects of Alien Status in Medieval English Law with Special Reference to Ireland', in D. Jenkins (ed.), *Legal History Studies* (Cardiff, 1975), pp. 129–35; H. G. Richardson, 'English Institutions in Medieval Ireland', *IHS*, 1 (1939), pp. 386–90; A. J. Otway-Ruthven, 'The Request of the Irish for English Law, 1277–1280', *IHS*, 6 (1949), pp. 261–70; 'The Native Irish and English Law in Medieval Ireland', *IHS*, 7 (1951), pp. 1–16; A. Gwynn, 'Edward I and the Proposed Purchase of English Law for the Irish, *c.* 1276–1280', *Transactions of the Royal Historical Society*, 10 (1960), pp. 111–27; G. J. Hand, *English Law in Ireland, 1290–1324* (Cambridge, 1967), pp. 198–201; J. Mills (ed.), *Calendar of the Justiciary Rolls in Proceedings in the Court of the Justiciar*, 3 vols. (Dublin, 1905–17), vol. 1, pp. vii–ix; B. Murphy, 'The Status of the Native Irish after 1331', *Irish Jurist*, 2 (1967), p. 125; Morley, pp. 263–6.

19 Hand, *English Law*, p. 199; see also Hand's 'The Status of the Native Irish in the Lordship of Ireland', *Irish Jurist*, 1 (1966), p. 109; also Davies, *Reports*, pp. 103–6; Davies used similar evidence in his *Brief Discovery*. See Morley, pp. 263–6. As Hand has suggested, Davies may have used Cambridge University Add. MS 3104, fos. 49–50; other English jurists in Jacobean Ireland also commented on the exception. See Huntington Library MS 7042, 'Laws of Ireland', fo. 1.

20 Nicholls, *Gaelicized Ireland*, pp. 57–60; Davies, *Reports*, pp. 134–7. Less useful are W. Sommer, *A Treatise of Gavelkind* (London, 1660) and S. Taylor, *The History of Gavelkind* (London, 1663). For a less antiquarian approach see C. I. Elton, *The Tenures of Kent* (London, 1867) and J. Wilson, *The Common Law of Kent, or the Custom of Gavelkind* (London, 1822).

21 A variant of the chief making a division occurred in Connaught and Thomand, where lands were redistributed annually at Mayday. Nicholls, 'Documents on Irish Law', pp. 106–7, and *Gaelicized Ireland*, pp. 60–4.

22 D. A. Binchy, 'Some Celtic Legal Terms', *Celtica*, 3 (1956), p. 221; see

also T. M. Charles-Edwards, 'The Heir-Apparent in Irish and Welsh Law', *Celtica*, 9 (1971), pp. 180–9.

23 J. Goody, 'Strategies of Heirship', *Comparative Studies in Society and History*, 15 (1973), p. 5; A. S. Diamond, *Primitive Law* (London, 1971), pp. 279–86.

24 Nicholls, *Gaelicized Ireland*, p. 26; G. A. Hayes McCoy, 'The Making of an O'Neill, a View of the Ceremony at Tullahoge, Co. Tyrone', *UJA*, 33 (1970), pp. 89–94; SP/63/112/fo. 150a; *CSPI, 1574–85*, p. 534: 'The custom of tanistry is the root of all the barbarism of Ireland'; *State Papers, Henry VIII*, 11 vols. (London, 1830–52), vol. 2, p. 5: 'Also the son of every the said captaines shall not succeed to his father without he being the strongest of all his nation; for there shall be none chief captain in any of the said regions by lawful succession but by fort main and election; and he that hath the strong arm and the hardest sword amongst them hath the best right and title'. See also Lam. Pal. MS 609, fo. 15b; *Cal. Car., 1515–74*, p. 339: 'The hope that every Irishman hath come in time to be elected captain of his nation is the cause why every of them keepeth idle men of war, that thereby he might be stronger, and so thought the worthiest to be elected.' For similar comments see Lam. Pal. MS 616, fos. 116a–117b; *Cal. Car., 1589–1600*, pp. 27–8.

25 Nicholls, *Gaelicized Ireland*, pp. 25–6; Davies, *Reports*, pp. 78–115.

26 Davies, *Brief Discovery*, in Morley, pp. 291–3. For the problems associated with the conflict of laws and defining native custom through the mechanism of metropolitan law see J. Montrose, 'The Use of Legal Categories in Problems Concerning Compilation of Customs and Codification', *Precedent in English Law and Other Essays* (Shannon, 1968), pp. 79–80.

27 E. Spenser, *A View of the State of Ireland: Written Dialogue-Wise between Eudoxus and Irenaeus*, in Morley, pp. 41–3.

28 Falkiner, 'Moryson's Commonwealth', in *Illustrations of Irish History*, p. 243.

29 H. Maine, *Early History of Institutions* (London, 1880), pp. 53–4; E. M. Hinton, *Ireland through Tudor Eyes* (Philadelphia, 1935), p. 16; Canny, *Elizabethan Conquest*, pp. 33–4.

30 J. F. Dimock (ed.), *Giraldi Cambrensis, Opera*, 8 vols. (London, 1867), vol. 5, pp. 315–20; C. C. J. Webb (ed.), *John of Salisbury's Metalogicon* (Oxford, 1924), pp. 217–18; Weckman, *Las Bulas Alejandrinas de 1493*, pp. 45–68; Muldoon, 'The Remonstrance of the Irish Princes', p. 312; J. A. Watt, 'Laudabiliter in Medieval Diplomacy and Propaganda', *IER*, 87 (1957), pp. 420–32; M. P. Sheehy, 'The Bull Laudabiliter: A Problem in Medieval Diplomatique and History', *Journal of the Galway Archaeological and Historical Society*, 29 (1960), pp. 45–70; see also Sheehy's *Pontifica Hibernica*, vol. 1, pp. 15–16; for papal designs on Ireland see C. Petrie, 'The Hispano-Papal Landing at Smerwick', *Irish Sword*, 9 (1969–70), pp. 82–94; see also *CSP – Rome*, vol. 2, pp. 22–5, 367, 416–17, 423–4, 443–5, 188–9; *CSP – Spain*, 1568–79, pp. 209–11, 293.

31 Lam. Pal. MS 623, fo. 48b, and MS 598, fo. 28b; *Cal. Car., Book of Howth*, pp. 100, 312.

32 Coke, *Fourth Institute*, p. 359.

33 See chapter nine of this study.

34 *Cal. Car., 1603–24*, pp. 30–1.

35 SP/63/201/fo. 115a; *CSPI, 1596–7*, p. 436; Lam. Pal. MS 612, fos. 45a–46a; *Cal. Car., 1589–1600*, pp. 122–3; SP/63/183/fo. 202a; *CSPI, 1592–6*, pp. 406–7; SP/63/183/fos. 233a–240a; *CSPI, 1592–6*, pp. 409–10. For the Spanish invasion at Kinsale see J. J. Silke, *Kinsale – The Spanish Intervention in Ireland at the End of the Elizabethan Wars* (New York, 1970).

36 SP/63/206/fo. 154a; *CSPI, 1599–1600*, p. 280; SP/63/183/fo. 317a; *CSPI, 1592–6*, p. 423. 'For now the Ulster men and these are joined in one action and one quarrel, striving for the maintenance of their tanist law an old Irish custom, under which they acknowledge little or no sovereignty to your majesty, and now these men term themselves the Pope's men and the traitor Tyrone's and in show of religion openly profess popery and massings, having roving wicked priests and titular Bishops, which daily resort to them from Rome and parts beyond the sea.' See also SP/63/186/fo. 179a; *CSPI, 1592–6*, p. 468: the Lord Deputy speaks of the 'disloyal resolution of the rebels to shake off her Majesty's government, and a settled wilfullness to bring in foreign rule'.

37 SP/63/215/fos. 40a–41a; *CSPI, 1603–6*, p. 13. The best treatment of the subject is N. P. Canny, 'The Treaty of Mellifont and the Reorganization of Ulster, 1603', *Irish Sword*, 9 (1969–70), pp. 249–62.

38 Hughes, *Unpublished Chapters of Fynes Moryson's Itinerary, Shakespere's Europe*, pp. 23–31.

39 Canny, 'Treaty of Mellifont', pp. 260–1.

40 BL Add. MS 4879, fos. 180a–b; for a general background to the O'Neill lordship see N. P. Canny, 'Hugh O'Neill, Earl of Tyrone and the Changing Face of Gaelic Ulster', *Studia Hibernica*, 10 (1970) pp. 7–35.

41 J. Morrin (ed.), *Calendar of the Patent and Close Rolls of Chancery In Ireland from the 18th to the 45th year of Queen Elizabeth* (1576–1602), 2 vols. (Dublin, 1862), vol. 2, p. 130.

42 SP/63/219/fo. 230a; *CSPI, 1606–8*, p. 51.

43 Canny, 'Treaty of Mellifont', p. 255.

44 T. W. Moody, *The Londonderry Plantation, 1609–41* (Belfast, 1939), p. 25.

45 N. P. Canny, 'The Flight of the Earls, 1607', *IHS*, 17 (1971), pp. 380–97; R. Bagwell, *Ireland under the Stuarts*, 3 vols. (London, 1963), vol. 1, p. 13; Moody *et al.*, *A New History of Ireland*, p. 372.

46 See the 'Confessions of Southampton and Danvers' in J. Bruce (ed.), *Correspondence of King James VI of Scotland with Sir Robert Cecil* (Camden Society, Westminster, 1861), pp. 101–7; F. Moryson, *An Itinerary of Ten Yeeres Travell* (London, 1617), pt. 2, p. 89; SP/14/18/fo. 19a; *CSPD, 1603–10*, p. 287; F. M. Jones, *Mountjoy, the Last Elizabethan Deputy* (Dublin, 1958), p. 180.

47 P. M. Handover, *The Second Cecil* (London, 1959), p. 159.

48 Lascelles, *Liber Munerum Publicorum Hiberniae*, vol. 1, pt. 2, pp. 75 and 182; 'The Diary of Sir Roger Wilbraham', *Camden Miscellany*, 10 (1902), p. 106; SP/63/219/fo. 173b; *CSPI, 1606–8*, p. 19.

49 SP/63/216/fo. 45a; *CSPI, 1603–6*, p. 160.

50 Morley, pp. 262 and 264.

51 See note 17.

52 PRO/31/8/201/fos. 131a–134a; *CSPI, 1603–6*, p. 299; Erck, pp. 182–4; J. Lodge (ed.), *Desiderata Curiosa Hibernica*, 2 vols. (Dublin, 1772), vol. 1, pp. 456–7. The most thorough treatment of the subject is N. P. Canny, 'The Career of Hugh O'Neill, Earl of Tyrone, 1603–07' (University College Galway, unpublished MA thesis, 1967), pp. 124–42.

53 Erck, pp. 182–4. There were in fact two separate commissions – one for the surrender of uncertain titles and one for the surrender of tanist lands only. See also Steele, *Proclamations*, vol. 2, p. 18, no. 186, p. 19, no. 196.

54 SP/63/217/fos. 155b and 156b; *CSPI, 1603–6*, p. 320; Canny, 'Flight of the Earls', p. 385; 'Treaty of Mellifont', pp. 256 and 258; see also C. Falls, 'Neill Garve: English Ally and Victim', *Irish Sword*, 1 (1950), pp. 1–7.

55 SP/63/217/fo. 155a; *CSPI, 1603–6*, pp. 318–19.

56 For the 1606 commission see Canny, 'Career of Hugh O'Neill', pp. 143–68; SP/63/218/fos. 207a and b; *CSPI, 1603–6*, p. 492; SP/63/219/fo. 3b; *CSPI, 1603–6*, p. 512.

57 Davies, *Reports*, p. 137; HMC, *Hastings MSS*, vol. 4, p. 153; HMC, *9th Rep. App. MSS of the Marquis of Drogheda*, p. 311.

58 SP/63/219/fos. 109b–110a; *CSPI, 1603–6*, p. 575; BL Add. MS 4793, fos. 53b–54a; Morley, pp. 376–7. The importance placed on the eldest co-heir or clan head in the Irish custom of gavelkind led many English observers to identify shared inheritance by gavelkind with succession by right of tanistry. In this sense Davies and the English judiciary may very well have considered the judicial resolution voiding gavelkind as applicable to the custom of tanistry as well.

59 BL Add. MS 4793, fo. 51a; Morley, p. 372; SP/63/219/fos. 106a and b; *CSPI, 1603–6*, p. 575.

60 BL Add. MS 4793, fo. 55b; Morley, p. 379; SP/63/219/fo. 109b; *CSPI, 1603–6*, p. 575; for a discussion of Cavan see R. J. Hunter, 'The Ulster Plantation in the Counties of Armagh and Cavan, 1608–41', 2 vols. (TCD, unpublished M. Litt. thesis, 1968), vol. 1, pp. 55–63.

61 SP/63/219/fo. 174a; *CSPI, 1606–8*, p. 20.

62 For a discussion of the Monaghan settlement see P. J. Duffy, 'Patterns of Landownership in Gaelic Monaghan in the Late Sixteenth Century', *Clogher Record*, 10 (1981), pp. 304–19.

63 BL Add. MS 4793, fos. 38b–39a; Morley, p. 351; SP/63/219/fo. 111b; *CSPI, 1603–6*, p. 575.

64 BL Add. MS 4793, fos. 38b–39a; Morley, p. 351; SP/63/219/fos. 94b–95a; *CSPI, 1603–6*, p. 575.

65 SP/63/222/fo. 8a; *CSPI, 1606–8*, p. 212.

66 For a discussion of the O'Cahan affair see Canny, 'Hugh O'Neill, Earl of Tyrone', pp. 12–14; J. O'Donovan (ed.), 'Henry Docwra's Narration', *Miscellany of the Celtic Society* (Dublin, 1849), pp. 271, 284. See in particular O'Cahan's petition to be exempted from Tyrone's rule: SP/63/221/fo. 49a; *CSPI, 1606–8*, pp. 110–11; SP/63/221/fos. 147a–149a; *CSPI, 1606–8*, pp. 155–7.

67 Bodl. Carte MS 61, fo. 344a; *CSPI, 1606–8*, p. 127; SP/63/222/fos. 12a and b; *CSPI, 1606–8*, p. 214; SP/63/222/fos. 14a and b; *CSPI, 1606–8*, pp. 215–17. For the nature of *termon* and *erenagh* lands see Nicholls, *Gaelicized Ireland*, pp. 105–13; see also J. Barry, 'The Coarb in Medieval

Times', *IER*, 89 (1958), pp. 24–35; 'The Erenagh in the Monastic Irish Church', *IER*, 89 (1958), pp. 424–32; 'The Lay Coarb in Medieval Times', *IER*, 91 (1959), pp. 27–39; 'The Coarb and the Twelfth-Century Reform', *IER*, 88 (1957), pp. 17–25.

68 SP/63/221/fo. 139a; *CSPI, 1606–8*, p. 151; SP/63/222/fo. 55b; *CSPI, 1606–8*, pp. 244–5.

69 BL Add. MS 4879, fo. 180a.

70 SP/63/135/fos. 77a–87a; *CSPI, 1586–8*, pp. 520–2; SP/63/129/fo. 112a; *CSPI, 1586–8*, p. 332; SP/63/219/fos. 174b–175b; *CSPI, 1606–8*, pp. 20–1; SP/63/221/fos. 214a–218a; *CSPI, 1606–8*, pp. 190–202.

71 SP/63/222/fos. 6b–7a; *CSPI, 1606–8*, p. 211.

72 It is interesting to note that Con O'Neill's patent makes no mention of these territories. Morrin, *Calendar of the Patent and Close Rolls, Henry VIII, Edward VI, Mary and Elizabeth*, p. 88. For the territories in question see the manuscript map drawn up in conjunction with the 1587 inquisition: MPF 307.

73 SP/63/222/fo. 6b; *CSPI, 1606–8*, p. 210.

74 SP/63/221/fo. 199a; *CSPI, 1606–8*, p. 193; SP/63/222/fo. 316a; *CSPI, 1606–8*, p. 376.

75 PRO/31/8/201/fo. 242; *CSPI, 1606–8*, p. 221.

76 Canny, 'The Flight of the Earls', pp. 390–9.

77 BL Add. MS 4819, fo. 186a; BL Cecil MS 117, fo. 162a; HMC, *Salisbury MSS*, vol. 18, p. 314.

78 SP/63/224/fos. 194a–195b; *CSPI, 1606–8*, pp. 606–7; SP/63/225/fo. 113a; *CSPI, 1608–10*, pp. 63, 65. The English Privy Council adopted a harder line: *CSPI, 1606–8*, p. 617; Davies continously called for a general rooting out of natives. SP/63/224/fo. 250b; *CSPI, 1608–10*, p. 17.

79 SP/63/229/fo. 171b; *CSPI, 1608–10*, p. 520.

80 Bodl. Carte MS 61, fos. 111a–123b; *CSPI, 1608–10*, pp. 553–68.

81 Bodl. Carte MS 61, fos. 126a–127b; *CSPI, 1608–10*, p. 569.

82 BL Add. MS 4793, fo. 45b; for Cavan see fos. 53b–54a; SP/63/219/fos. 109b–110a; *CSPI, 1603–6*, p. 575.

83 BL Harl. MS 697, fo. 20a; from the Presidency Court the defendant Cahir petitioned unsuccessfully to have the case referred to Chancery. PROI, Chancery Pleadings, G73.

84 BL Add. MS 47,172, fos. 135a–136b; HMC, *Egmont MSS*, p. 30.

85 W. F. T. Butler, *Gleanings from Irish History* (London, 1925), pp. 78–97; H. W. Gillman, 'The Chieftains of Pobul-Callaghan', *Journal of the Cork Historical and Archaeological Society*, 3 (1897), pp. 201–20; Lam. Pal. MS 631, fo. 70a; *Cal. Car., 1589–1600*, p. 69; here the land in question is described: 'Dowallie is equallie divided into three parts, viz. one part called Clan Cartie of Dowallie; the second O'Calchans country; the third part is MacAlies, O'Kiffes and O'Kirkes countries'; see appendix to this chapter.

86 Davies, *Reports*, pp. 81–6; also F. H. Newark, 'The Case of Tanistry', *NILQ*, 9 (1950), pp. 215–21.

87 Davies, *Reports*, p. 94.

88 The case also raised doubts over the accuracy of official sources recording common law tenures in Gaelic or Anglicized districts where, in fact,

the older Gaelic customs prevailed. In the early seventeenth century, for example, a Chancery suit between the extended kin group of the McKiernan family from county Cavan and an English adventurer, James Craig, further illustrates the point. In this instance, Brian McKiernan, who had surrendered his family's land for a common law title, 'being the chief and eldest of his sept', sold the lands of his kin group to Craig. Five members of the McKiernan family petitioned Craig for the return of the family lands. Since Brian McKiernan held the family estate by English patent under common law, the case illustrates the fascinating problem of the survival of Gaelic practice under the guise of a common law estate. PROI, Chancery Pleadings, N153.

89 Davies, *Reports*, p. 86. In the end, Davies' client Cahir O'Callaghan, whose title rested on the common law settlement made by Donough MacTeige in 1574, obtained seisin of the castle with its adjacent lands. However a badly damaged Chancery document, PROI, Chancery Pleading R14, mentions an equitable partition between the claimants. There is an interesting footnote to the story. In 1631 the rival claims to Castle Dromaneen merged when Eleanor, granddaughter and surviving descendant of Conogher of the Rock, and Donough, the son and heir of Cahir O'Callaghan, the defendant, were married. During the protectorate, Donough was banished to Clare where the Cromwellian government awarded him a lease of land at a peppercorn rent for 1,000 years until such time as he would return to Dromaneen. Donough, however, fared ill in the Restoration Settlement, and the family remained in Clare where its descendants live to this day. Griffith, p. 200; Butler, *Gleanings*, p. 92.

90 Butler, *Gleanings*, p. 91.

91 BL Cott. MS Titus B.x, fos. 202a–b; SP/63/229/fos. 128a–130a; *CSPI, 1608–10*, p. 498; Morley, p. 384.

92 BL Cott. MS Titus B.x, fos. 202a–205b; SP/63/229/fos. 128a–130a; *CSPI, 1608–10*, pp. 497–501.

93 BL Cott. MS Titus B.x, fos. 202b–203a; Morley, p. 387.

94 BL Cott. MS Titus B.x, fos. 203a and b; SP/63/229/fos. 128b–129a; Morley, p. 386; *CSPI, 1608–10*, p. 498. In another dispute over tanistry between Dr Charles Dunne, one of the Masters of Chancery, and his brother Thadie resolved in the Court of Chancery on 9 December 1612, the judges concluded that: 'The custom of Tanistry is utterlie voide in lawe so as all the said parties have occupied as intruders upon the King's Majesties' posssession.' Dublin: Marsh's Library, MS Z.4.2.19, fo. 402.

95 SP/63/229/fo. 129a; *CSPI, 1608–10*, p. 499.

96 SP/63/226/fos. 163a–165a; *CSPI, 1608–10*, pp. 181–4; SP/63/227/fos. 60a–61b; *CSPI, 1608–10*, pp. 255–6; SP/63/227/fos. 104a–106a; *CSPI, 1608–10*, pp. 285–7; SP/63/227/fo. 94a; *CSPI, 1608–10*, pp. 280–1; SP/63/227/fo. 180a; *CSPI, 1608–10*, pp. 282–3; SP/63/227/fo. 117a; *CSPI, 1608–10*, pp. 292–3.

97 SP/63/228/fos. 138a–146b; *CSPI, 1608–10*, pp. 403–4; Bodl. Carte MS. 61, fos. 118b, 122a, 125a; *CSPI, 1608–10*, pp. 561, 564–5, 567. For the disposition of *termon* and *erenagh* lands see Hunter, 'Ulster Plantation', vol. 1, p. 18.

98 G. Keating, *The History of Ireland* (Irish Texts Society, 1, London, 1902), pp. 67–71; Nicholls, *Gaelicized Ireland*, pp. 57–65, 21–44.

99 See P. W. Joyce, *A Social History of Ancient Ireland*, 2 vols. (London, 1903), vol. 1, pp. 184–96; see also D. Coghlan, *The Ancient Land Tenures of Ireland* (Dublin, 1933), pp. 60–76. The myth of collective ownership was later demolished by Eoin MacNeill in his 'Communal Ownership in Ancient Ireland', *Irish Monthly*, 47 (1919), pp. 407–15, 463–74; MacNeill interpreted the growth of tanistry as a response to the Norman invasion. See *Early Irish Law and Institutions* (Dublin, 1935), pp. 148–9; more recent research has conclusively shown the custom to be pre-conquest and Gaelic in origin. See Binchy, 'Some Celtic Legal Terms', pp. 221–3.

100 D. Mathew, *The Celtic Peoples and Renaissance Europe: A Study of the Celtic and Spanish Influences on Elizabethan History* (New York, 1933), p. 460.

101 Nicholls, 'Documents on Irish Law', pp. 105–29.

102 Lam. Pal. MS 617, fos. 113a–117a; *Cal. Car., 1603–24*, p. 299; Lam. Pal. MS 605, fo. 224a; *Cal. Car., 1603–24*, p. 370; Lam. Pal. MS 605, fo. 225b; *Cal. Car., 1603–24*, p. 332, Lam. Pal. MS 613, fo. 89b; *Cal. Car., 1603–24*, p. 378.

103 Lam. Pal. MS 605, fos. 225a–226a; *Cal. Car., 1603–24*, p. 331; Lam. Pal. MS 613, fo. 89b; *Cal. Car., 1603–24*, p. 378.

104 Lam. Pal. MS 629, fo. 31a; *Cal. Car., 1603–24*, p. 157.

105 A useful summary can be found in F. H. Newark, 'The Case of Tanistry', *NILQ*, 9 (1950–2), pp. 215–21.

106 Morrin, *Calendar of the Patent and Close Rolls of Chancery in Ireland, 18th to the 45th Year of Queen Elizabeth*, vol. 2, pp. 260–2; see also Fiants 5903 and 5908 for Conogher's surrender and regrant. *The Sixteenth Report of the Deputy Keeper of the Public Records in Ireland* (Dublin, 1884), pp. 261–2; PROI, Salved Chancery Pleadings, I222, 223; BL Harl. MS 697, fo. 20a.

5 The case of the Bann fishery

1 Davies, *Reports*, pp. 149–58.

2 John Lodge, *The Peerage of Ireland*, 5 vols. (London, 1754), vol. 1, pp. 211–20. For the MacDonnells generally see George Hill, *An Historical Account of the MacDonnells of Antrim* (Belfast, 1873).

3 Gibbs, *Complete Peerage*, vol. 1, p. 174.

4 Erck, pp. 8, 52, 137; Griffith, pp. 30, 58 and 91.

5 This chapter follows closely the path laid down by the Irish nationalist MP T. M. Healy at the beginning of this century. Although the book is carefully researched and well argued, Healy's nationalist bias led him to commit several minor errors in fact and more serious deficiencies in interpretation. Nevertheless, this revision owes much to Healy's pioneer work. See the following: T. M. Healy, *Stolen Waters* (London, 1913); *The Great Fraud of Ulster* (Dublin, 1917); there is also a condensed version: *The Planter's Progress* (Dublin, 1921).

6 Before the Tudor conquest, it appears that cadet branches and client septs

of the O'Neill family shared the fishing rights to the Bann between themselves. Although the crown occasionally adjudicated disputes over the river, it does not appear that the Dublin government ever pressed a definitive claim to riparian rights prior to 1603. At the end of the Nine Years War, it seems that fishing rights to the Bann devolved to Hugh O'Neill, Earl of Tyrone, and to Sir Randall MacDonnell. It could be said, however, that the crown maintained the requisite *animus* to sustain a superior right over the river. In 1543 the Dublin government negotiated a bitter feud over fishing rights to the Bann between the McQuillans and O'Cahans in which the disputants renounced their claims in return for crown pensions. Fishing rights were subsequently leased to John Travers, the Master of the Ordnance, for 41 years. Bradshaw, *Irish Constitutional Revolution*, p. 220; Morrin, *Calendar of the Patent and Close Rolls, Henry VIII, Edward VI, Mary and Elizabeth*, p. 12; in the late sixteenth century, the fiants and patent rolls show a number of grants and conveyances extending a limited but derivative title to the river. The first grant was made to William Piers of Carrickfergus on 24 March 1571 for a lease of 21 years. Piers, in return, agreed to pay an annual rent of £10 to be increased to £40 per year 'should he be able to enjoy [the river] peaceably without interruption for a year'. Nevertheless the frequency of such 21-year leases to Charles Russell in 1586, to Charles Howard Lord High Admiral in 1587 and to Sir William Godolfin in 1600 suggests that the Gaelic fastness of Ulster did not readily lend itself to exploitation by colonial adventurers. Irish Fiants: 1796, 4827, 5040, 6413; Morrin, *Calendar of the Patent and Close Rolls of Chancery* (1576–1602), p. 562.

7 As cited in Moody, *The Londonderry Plantation*, p. 44.

8 T. W. Moody and J. G. Simms, *The Bishoprics of Derry and the Irish Society of London, 1602–1705* (Dublin, 1968), p. 9; see also *A Concise View of the Origin Constitution and Proceedings of the Honorable Society of the Governor and Assistants of London, of the New Plantation in Ulster* (London, 1822), p. clxxvii.

9 SP/63/201/fos. 132a–133a; *CSPI, 1596–7*, p. 444; F. J. Bigger, 'Sir Arthur Chichester, Lord Deputy of Ireland – With Some Notes on the Plantation of Ulster', *UJA*, 10 (1904), p. 6; Sir Alexander Palmer Bruce Chichester, *History of the Family Chichester* (London, 1871), p. 53.

10 For the career of Phillips see T. W. Moody, 'Sir Thomas Phillips of Limavady, Servitor', *IHS*, 1 (1939), pp. 251–72.

11 SP/63/216/fo. 105a; *CSPI, 1603–6*, p. 194.

12 SP/63/216/fo. 105a; *CSPI, 1603–6*, p. 194.

13 SP/63/217/fo. 72b; *CSPI, 1603–6*, p. 276.

14 SP/63/217/fo. 72a; *CSPI, 1603–6*, p. 275.

15 SP/63/218/fo. 219b; *CSPI, 1603–6*, p. 502.

16 SP/63/218/fos. 219b–222a; *CSPI, 1603–6*, p. 503.

17 SP/63/219/fo. 78b; *CSPI, 1603–6*, p. 569.

18 SP/63/219/fo. 76a; *CSPI, 1603–6*, p. 566.

19 SP/63/219/fo. 16a; *CSPI, 1603–6*, p. 518.

20 SP/63/219/fo. 16b; *CSPI, 1603–6*, p. 518.

21 T. O. Ranger, 'Richard Boyle and the Making of an Irish Fortune, 1588–1614', *IHS*, 10 (1957), pp. 288–9. Valuations of land were usually

notional, bearing no relation to the extent or real value of the property conveyed.

22 T. O. Ranger, 'The Career of Richard Boyle, First Earl of Cork in Ireland, 1588–1643' (University of Oxford, unpublished D. Phil. thesis, 1958).

23 Erck, pp. 28, 194.

24 *Ibid.*, pp. 289–301; quote taken from Ranger, 'Richard Boyle', p. 295.

25 SP/63/222/fos. 315a–316a; *CSPI, 1606–8*, p. 378.

26 SP/63/228/fo. 253a; *CSPI, 1608–10*, p. 435; for this commission the Dublin government derived a separate though contiguous body to receive and regrant lands held by tanistry. Bodl. Carte MS 61, fo. 152a; Steele, *Proclamations*, vol. 2, p. 18, no. 186, p. 19, no. 196.

27 Ir. St. 10 Ch. I Ses. 2, c. 1. For typical problems associated with the use in Ireland see SP/63/131/fo. 33a; *CSPI, 1586–8*, p. 400; SP/63/132/fo. 101a; *CSPI, 1586–8*, p. 453.

28 Erck, pp. 23, 127–8.

29 *Ibid.*, p. 23. The most recent account of the Chichester estates is P. Roebuck, 'The Making of an Ulster Great Estate: The Chichesters, Barons of Belfast and Viscounts of Carrickfergus, 1597–1648', *RIA Proc.*, Section C, 79 (1979), pp. 22–5. For the fate of the family's estates in the nineteenth century see W. A. Maguire, 'Lord Donegall and the Sale of Belfast: A Case History from the Encumbered Estates Court', *Economic History Review*, 2nd series, 29 (1976), pp. 570–84; 'The 1822 Settlement of the Donegall Estates', *Irish Economic and Social History*, 3 (1976), pp. 17–32.

30 Erck, p. 199.

31 D. A. Chart, 'The Break-up of the Estate of Con O'Neill', *RIA Proc.*, Section C, 10 (1942), pp. 119–51; M. Perceval-Maxwell, *The Scottish Migration to Ulster in the Reign of James I* (London, 1973), pp. 55–60; Hill, *MacDonnells of Antrim*, pp. 21–3.

32 Bodl. Carte MS 61, fo. 145a; *CSPI, 1603–6*, p. 271.

33 SP/63/217/fo. 112b; *CSPI, 1603–6*, p. 295; SP/63/217/fos. 122a and b; *CSPI, 1603–6*, p. 300; Chart, 'The Break-up', p. 124.

34 Erck, p. 199, Griffith, p. 200; Roebuck, 'The Making', p. 9.

35 PROB/11/109/fos. 322–3; Griffith, p. 5.

36 Erck, pp. 28, 280, 281; Griffith, p. 71; Bodl. Carte MS 61, fo. 85b; SP/63/223/fo. 96b (uncalendared).

37 Griffith, p. 200. Title to the other moiety was in dispute between Hamilton and Tyrone.

38 SP/63/227/fo. 145a; *CSPI, 1608–10*, pp. 301–2.

39 SP/63/227/fo. 145a; *CSPI, 1608–10*, pp. 301–2; Bodl. Carte MS 61, fo. 85b.

40 PRO/31/8/199/fos. 457a–458b; *CSPI, 1608–10*, p. 199.

41 Bodl. Carte MS 61, fo. 85b; *CSPI, 1608–10*, p. 564.

42 SP/63/223/fo. 183a; *CSPI, 1606–8*, pp. 468–9.

43 SP/63/222/fo. 315a; *CSPI, 1606–8*, p. 375.

44 Bodl. Carte MS 61, fo. 85b; after Tyrone's departure from Ireland in 1607, the state contested the Wakeman–Hamilton claim to Tyrone's moiety of the fishery, validating its claim by virtue of Tyrone's attainder.

The deed drawn up on 3 April 1611 to record Chichester's interest in the Bann was adjusted to account for the state's seizure of Tyrone's portion of the river; Griffith, p. 200.

45 SP/63/222/fo. 82a; *CSPI, 1606–8*, p. 252; PRO/31/8/201/fo. 227; *CSPI, 1606–8*, p. 134.

46 SP/63/222/fo. 82a; *CSPI, 1606–8*, p. 252.

47 PRO/31/8/201/fo. 227a; *CSPI, 1606–8*, p. 134.

48 SP/63/223/fo. 96a; *CSPI, 1606–8*, p. 428.

49 SP/63/223/fo. 96a; *CSPI, 1606–8*, p. 428.

50 SP/63/223/fo. 97a; *CSPI, 1606–8*, p. 428.

51 SP/63/224/fo. 55a; *CSPI, 1606–8*, p. 524.

52 SP/63/224/fo. 55a; *CSPI, 1606–8*, p. 524.

53 Lam. Pal. MS 630, fo. 109b; *Cal. Car., 1603–24*, p. 152.

54 SP/63/224/fo. 270a; *CSPI, 1608–10*, p. 21.

55 *Cal. Car., 1603–24*, p. 37; *CSPI, 1608–10*, p. 136.

56 SP/63/227/fo. 94b; *CSPI, 1608–10*, p. 281.

57 SP/63/229/fo. 66a; *CSPI, 1608–10*, p. 477.

58 SP/63/228/fo. 24a; *CSPI, 1608–10*, p. 353.

59 PRO/31/8/199/fo. 453a; *CSPI, 1608–10*, p. 199.

60 Davies, *Reports*, p. 154.

61 For the significance of argument from continental law in early modern law and jurisprudence see chapter nine of this study.

62 Davies, *Reports*, p. 154.

63 *Ibid.*, pp. 154–5.

64 *Ibid.*, pp. 151–2; Davies' claim to navigable waterways and to the high sea bordering Britain anticipated by twenty years the famous debate between the Dutch jurist Hugo Grotius and the English legal scholar John Selden. As a good Dutchman, Grotius argued for free trade on the high seas as a public waterway lying outside the dominion of national states. Selden, on the other hand, argued that the sea could be appropriated and occupied, and that English rule over the ocean extended to foreign coastlines. See Hugo Grotius, *The Freedom of the Seas* (New York, 1916), pp. 7–11; John Selden, *Mare Clausam* (London, 1613), pp. 61–72; for Grotius' rejoinder see H. F. Wright (ed.), 'Some Lesser Known Works of Hugo Grotius', *Bibliotheca Visseriana Dissertationum Ius Internationale Illustrantium*, 7 (1928), pp. 154–205; for a general review see W. Senior, 'Early Writers on Maritime Law', *LQR*, 37 (1921), pp. 323–36.

65 Davies, *Reports*, pp. 157–8; Jacques Cujas, *Corporis Iuris Civilis*, 2 vols. (Amsterdam, 1681), vol. 2, p. 741; for his career see D. R. Kelley, *Foundations of Modern Historical Scholarship: Language, Law and History in the French Renaissance* (New York, 1970), pp. 112–15.

66 Davies, *Reports*, p. 157; Renattus Choppinus, *De Domanio Franciae* (Frankfurt, 1701), pp. 111–15; for his career see J. F. Michaud and L. G. Michaud (eds.), *Biographie Universelle, Ancienne et Moderne*, 85 vols. (Paris, 1811–62), vol. 1, p. 199.

67 Davies, *Reports*, p. 157.

68 Healy, *Stolen Waters*, pp. 468–85.

69 Healy erroneously attributed the decision arising from the case of the Bann to the Court of Castle Chamber. *Ibid.*, pp. 181–3.

70 Perceval-Maxwell, *The Scottish Migration*, p. 62.
71 In 1637, Sir Henry Marten, Judge of the English Court of Admiralty, cited Davies' report of the Bann fishery as binding authority to establish a prerogative right to collect all ferry tolls over navigable rivers in Ireland. SP/63/256/fos. 3a and 40a; *CSPI, 1633–47*, pp. 144, 150.

6 *The mandates controversy and the case of Robert Lalor*

1 SP/63/215/fo. 109a; *CSPI, 1603–6*, p. 34; SP/63/215/fo. 114a; *CSPI, 1603–6*, pp. 36–7; SP/63/215/fos. 116a–117a; *CSPI, 1603–6*, pp. 37–8; SP/63/215/fo. 122b; *CSPI, 1603–6*, pp. 39–42.
2 SP/63/215/fo. 126a; *CSPI, 1603–6*, p. 42; SP/63/215/fos. 127a–128a; *CSPI, 1603–6*, pp. 43–4; Charles Smith, *The Antient and Present State of the County and City of Waterford* (Dublin, 1746), pp. 143–5.
3 Moryson, *Itinerary*, pp. 293–7; SP/63/215/fos. 177a and 181a; *CSPI, 1603–6*, pp. 65–6; SP/63/215/fo. 271a; *CSPI, 1603–6*, p. 68; Meade was tried on two charges: denial of the king's lawful title to the English crown and levying of war. BL Add. MS 47, 172, fos. 130a–132a; HMC, *Egmont MSS*, vol. 1, pt. 1, p. 28. In 1611 Meade wrote a tract entitled 'Advice to Catholics of Munster' in which he argued that the Irish penal laws imposed by the Irish statute of 2 Elizabeth expired on the death of the queen. BL Cott. MS Titus B. X, fo. 292a, and Bodl. Laudian MS 612, fo. 143a.
4 BL Cecil MS 186, fo. 41a; HMC, *Salisbury MSS*, vol. 13, p. 609. In Gaelic areas the government placed the religious problem within the larger context of Anglicizing Gaelic society. Here the government launched a programme of evangelism and conversion that hinged on publishing the New Testament and Book of Common Prayer in Gaelic, and on staffing at least some benefices with preachers learned in the Irish tongue. The New Testament and Book of Common Prayer were translated into Gaelic by William Daniel, the Lord Archbishop of Tuam. SP/63/217/fo. 263b; *CSPI, 1603–6*, p. 357. See also C. Litton Falkiner, 'William Farmer's Chronicles of Elizabeth Queen of Ireland', *EHR*, 22 (1907), p. 535. For the appointment of Gaelic-speaking clerics see SP/63/215/fo. 217a; *CSPI, 1603–6*, p. 86; Erck, p. 30. Due to the government's insistence on filling the church with Englishmen, such linguistic skills were obviously in short supply. As late as 1618, the Earl of Thomond complained of the general inability of Protestant clerics to reach the mass of Gaelic-speaking natives. Lam. Pal. MS 207, fo. 211a; *Cal. Car., 1603–24*, p. 376.
5 SP/63/212/fo. 331a; *CSPI, 1601–3*, p. 569. Attempts to revive the commission in the first decade of the seventeenth century were cancelled because the commissioners were more interested in levying fines than enforcing religious conformity. Bodl. Carte MS 30, fos. 75a–78a.
6 For Wilbraham's diary entry see *Camden Miscellany*, 10 (1902), p. 66.
7 Barnaby Rich, *A New Description of Ireland* (London, 1610), p. 67.
8 SP/63/215/fos. 149a and b; *CSPI, 1603–6*, p. 212–13.
9 Ir. St. 28 Hen. VIII c. 13; 2 Eliz. c. 1 and c.2; the Henrician Act and Oath of Supremacy were abolished by Mary but later introduced in 1560 by

Elizabeth. The English Act of Uniformity was extended to Ireland by Edward VI and subsequently passed by the Irish parliament in 1560. For the limited inroads made by the Reformation in Ireland see Bradshaw, 'Sword, Word and Strategy', pp. 475–502; for another view see Canny, 'Why the Reformation Failed in Ireland', pp. 423–50.

10 SP/63/216/fo. 162b; *CSPI, 1603–6*, p. 219. At that time Saxey, who had practised law for 46 years, 12 of them in Ireland, was petitioning Salisbury for promotion to replace Sir Edward Pelham as Chief Baron of the Exchequer. BL Cecil MS 119, fo. 90a; HMC, *Salisbury MSS*, vol. 18, pp. 154–5; SP/63/216/fo. 161b; *CSPI, 1603–6*, p. 218.

11 SP/63/215/fos. 160a and b; *CSPI, 1603–6*, pp. 58–9; SP/63/215/fos. 177a–178b; *CSPI, 1603–6*, pp. 65–8.

12 Bodl. Carte MS 61, fo. 180a; *CSPI, 1603–6*, p. 190. As the patentee officer responsible for the collection of fee farm duties on wine, Brouncker had a very active intelligence network to focus on the movements of the recusant clergy. Erck, pp. 1, 73. For some of the tactics employed by the recusant clergy see BL Lansdowne MS 159, fo. 270a.

13 SP/63/217/fo. 127a; *CSPI, 1603–6*, pp. 300–1.

14 SP/63/217/fo. 212a; *CSPI, 1603–6*, p. 346.

15 SP/63/217/fos. 254a–256a; *CSPI, 1603–6*, pp. 370–2.

16 TCD MS 852 (G.3.1), fo. 89a; *CSPI, 1603–6*, pp. 348–9, 353.

17 SP/63/219/fo. 103a; *CSPI, 1603–6*, p. 551; Bodl. Carte MS 61, fos. 83a and b; *CSPI, 1606–8*, p. cv.

18 SP/63/221/fo. 171a; *CSPI, 1606–8*, p. 188; PRO/31/8/210/fo. 246; *CSPI, 1606–8*, p. 222.

19 *CSPI, 1606–8*, pp. xcvi–xcvii.

20 SP/63/217/fos. 246a and b; *CSPI, 1603–6*, p. 367; SP/63/217/fos. 231a–234a; *CSPI, 1603–6*, pp. 362–5.

21 SP/63/217/fo. 6a; *CSPI, 1603–6*, p. 367; Bagwell, *Ireland under the Tudors*, vol. 2, pp. 327–9.

22 Lam. Pal. MS 600, fo. 226a; *CSPI, 1611–14*, p. 394; *DNB*, vol. 1, pp. 1181–2.

23 SP/63/217/fo. 6a; *CSPI, 1603–6*, p. 172.

24 SP/63/217/fo. 267a; *CSPI, 1603–6*, p. 374.

25 SP/63/217/fo. 267a; *CSPI, 1603–6*, p. 374.

26 SP/63/217/fo. 267a; *CSPI, 1603–6*, p. 374; SP/63/218/fo. 88a; *CSPI, 1603–6*, p. 438. Barnewall also accused Ley of doubling fees in the Court of King's Bench.

27 SP/63/217/fo. 267a; *CSPI, 1603–6*, p. 374.

28 SP/63/218/fo. 126b; *CSPI, 1603–6*, p. 447; SP/63/217/fo. 256a; *CSPI, 1603–6*, p. 372.

29 SP/63/217/fo. 256a; *CSPI, 1603–6*, pp. 370–2; also SP/63/221/fo. 63a; *CSPI, 1606–8*, p. 117.

30 SP/63/218/fo. 192a; *CSPI, 1603–6*, p. 488; SP/63/218/fo. 152a; *CSPI, 1603–6*, p. 463.

31 Bodl. Carte MS 3, fo. 82a; *CSPI, 1603–6*, p. 509.

32 SP/63/219/fo. 3a; *CSPI, 1603–6*, pp. 509–10; PRO/31/8/199/fo. 118; *CSPI, 1603–6*, p. 547.

33 SP/63/219/fo. 3a; *CSPI, 1603–6*, pp. 509–10.

34 SP/63/217/fo. 254a; *CSPI, 1603–6*, p. 370.

35 Bodl. Carte MS 61, fo. 151a; *CSPI, 1603–6*, p. 350.

36 Bodl. Carte MS 61, fo. 151a; *CSPI, 1603–6*, p. 351; A. G. Petti, 'Recusant Documents from the Ellesmere Manuscripts', *Catholic Record Society*, 60 (1968), p. 177.

37 TCD MS 843 (F.3.17), fos. 397–8; *CSPI, 1603–6*, pp. 584–9.

38 TCD MS 843 (F.3.17), fo. 401; *CSPI, 1603–6*, p. 588.

39 TCD MS 843 (F.3.17), fo. 401; *CSPI, 1603–6*, p. 588.

40 PRO/31/8/199/fos. 197–8; *CSPI, 1606–8*, pp. 49–50; PRO/31/8/199/fos. 118–19; *CSPI, 1603–6*, p. 547; for Chief Justice Popham's certification see SP/14/24/fo. 51b; *CSPD, 1603–10*, p. 339.

41 PRO/31/8/199/fo. 198; *CSPI, 1606–8*, p. 50.

42 SP/63/218/fo. 38a; *CSPI, 1603–6*, p. 408; there is a manuscript report of Lalor's case in the British Museum. See Royal MS 18.C.xv: 'The Case of Praemunire', fos. 1a–22b.

43 SP/63/218/fo. 57b; *CSPI, 1603–6*, p. 416.

44 Petti, 'Recusant Documents', p. 165; SP/63/218/fo. 57b; *CSPI, 1603–6*, p. 416.

45 SP/63/222/fos. 6a and b; *CSPI, 1606–8*, pp. 209–10; BL Cecil MS 112, fo. 156a; HMC, *Salisbury MSS*, vol. 17, p. 476; the Countess of Kildare is represented as being a 'teat to give such nourishment to all Romish rebels'.

46 Petti, 'Recusant Documents', p. 166.

47 *Ibid.*

48 SP/63/218/fo. 127b; *CSPI, 1603–6*, p. 448.

49 J. H. Baker, 'The Common Lawyers and the Chancery: 1616', *Irish Jurist*, 4 (1969), pp. 383–4; see also J. P. Dawson, 'Coke and Ellesmere Disinterred: The Attack on the Chancery in 1616', *Illinois Law Review*, 36 (1941), p. 136.

50 Davies, *Reports*, p. 243; Petti, 'Recusant Documents', p. 173.

51 Davies, *Reports*, p. 242; Petti, 'Recusant Documents', p. 173.

52 Davies, *Reports*, p. 270; Petti, 'Recusant Documents', p. 189.

53 Davies, *Reports*, p. 270; Petti, 'Recusant Documents', p. 189.

54 Davies, *Reports*, pp. 271–2; Petti, 'Recusant Documents', pp. 189–90.

55 Davies, *Reports*, p. 272; Petti, 'Recusant Documents', p. 190.

56 Davies, *Reports*, p. 273; Petti, 'Recusant Documents', p. 191.

57 Davies, *Reports*, p. 274; Petti, 'Recusant Documents', p. 191.

58 Petti, 'Recusant Documents', p. 193.

59 SP/63/222/fo. 6a; *CSPI, 1606–8*, p. 210; SP/63/218/fo. 163a; *CSPI, 1603–6*, p. 476.

60 Bagwell, *Ireland under the Stuarts*, vol. 1, p. 29; Aidan Clarke, 'Plantation and Toleration', in Moody *et al.*, *A New History of Ireland*, p. 192; Cregan, 'Irish Recusant Lawyers', p. 312; W. E. H. Lecky, *A History of Ireland in the Eighteenth Century*, 5 vols. (London, 1913), vol. 1, p. 35; E. Curtis, *A History of Ireland* (London, 1945), p. 224.

61 PRO/31/8/199/fos. 221–2; *CSPI, 1606–8*, p. 137.

62 PRO/31/8/199/fos. 69–70; *CSPI, 1603–6*, p. 461.

63 PRO/31/8/199/fo. 218; *CSPI, 1606–8*, p. 138.

64 PRO/31/8/199/fo. 222; *CSPI, 1606–8*, p. 137.

65 BL Add. MS 47, 172, fo. 148a; HMC, *Egmont MSS*, p. 32; SP/63/221/fo. 92a; *CSPI, 1606–8*, p. 131; SP/63/222/fo. 68a; *CSPI, 1606–8*, p. 250.
66 Alfred J. Loomie (ed.), 'Spain and the Jacobean Catholics', *Catholic Record Society*, 64 (1973), pp. xv–xx; see also SP/63/225/fo. 269a; *CSPI, 1608–10*, p. 122; remission of fines was sued for by all the Munster towns in late 1608 and subsequently granted in early 1609. PRO/31/8/199/fo. 419; *CSPI, 1608–10*, p. 129.

7 The case of customs payable for merchandise

1 The involvement of Cecil and a group of London merchants in the proposed farm of the Irish customs has been fully explored elsewhere. Particularly useful are A. F. Upton, *Sir Arthur Ingram* (Oxford, 1961), pp. 14–15, 85–6; H. F. Kearney, *Strafford in Ireland* (Manchester, 1959), pp. 161–2; R. H. Tawney, *Business and Politics in the Reign of James I* (Cambridge, 1958), pp. 86–7, 97; Menna Prestwich, *Cranfield, Politics and Profits under the Early Stuarts* (Oxford, 1966), pp. 126–8; V. Treadwell, 'The Establishment of the Farm of the Irish Customs', *EHR*, 93 (1978), pp. 585–6.
2 Arthur Collins (ed.), *Letters and Memorials of State*, 2 vols. (London, 1746), vol. I, p. 24.
3 V. R. Treadwell, 'Irish Financial Administrative Reform under James I: The Customs and State Regulation of Trade' (Queen's University, Belfast, unpublished Ph. D. thesis, 1961), p. 362; see also the preamble to the Elizabethan Trade Acts: Ir. St. 11 Eliz. c. 1 and c. 2.
4 Canny, *Elizabethan Conquest*.
5 Morley, p. 234.
6 SP/63/167/fo. 36a; *CSPI, 1592–6*, p. 10.
7 SP/63/205/fo. 429b; *CSPI, 1599–1600*, p. 201.
8 SP/63/210/fo. 64a; *CSPI, 1601–3*, p. 280.
9 SP/63/210/fo. 190a; *CSPI, 1601–3*, p. 337; Lam Pal. MS 615, fo. 484a; *Cal. Car., 1601–3*, p. 390.
10 Moryson, *Itinerary*, pt. 2, pp. 247–8.
11 A. P. Newton, 'The Establishment of the Great Farm of the English Customs', *Transactions of the Royal Historical Society*, 4th series, I (1918), pp. 129–55; R. Ashton, 'Revenue Farming under the Early Stuarts', *Economic History Review*, 2nd series, 8 (1956), pp. 310–22.
12 Upton, *Sir Arthur Ingram*, pp. 14–15.
13 Leeds Public Library: MS TN/PO 7, 'Irish Customs', II (1); HMC, *Various Collections*, vol. 8, pp. 49–50.
14 Tawney, *Business and Politics*, pp. 83–5; Upton, *Sir Arthur Ingram*, pp. 14–15, 54–61; HMC, *Sackville MSS* vol. I, p. 49; Treadwell, 'Farm of the Irish Customs', p. 586.
15 SP/63/221/fo. 1a; *CSPI, 1606–8*, pp. 74–5.
16 SP/31/8/199/fo. 191a; *CSPI, 1606–8*, pp. 105–6; Cogan and Waad were paid £476 out of the English Exchequer for their expenses. SP/14/192/13.
17 Lascelles, *Liber Munerum Publicorum Hiberniae*, vol. 2, p. 137.
18 BL Lansdowne MS 156, fos. 204a–205a; SP/63/221/fos. 123a–124a; *CSPI, 1606–8*, p. 147.

19 BL Lansdowne MS 156, fos. 203a–205a; Lam. Pal. MS 629, fos. 74a–76b; *Cal. Car., 1603–24*, pp. 85–6; SP/63/221/fos. 119a–120a, 123a–124a; *CSPI, 1606–8*, pp. 146–7.

20 BL Lansdowne MS 156, fos. 203a–205a.

21 Seamus Pender, *Waterford Merchants Abroad* (National University of Ireland, O'Donnell Lecture, Tralee, 1964), pp. 3–4.

22 Davies, *Reports*, p. 18.

23 SP/63/222/fos. 8b–9a; *CSPI, 1606–8*, p. 213; BL Harl. MS 2058, fos. 59a, 62b, 63a; PROI, Ferguson MS 27, fos. 1–2.

24 V. Treadwell, 'The Irish Customs Administration in the Sixteenth Century', *IHS*, 21 (1977), p. 388; 'Irish Financial Administrative Reform', pp. 3–4; Davies, *Reports*, pp. 20–34; Davies, *The Question Concerning Impositions*, pp. 168–9.

25 For a discussion of the medieval origins and administration of these duties see Mary Donovan O'Sullivan, 'Italian Merchant Bankers and the Collection of Customs in Ireland, 1275–1311', in J. A. Watt (ed.), *Medieval Studies Presented to Aubrey Gwynn* (Dublin, 1961), pp. 168–9.

26 Davies, *Reports*, p. 31; Morley, pp. 243–4.

27 Ir. St. 14 Ed. IV c. 2; 15 Ed. IV c. 56; 16 Ed. IV c. 14; 19 Ed. IV c. 24 and c. 27.

28 Ir. St. 10 Hen. VII c. 8; Davies, *Reports*, p. 31.

29 Ir. St. 15 Hen. VII c. 1.

30 Treadwell, 'Irish Customs Administration', p. 388.

31 Davies, *Reports*, p. 34; Treadwell, 'Irish Customs Administration', pp. 391–2.

32 Treadwell, 'Irish Customs Administration', pp. 392–3.

33 *Ibid.*, pp. 406–7.

34 SP/63/221/fos. 8b–9a; *CSPI, 1606–8*, p. 213.

35 CSPI, 1606–8, p. 249; SP/31/8/199/fos. 241–2.

36 BL Lansdowne MS 156, fos. 200a–202a.

37 Davies, *Reports*, pp. 18–19.

38 *Ibid.*, p. 19.

39 *Ibid.*

40 *Ibid.*, p. 20.

41 Davies, *The Question Concerning Impositions*, pp. 1–9.

42 Davies, *Reports*, p. 33; it is difficult to determine the precise foundation for this statement in Roman law. Very similar statements occur in *C.* 4.61.10, 13; *D.* 50.16.16–17.

43 Davies, *Reports*, p. 34.

44 *Ibid.*, pp. 35–6.

45 *Ibid.*, p. 36.

46 *Ibid.*, p. 37. Mr Kenneth Nicholls has recently informed me that in Anglo-Irish usage coquet was meant to imply the great custom, and was adopted into Irish as *coicéad*.

47 *Ibid.*, p. 37.

48 *Ibid.*, p. 41.

49 *Ibid.*

50 *Ibid.*, pp. 41–2; SP/31/8/199/fos. 378–9; *CSPI, 1606–8*, p. 579.

51 BL Lansdowne MS 156, fo. 186a; Griffith, p. 133; BL Cecil MS 123,

fo. 69a; HMC, *Salisbury MSS*, vol. 19, p. 349; *CSPD, 1603–10*, p. 384.

52 SP/63/225/fo. 173a; *CSPI, 1608–10*, p. 93.
53 SP/31/8/201/fo. 221a; *CSPI, 1606–8*, p. 330.
54 SP/31/8/201/fo. 221a; *CSPI, 1606–8*, p. 330.
55 SP/14/34/fo. 8a; *CSPD, 1603–10*, p. 437.
56 SP/31/8/201/fo. 308a; *CSPI, 1606–8*, p. 579.
57 Davies, *Reports*, p. 42.
58 *Ibid.*, p. 43.
59 *Ibid.*; BL Harl. MS 2138, fos. 21a–b; J. T. Gilbert (ed.), *Calendar of the Ancient Records of Dublin, in the Possession of the Corporation*, 17 vols. (Dublin, 1889–95), vol. 3, pp. 542–6.
60 Davies, *Reports*, p. 43.
61 BL Harl. MS 2138, fo. 21a; Gilbert, *Cal. Anc. Rec. Dublin*, vol. 3, p. 544.
62 BL Harl. MS 2138, fo. 21b; Gilbert, *Cal. Anc. Rec. Dublin*, vol. 3, p. 545.
63 BL Harl. MS 2138, fos. 23a–b.
64 *Ibid.*, fo. 23a.
65 *Ibid.*
66 *Ibid.*, fo. 23b.
67 *Ibid.*
68 *Ibid.*
69 *Ibid.*
70 *Ibid.*
71 *Ibid.*
72 *Ibid.*, fo. 24a.
73 *Ibid.*
74 *Ibid.*
75 *Ibid.*
76 SP/31/8/199/fo. 449; *CSPI, 1608–10*, p. 190.
77 SP/31/8/199/fos. 446a–447a; *CSPI, 1608–10*, p. 128.
78 SP/31/8/199/fo. 417a; *CSPI, 1608–10*, p. 133. On 19 January 1609, Galway was exempted from all customs except for the coquet of hides. The town, like the city of Drogheda, was also made a county. The corporation of Limerick was exempted from poundage and granted the great custom. SP/31/8/199/fo. 428; *CSPI, 1608–10*, p. 139. See also SP/63/227/fo. 66a; *CSPI, 1608–10*, p. 257. On account of its adherence to the Protestant religion, Youghal was granted the coquet custom and custom of poundage for the repair of city walls. In the proposed division of county Cork, Youghal was designated the seat of the new shire, the Mayor and Recorder being assigned as justices of the peace for the town and county. See Davies' letter to Chichester on the grant of the coquet custom to the Munster towns. SP/31/8/199/fo. 509.
79 SP/31/8/199/fo. 447; *CSPI, 1608–10*, p. 129.
80 Bodl. University College MS 103, fos. 74–80; BL Lansdowne MS 156, fos. 289a–292a; BL Add. MS 11,402, fo. 136a; Treadwell, 'Farm of the Irish Customs', pp. 494–5.
81 SP/63/229/fo. 34a; *CSPI, 1608–10*, p. 451.

82 SP/31/8/199/fo. 452; *CSPI, 1611–14*, p. 21; *Cal. Car., 1603–24*, pp. 64–5.

83 Treadwell, 'Farm of the Irish Customs', p. 596; Upton, *Sir Arthur Ingram*, p. 15; Prestwich, *Cranfield*, pp. 86–7; HMC, *Sackville MSS*, vol. 1, pp. 257–9.

84 BL Cecil MS 196, fo. 46a; HMC, *Salisbury MSS*, vol. 21, pp. 304–5.

85 Lam. Pal. MS 629, fos. 82a and b; *Cal. Car., 1603–24*, p. 93; *CSPI, 1611–14*, p. 410.

86 Treadwell, 'Farm of the Irish Customs', p. 598; Lam. Pal. MS 629, fos. 62a–b; *Cal. Car., 1603–24*, pp. 174–6.

87 See Davies' uncalendared 'Propositions for the Increase of his Majesties' Revenue in Ireland', Bodl. Carte MS 61, fo. 140b; *CSPI, 1611–14*, p. 144; PRO/31/8/199/fo. 515; *CSPI, 1611–14*, p. 230; Griffith, p. 208.

88 The 1611 proclamation banning massing priests and Jesuits was the same as the one issued in 1604. See chapter six of this work. Lam. Pal. MS 629, fos. 139a–140a; *Cal. Car., 1603–24*, p. 74; Griffith, p. 255.

89 Treadwell, 'Farm of the Irish Customs', p. 599; Lascelles, *Liber Munerum Publicorum Hiberniae*, vol. 1, pt. 2, pp. 146–67; see in particular Dublin, Drogheda, Wexford, Cork, Kinsale, Limerick, Waterford, Youghal and Galway.

90 Spedding, *Works of Francis Bacon*, vol. 4, pp. 358–60.

91 Leeds Public Library: MS TN/PO 7, III (3); Treadwell, 'Farm of the Irish Customs', pp. 600–1.

92 Treadwell, 'Irish Financial Administrative Reform', p. 358.

93 *Ibid.*, pp. 358 and 406.

94 Revenue from crown lands in Ireland has not yet received the attention it deserves. For Irish wardship see H. F. Kearney, 'The Court of Wards and Liveries in Ireland, 1622–41', *RIA Proc.*, Section C, 57 (1956), pp. 29–68; V. Treadwell, 'The Irish Court of Wards under James I', *IHS*, 12 (1961), pp. 1–27.

95 Peter Gale, *An Enquiry into the Ancient Corporate System of Ireland* (London, 1834), pp. 44–5; J. J. Webb, *Municipal Government in Ireland, Medieval and Modern* (Dublin, 1918), pp. 141–2.

96 Treadwell, 'Farm of the Irish Customs', p. 593.

97 SP/63/231/fo. 62a; *CSPI, 1611–14*, p. 21; it is interesting to note that on 29 May 1609 the resolution of the judges in England was enrolled in the Irish Court of Exchequer, PROI, Ferguson MS 11, fo. 176; Davies, *Reports*, p. 47.

98 Lam. Pal. MS 629, fos. 56a and b; *Cal. Car., 1603–24*, p. 83.

99 Lam. Pal. MS 629, fo. 84b; *Cal. Car., 1603–24*, p. 97; SP/63/232/fo. 24b; *CSPI, 1611–14*, p. 250.

100 SP/63/232/fo. 24b; *CSPI, 1611–14*, p. 250; Lam. Pal. MS 629, fo. 30b; *Cal. Car., 1603–24*, pp. 156, 161.

101 See also the fragmentary journal of the proceedings in the Irish House of Lords. BL Add. MS 4792, fo. 94a; V. Treadwell, 'The House of Lords in the Irish Parliament of 1613–15', *EHR*, 70 (1965), p. 100.

102 *The Journal of the House of Commons of the Kingdom of Ireland*, 23 vols. (Dublin, 1763–86), vol. 1, p. 16.

103 *Ibid.*, p. 17.

8 *The case of mixed money*

1 SP/63/208/pt. 2/fos. 76a–101a; *CSPI, 1600–1*, p. 350; Lam. Pal. MS 617, fo. 204a; *Cal. Car., 1601–3*, pp. 67–8.

2 Dr C. E. Challis devotes several pages to Elizabeth's Irish debasement in his recent study: *Tudor Coinage* (Manchester, 1978), pp. 268–74.

3 SP/63/215/fo.86a; *CSPI, 1603–6*, p. 26.

4 SP/63/215/fo. 261b; *CSPI, 1603–6*, p. 112.

5 Davies, *Reports*, p. 50. The case of mixed money may also be found in Howell, *State Trials*, vol. 2, pp. 114–30.

6 Dietz, *English Public Finance* (New York, 1932), pp. 432–3.

7 BL Lansdowne MS 156, fo. 253.

8 BL Cecil MS 92, fo. 68a; HMC, *Salisbury MSS*, vol. 15, pp. 1–2.

9 C. E. Challis, 'The Tudor Coinage in Ireland', *BNJ*, 40 (1971), pp. 97–119; M. Dolley, 'Anglo-Irish Monetary Policies, 1172–1637', *Historical Studies*, 7 (1969), pp. 45–64; also M. Dolley, 'The Irish Coinage 1534–1691', in Moody *et al.*, *A New History of Ireland*, p. 408.

10 Ir. St. 38 Hen. VI c. 11; Dolley, 'Anglo-Irish Monetary Policies', pp. 52–3.

11 Challis, *Tudor Coinage*, pp. 101–9; Dolley, in Moody *et al.*, *A New History of Ireland*, pp. 408–11.

12 Dolley, in Moody *et al.*, *A New History of Ireland*, p. 412. The whole range of Irish coins from the middle ages to the present may be seen in the Ulster Museum in Belfast.

13 SP/63/207/pt. 2/fo. 67a; *CSPI, 1600–1*, p. 26.

14 SP/63/213/fo. 151a; *CSPI, 1601–3*, p. 629.

15 Wilbraham's observations on Cecil can be found in his diary, which is printed in *Camden Miscellany*, 10 (1902), p. 106.

16 For Hayes' plan to alter the coinage see SP/63/209/fos. 352a–b; *CSPI, 1601–3*, p. 225; SP/63/212/fo. 244a; *CSPI, 1601–3*, pp. 543–4; BL Harl. MS 38, fos. 225a–236a.

17 'Wilbraham's Diary', *Camden Miscellany*, pp. 37–41; for other deliberations see SP/63/209/fos. 354a–360b; *CSPI, 1601–3*, pp. 225–34.

18 SP/63/208/pt. 1/fo. 43a; *CSPI, 1600–1*, p. 158; SP/63/207/pt. 6/fo. 321a; *CSPI, 1600–1*, p. 126; SP/63/208/pt. 1/fo. 41a; *CSPI, 1600–1*, p. 158.

19 SP/63/208/pt. 1/fo. 43a; *CSPI, 1600–1*, p. 158.

20 SP/63/216/fos. 167b–168a; *CSPI, 1603–6*, pp. 223–4.

21 SP/63/209/pt. 2/fos. 435a and b; *CSPI, 1601–3*, p. 251.

22 Challis, *Tudor Coinage*, p. 272, for production costs see Carey's accounts: PRO E351/239; E351/239/266; A.O.1/289/1086. See also SP/63/209/pt. 2/fo. 425a; *CSPI, 1601–3*, p. 248.

23 SP/63/208/pt. 2/fo. 82a; *CSPI, 1600–1*, p. 350; Lam. Pal. MS 617, fo. 204a; *Cal. Car., 1601–3*, pp. 67–8.

24 SP/63/210/fo. 65a; *CSPI, 1601–3*, p. 280.

25 These figures differ slightly from those provided by Dr Challis. See E351/239.

26 *Ibid.*; E351/266; A.O.1/289/1086; A.O.1/288/1082.

27 SP/63/210/fo. 65a; *CSPI, 1601–3*, p. 281.

28 SP/63/210/fo. 65b; *CSPI, 1601–3*, p. 281.

29 SP/63/211/fo. 205a; *CSPI, 1601–3*, p. 432.
30 SP/63/210/fo. 64a; *CSPI, 1601–3*, p. 280.
31 SP/63/211/fo. 139a; *CSPI, 1601–3*, pp. 407–9; Lam. Pal. MS 617, fo. 264a; *Cal. Car., 1601–3*, pp. 246–7.
32 SP/63/212/fo. 148a; *CSPI, 1601–3*, p. 511.
33 SP/63/212/fo. 146b; *CSPI, 1601–3*, p. 509; BL Cecil MS 91, fo. 139a; HMC, *Salisbury MSS*, vol. 12, p. 646.
34 SP/63/212/fo.147a; *CSPI, 1601–3*, pp. 509–10.
35 SP/63/212/fo. 147b; *CSPI, 1601–3*, p. 510.
36 Lam. Pal. MS 607, fos. 219a–221a; *Cal. Car., 1601–3*, pp. 409–14.
37 SP/63/212/fo. 299a; *CSPI, 1601–3*, p. 561; BL Cecil MS 91, fos. 122a and 139a; HMC, *Salisbury MSS*, vol. 12, pp. 624 and 646.
38 SP/63/212/fo. 269a; *CSPI, 1601–3*, p. 551; for further complaints by the Dubliners see Gilbert, *Cal. Anc. Rec. Dublin*, vol. 2, p. 283.
39 SP/63/212/fo. 298b; *CSPI, 1601–3*, p. 560.
40 SP/63/212/fos. 335a and b; *CSPI, 1601–3*, p. 571.
41 SP/63/215/fo. 86a; *CSPI, 1603–6*, p. 26.
42 SP/14/1/28; *CSPD, 1603–10*, p. 3; *CSPI, 1603–6*, p. 87; BL Cecil MS 99, fo. 118a; HMC, *Salisbury MSS*, vol. 15, pp. 49–50.
43 Dolley, 'Anglo-Irish Monetary Policies', p. 59; Dolley, 'The Irish Coinage', pp. 414–15.
44 SP/63/215/fo. 265b; *CSPI, 1603–6*, p. 115.
45 For problems over the precise value ascribed to sterling money in Ireland see James Simon, *An Essay towards an Historical Account of Irish Coins* (Dublin, 1749), p. 110.
46 The proclamation may be found in the above, p. 116.
47 SP/63/210/fo. 295a; *CSPI, 1601–3*, pp. 355 and lxix; Davies, *Reports*, p. 49; see also PROI, Salved Chancery Pleadings, I245, B92.
48 Davies, *Reports*, p. 49.
49 *Ibid.*, pp. 49–50.
50 René Budelius, *De Monetis et Re Nummaria* (Cologne, 1591). For Budelius see *Biographie Universelle, Ancienne et Moderne*, vol. 6, p. 112.
51 Davies, *Reports*, p. 60; J. F. Von Schulte, *Die Geschichte der Quellen und Literatur des Canonischen Rechts*, 3 vols. (Stuttgart, 1875–80), vol. 3, p. 721; Leyva Covarruvius, *Veterum Collatio Numismatum Cum His, Quae Modo Expendatur Publicae & Regia Authoritate Percusa* (Salamanca, 1562), pp. 51–2.
52 Davies, *Reports*, p. 54.
53 *Ibid.*, pp. 61–9.
54 *Ibid.*, pp. 61–2; Covarruvius, *Veterum Collatio*, p. 9; Choppinus, *De Domanio Franciae*, pp. 158–9. For the place of Choppinus in French legal scholarship see Kelley, *Foundations of Modern Historical Scholarship*, p. 193. For biographical details see *Biographie Universelle, Ancienne et Moderne*, vol. 8, p. 199.
55 Davies, *Reports*, pp. 62–4.
56 *Ibid.*, p. 67; Davies also cites Charles Dumoulin, the great French legal humanist, and Marquard Freherus, another well-known sixteenth-century French civilian. See Budelius, *De Monetis*, pp. 485 and 526. For Dumoulin's position in French humanist scholarship see Kelley,

Foundations of Modern Historical Scholarship, pp. 189–94; also Marquard Freherus, *De Re Monetaria Veterum Romanorum et Hodierni Apud Germanes Imperii* (Lyons, 1605), p. 47. For Freherus' career as a civil lawyer see *Biographie Universelle, Ancienne et Moderne*, vol. 15, p. 132.

57 Davies, *Reports*, pp. 49 and 73.

58 *Ibid.*, p. 73; Budelius, *De Monetis*, p. 194.

59 Davies, *Reports*, p. 75; William Lyndwood, *Provinciale, Seu Constitutiones Angliae* (Oxford, 1679), p. 171. Lyndwood's comments appear to be a gloss on *C*.11.11.10.

60 Davies, *Reports*, p. 76.

61 *Ibid.*; Budelius, *De Monetis*, p. 215.

62 Davies, *Reports*, p. 77.

63 Government allegations of fraud were subsequently levelled at Carey himself and continued against his heirs until 1637. PRO/31/8/199/fos. 301–2; *CSPI, 1606–8*, p. 396; for official charges against Carey for alleged misconduct over the exchange see PRO E/126/3/fos. 352a–354a. As early as 1603, Chief Justice Popham expressed an awareness of Carey's misdeeds: BL Cecil MS 96, fo. 128a; HMC, *Salisbury MSS*, vol. 12, pp. 522–3.

64 J. W. Wallace, *The Reporters Arranged and Characterized with Incidental Remarks* (Edinburgh, 1882), pp. 234–6.

9 Sir John Davies, the ancient constitution and civil law

1 J. G. A. Pocock, *The Ancient Constitution and the Feudal Law* (Bath, 1974), p. 90.

2 B. Levack, *The Civil Lawyers in England, 1603–41* (Oxford, 1973), pp. 145–6.

3 Abbott, *Law Reporting in England*, pp. 190–1.

4 3 *Coke Rep.*, pref., p. xxb.

5 D. S. Bland, 'Rhetoric and the Law Student in Sixteenth-Century England', *Studies in Philology*, 54 (1957), pp. 498–508; R. J. Schoeck, 'Rhetoric and Law in Sixteenth-Century England', *Studies in Philology*, 50 (1953), pp. 119–27; Louis Knafla, 'The Matriculation Revolution and Education at the Inns of Court in Renaissance England', in A. J. Slavin (ed.), *Tudor Men and Institutions* (Baton Rouge, La., 1972), p. 252; also 'The Law Studies of an Elizabethan Student', *HLQ*, 32 (1969), pp. 227 and 231–4.

6 L. Knafla, *Law and Politics in Jacobean England* (Cambridge, 1977), p. 49.

7 W. Fulbecke, *Directive or Preparataive to the Study of the Law* (London, 1602), pp. 26–9.

8 For Dodderidge and Whitelock see E. Foss, *A Biographical Dictionary of the Judges of England* (London, 1870), pp. 223, 721–2.

9 F. W. Maitland, *Select Passages from the Works of Bracton and Azo* (Selden Society, 8, London, 1894), p. xxx.

10 See Ulpian on *ius naturale* in *D*.1.1.1.3; *Inst.* 1.2.2; 'natural law' was identified with the instincts all men share with other creatures. The law of nations or *ius gentium* was seen as a component part of the natural law, but was for the most part used interchangeably with natural law.

See J. A. C. Thomas, *Textbook of Roman Law* (New York, 1976), pp. 62–5.

11 G. W. Prothero, *Select Statutes and Other Constitutional Documents Illustrative of the Reigns of Elizabeth and James I* (Oxford, 1898), pp. 351–2; S. R. Gardiner, *Parliamentary Debates in 1610* (Camden Society, 81, 1867), pp. 89, 90 and 119.

12 BL Harl. MS 278, fos. 411a–412a, 418b–422b; Davies, *The Question Concerning Impositions*, pp. 1–9; *Reports*, p. 34.

13 PRO Wards 15.6.1 as cited in C. Russell, *The Crisis of Parliaments, 1509–1660* (Oxford, 1977), p. 255.

14 *House of Lords Journal*, vol. 3, p. 758.

15 I am indebted to Professor Brian Levack for calling my attention to this manuscript. BL Harl. MS 5220, fo. 4b.

16 T. Craig, *De Unione Regnorum Britanniae Tractatus* (Scottish History Society, 60, 1909), pp. 312, 326–7. Also Peter Stein, 'The Influence of Roman Law in the Law of Scotland', *Juridical Review*, new series, 8 (1962–3), p. 219.

17 Charles Donahue, 'The Civil Law in England', *Yale Law Journal*, 84 (1974), p. 180.

18 F. W. Maitland, *English Law and the Renaissance* (Cambridge, 1901); see also C. H. McIlwain, *The Political Works of James I* (Cambridge, Mass., 1918), pp. xl–xli.

19 Maitland's reception thesis was thoroughly demolished in 1966 by Professor Thorne. See 'English Law and the Renaissance', *La Storia del Diritto nel Quadro delle Scienza Storiche* (Florence, 1966), pp. 437–45.

20 G. R. Elton, 'The Political Creed of Thomas Cromwell', *Transactions of the Royal Historical Society*, 15 (1965), p. 78.

21 John Cowell, *The Interpreter* (Cambridge, 1607). See especially 'Prerogative of the King'; A. Gentili, *Regales Disputationes Tres; id est de Potestate Regis Absoluta* (London, 1605), pp. 3–58.

22 For Bacon see *An Offer to the King of a Digest to be of the Laws of England* in Spedding, *Works of Francis Bacon*, vol. 7, pp. 358–62. See also his *Elements of the Common Lawes of England Containing a Collection of Some Principall Rules and Maxims of the Common Law, with their Latitude and Extent* (London, 1630), p. 139. Bacon's influence can be seen in James I's proposal for law reform. See McIlwain, *The Political Works of James I*, pp. 292–3, 311–12 and 332. Also D. Veall, *The Popular Movement for Law Reform 1640–1660* (Oxford, 1970), pp. 65–74; see also Brian Levack, 'The Proposed Union of English Law and Scots Law in the Seventeenth Century', *Juridical Review*, pt. 2, new series, 20 (1975), pp. 103–10.

23 2 *Coke Rep.*, pref., pp. vii and viii.

24 Coke, *Institutes*, vol. 2, proeme, p. vi.

25 S. E. Thorne, *A Catalogue of the Library of Sir Edward Coke* (New Haven, 1950), pp. 38–51.

26 T. E. Scrutton, 'Roman Law Influences in Chancery, Church Courts, Admiralty and Law Merchant', in *Select Essays in Anglo-American Legal History*, 3 vols. (Cambridge, 1907), vol. 1, pp. 209–10.

27 Peter Stein, *Regulae Iuris from Iuristic Rules to Legal Maxims* (Edinburgh, 1966), p. 101.

28 Spedding, *Works of Francis Bacon*, vol. 13, p. 65.

29 Knafla, *Law and Politics in Jacobean England*, p. 298.

30 John Holliday, *The Life of William Late Earl of Mansfield* (London, 1797), p. 90.

31 Peregrine Bingham, *Reports of Cases Argued and Determined in the Court of Common Pleas, 1822–1834*, 10 vols. (London, 1834), vol. 2, p. 296; James Stephen, *A History of the Criminal Law of England*, 3 vols. (London, 1883), vol. 2, p. 205.

32 Of the several editions of the *Reports*, the introduction may only be found in: Sir John Davies, *Le Primer Report des Cases in les Courts del Roy* (Dublin, 1615); *Le Primer Report des Cases & Matters en Ley Resolves & Adjudges en les Courts del Roy en Ireland* (London, 1628); and *Les Reports des Cases & Matters en Ley Resolves & Adjudges en les Courts del Roy en Ireland* (London, 1674).

33 Davies, *Le Primer Report* (1615), p. 6b.

34 *Ibid.*, pp. 5a–b; for Gomez see Von Schulte, *Die Geschichte der Quellen und Literatur*, vol. 3, p. 554; an Irish civilian picked up the cudgel in defence of his profession. See William Clerk, *An Epitome of Certaine Late Aspersions Cast at Civilians, the Civil and Ecclesiastical Laws, the Courts Christian, and at Bishops and their Chancellors* (Dublin, 1631), p. 6.

35 There are 98 statute citations (English and Irish) and 85 Roman and canon law citations.

36 Carte MS 62, fos. 590a–b; Wood, *Athenae Oxoniensis*, vol. 1, pp. 505–8; T. Ashton, 'Oxford's Medieval Alumni', *P & P*, 74 (1977), pp. 13–16.

37 In the case of commendams, for example, Davies cites materials from the library of New College. See *Reports*, pp. 193, 195.

38 For Merula see J. W. Wessels, *History of Roman Dutch Law* (Grahamstown, 1908), p. 234.

39 Bodl. Lib. D'Orville MS 52, fos. 49–50; BL Cotton MS Julius C. V, fo. 49; it has also been suggested that Davies may have accompanied one of the expeditions to the Azores. P. Finklepearl, *John Marston of the Middle Temple* (Cambridge, 1969), pp. 50–4.

40 D. E. C. Yale, 'Notes on the Jurisdiction of the Admiralty in Ireland', *Irish Jurist*, 3 (1968), pp. 146–62; see also Archbishop Usher's treatise on the 'Reception of the Imperial Laws in Ireland', Bodl. Lib. Tanner MS 458, fo. 21a; Delaney, 'A Note on the History of Legal Education in Ireland', p. 217; K. W. Nicholls has shown that the municipal code of Galway was derived from the Roman law. See his *Gaelicized Ireland*, p. 49. In 1578 the famous Jesuit Edmund Campion, while visiting the Recorder of Dublin – Sir Richard Stanyhurst – described certain schools in Gaelic districts where students memorized Justinian's *Institutes*. E. Campion and M. Hamner, *Two Histories of Ireland* (Dublin, 1633), p. 18. In 1609, the classical training of the professional scholars surprised even Davies, who remarked: 'for the jurors, being fifteen in number, thirteen spake good Latin, and that very readily'. SP/63/227/fo. 94a; in 1608, John Leigh, the High Sheriff of Tyrone, complained that legal matters were being settled in his district by 'Breghans or judges according to the rule of the Popish canons'. Lam. Pal. MS 607, fos. 166a and b; *Cal. Car., 1603–24*, pp. 30–1.

41 D. Sutherland, 'Conquest and Law', *Studia Gratiana*, 15 (1972), pp. 33–51; the origin of this tradition is of course in the *ius gentium* of the classical Roman law. The notion that a violent conquest could generate just title may be found in the following selections from Justinian's *Corpus: D.* 11.7.36; *D.* 41.2.18.4; *D.* 41.2.1.1; *D.* 49.15.4; *Inst.* 2.1.17; see also the marginal gloss on each of the above in *Digestum Vetus Seu Pandectorum Iuris Civilis Commentariis Accursii & Multorum Insuper Aliorum Tam Veterum* (Lyons, 1569). It is interesting to note that the medieval *Book of Feuds* defines a conquest feud as superior to any held by succession. Thomas Craig, *The Jus Feudale*, ed. J. S. Clyde, 2 vols. (Edinburgh, 1934), vol 1, p. 164.

42 Hugo Grotius, *De Iure Belli et Pacis*, ed. S. P. Scott (Indianapolis, 1926), bk. 3.6.11.1; bk. 3.6.4.1; Alberico Gentili, *De Iure Belli Libri Trees*, 2 vols. (Oxford, 1933), vol. 2, pp. 307, 381 and 385; Richard Zouche, *Iuris et Iudicii Fecialis, Sive Iuris Inter Gentes et Quaestionam de Eodem Explicatio* (Washington, DC, 1921), p. 138. It is interesting to note that Edmund Borlase, an Irish polemicist, grounded an English title to Ireland by right of conquest 'as Grotius in his excellent piece, *De Iure Belli & Pacis* notably well argues'. Edmund Borlase, *The Reduction of Ireland to the Crown of England* (London, 1675), pp. A2–A3.

43 Patrick Finglas, 'A Breviate of the Getting of Ireland and the Decaie of the Same', in W. Harris (ed.), *Hibernia, or Some Antient Pieces Relating to Ireland, Never Hitherto Made Publick* (Dublin, 1747), p. 88.

44 *L & P Henry VIII*, vol. 7, p. 1211; *L & P Henry VIII*, vol. 8, p. 527; *State Papers, Henry VIII*, vol. 2, pp. 341–2; for a general discussion see R. D. Edwards, 'The Irish Reformation Parliament of Henry VIII, 1536–7', *Historical Studies*, 6 (1968), p. 61; Dr Brendan Bradshaw has elucidated further the development of Henrician religious policy. See 'The Opposition to the Ecclesiastical Legislation', pp. 285–303.

45 BL Harl. MS 35, fo. 197b.

46 7 *Coke Rep.*, pp. 30, 38–9; *Fourth Institute*, p. 559; Knafla, *Law and Politics in Jacobean England*, p. 232; Davies, *Reports*, pp. 110–14.

47 Pocock, *Ancient Constitution*, p. 53; Blackstone explicitly states that Ireland's status is directly related to the law and right of conquest. See Blackstone, *Commentaries on the Laws of England*, vol. 1, p. 100.

48 A. G. Donaldson, 'The Application in Ireland of English and British Legislation Made before 1801' (Queen's University, Belfast, unpublished Ph.D. thesis, 1952), pp. 321–3.

49 Levack, *Civil Lawyers*, pp. 145–6.

50 25 Hen. VIII c. 19; 27 Hen. VIII c. 15 and c. 20; 35 Hen. VIII c. 16; D. Logan, 'The Henrician Canons', *BIHR*, 47 (1974), pp. 99–103.

51 J. Spalding, 'The Reformatio Legum Ecclesiasticarum of 1552 and the Furthering of Discipline in England', *Church History*, 39 (1970), pp. 162–71.

52 William Stubbs, 'The History of the Canon Law in England', in *Select Essays in Anglo-American Legal History*, vol. 1, pp. 263–5; *Seventeen Lectures on the Study of Medieval and Modern History* (Oxford, 1900), pp. 354–6; also his introduction to Report of the Commissioners, *The Constitution and Working of the Ecclesiastical Courts* (London, 1883), pp.

24–5; J. W. Gray, 'Canon Law in England: Some Reflections on the Stubbs–Maitland Controversy', *Studies in Church History*, 3 (1966), pp. 48–68; and C. Donahue, 'Roman Canon Law in the Medieval English Church: Stubbs vs. Maitland Re-examined after 75 Years in the Light of Some Records from the Church Courts', *Michigan Law Review*, 72 (1974), pp. 647–715.

53 Davies, *Reports*, pp. 185–229; the case dealt with a dispute between a local incumbent, Cyprian Horsefall, and a royal appointee, Robert Wale, to a vicarage in the diocese of Ossory. James Ware, *The History and Antiquities of Ireland*, trans. by Richard Harris, 2 vols. (Dublin, 1764), vol. 1, p. 419; *Irish Fiants*: 4256 and 6706.

54 Davies argued that the Pope's decretals were never entirely received in any European country outside the Pope's temporal authority. In other words, England would only use those canons which 'by such acceptance and usage obtained the force of laws in such particular realm of state and became part of the ecclesiastical law of such nation'. Davies, *Reports*, p. 196.

55 *Ibid.*, pp. 1–17.

56 SP/63/234/fo. 140a; SP/63/234/fo. 142a; the difficulty with procurations seems to have troubled Davies for several years. See his letter to Salisbury concerning Beeston's case in 1608; SP/63/223/fo.122a; *CSPI, 1606–8*, p. 436; *CSPI, 1608–10* (Philadelphia Papers), p. 247; *Cal. Pat. Rolls James I*, p. 105; O'Brien, *Advertisements for Ireland*, p. 17; PROI, Chancery Decrees A.1; Ferguson MS 11, fos. 42, 49 and 65; 27, fo. 16.

57 Joannes Paulus Lancelloti, *Institutiones Iuris Canonici, Quibus Ius Pontificum Singulari Methodo Libris Quatuor Comprehenditur* (Louvain, 1578), pp. 406–7; Davies, *Reports*, pp. 5, 7, 17; for biographical details on Lancelloti see Von Schulte, *Die Geschichte der Quellen und Literatur*, vol. 3, p. 451, and A. G. Cocognani, *Canon Law* (Westminster, 1949), p. 320; Barthélemy de Chassaneux, *Catalogus Gloriae Mundi* (Lyons, 1546), p. 119; for Chassaneux see *Biographie Universelle, Ancienne et Moderne*, vol. 7, pp. 699–700. I owe a debt of gratitude to Dr Richard Fraher of Harvard University who assisted me with identifying these canon law citations.

58 John Godolphin, *Repertorium Canonicum or an Abridgement of the Ecclesiastical Laws* (London, 1678), pp. 75–9.

59 Like the case of proxies, the case of the dean and chapter of Fernes represents one illustration of a general programme to recover the patrimony of the church. For the property in question see *Irish Fiants*: 6471, 6237 and 6243; Ware, *History and Antiquities*, vol. 1, pp. 446–8; Lancelloti, *Institutiones Iuris Canonici*, pp. 25 and 28; Nicolas de Tudeschi, *Omnia Quae Extant Commentaria Primae Partis in Primum et Decretalium Librum*, 7 vols. (Venice, 1588), vol. 6, pp. 99–100; Davies, *Reports*, pp. 129–32; for Tudeschi see Von Schulte, *Die Geschichte der Quellen*, vol. 2, pp. 312–13; and Cocognani, *Canon Law*, p. 336.

60 Edmund Gibson, *Codex Juris Ecclesiastici Anglicani or the Statutes, Constitutions, Canons and Rubricke Articles of the Church of England*, 2 vols. (London, 1713), p. 781.

61 F. W. Maitland, *Roman Canon Law in the Church of England* (London,

1898), pp. 1–50. This was elaborated in a second chapter entitled 'Church, State and Decretals', pp. 51–99.

62 Davies, *Reports*, pp. 164–5; Baldus de Ubaldis, *Opera Omnia*, 7 vols. (Venice, 1577), vol. 5, p. 79; for Baldus see Walter Ullman, *Law and Politics in the Middle Ages* (London, 1975), pp. 111–12.

63 Nat. Lib. Dublin, MS 11,044. This document was found in a tin box of roughly 300 unfoliated papers, most of which date after 1660.

64 Davies, *Reports*, p. 158.

65 Cujas, *Corporis Iuris Civilis*, vol. 2, p. 741; Choppinus, *De Domanio Franciae*, pp. 111–15. For biographical details on Cujas see Kelley, *Foundations of Modern Historical Scholarship*, pp. 112–15; for Choppinus see *Biographie Universelle, Ancienne et Moderne*, vol. 8, p. 199.

66 Budelius, *De Monetis*; for Budelius see *Biographie Universelle, Ancienne et Moderne*, vol. 6, p. 112.

67 Davies, *Reports*, p. 54: 'Monetandi jus principium ossibus inhaeret. Jus Monetae comprehenditur in regalibus quae nunquam a regio sceptro abdicantur.'

68 Davies, *Reports*, p. 54.

69 SP/63/226/fo. 18a; *CSPI, 1608–10*, p. 135.

70 K. Sharpe and C. Brooks, 'English Law and the Renaissance', *P & P*, 72 (1976), pp. 133–47; see Kelley's rejoinder, pp. 143–6 of the same issue of *P & P*. The controversy was sparked by D. R. Kelley, 'History, English Law and the Renaissance', *P & P*, 65 (1974), pp. 24–51; see also Kelley's book, *Foundations of Modern Historical Scholarship*.

71 J. W. Whittaker, *The Mirror of Justices* (Selden Society, 7, London, 1893), pp. ix–xi, 3.

72 K. Sharpe, C. Brooks and D. R. Kelley, 'English Law and the Renaissance', p. 146.

Select bibliography

Manuscripts

Cambridge
Add. Ms 3104; MS Ff. III.

Dublin
King's Inns: Black Book of the King's Inns.
Marsh's Library; MS Z3.1.12; MS Z3.2.21; MS Z3.1.9; MS Z4.2.19.
National Library of Ireland: MS 11,044; MS D.2007; MS D.3142; MS D. 3637.
Public Record Office of Ireland: Ferguson MSS, vols. 1–8, 9, 11 and 27; Lodge
    MSS, vols. 1–6; Calendar of Salved Chancery Bills, vols. 1–5; Salved
    Chancery Pleadings, A32, 206, 240; B92; G221, 271; I38, 39, 222, 223,
    226, 245; N153; R14; Chancery Decrees, A1, RC6/1–3, 9 and 11.
Royal Irish Academy: MS 12.D.4; MS 12.D.17; MS 12.D.19; MS 12.D.21;
    MS 12.D.38; MS 12.G.1–2; MS 12.P.4; MS 24.H.17; MS 12.S.3.
Trinity College, Dublin: MS 647 (F.1.7); MS 651 (F.4.8.); MS 657 (F.4.26);
    MS 842 (F.3.16); MS 843 (F.3.17); MS 852 (G.3.1); MS 853 (G.3.2).

Leeds
Leeds Public Library: Temple Newsham MSS, TN/PO 7, vols. 1–3.

London
British Library
Additional MSS: 4209; 4756; 4763; 4786; 4793; 4794; 6363; 11,402; 11,721;
    33,496; 34,324; 35,838; 36,775; 47,172.
Cecil MSS: (Microfilm of Hatfield MSS) vols. 90, 91, 92, 96, 99, 117, 119,
    123, 186, 196.
Cotton MSS: Titus B.x; Titus B.xI; Titus B.xII; Julius C.III; Julius C.v.
Egerton MSS: vols. 75, 76, 80, 2822.
Hargrave MSS: vols. 128, 278.
Harleian MSS: vols. 35, 38, 158, 251, 278, 697, 758, 1576, 2048, 2058, 2105
    2138, 4261, 4761, 4943, 5220, 5353.
Lansdowne MSS: 88, 156, 159, 253, 1208.
Royal MSS: 18.C.xv; 17.C.xxxII.
Sloane MSS: 1008, 3078, 3827.
Stowe MSS: 297.

Lambeth Palace
Carew MSS: 600, 605, 607, 609, 612, 613, 615, 619, 629, 630, 635.
Public Record Office
Auditor's Office: A.O.1/289/1086, 1082.
Chancery: C.66/1685; C.82/1694.
Exchequer: E/351/239, 266; E/126/3; E/134/22 Jas. I; E134/12 Chas. I.
King's Bench: KB140/15; KB29/243–51.
Maps: MPF 91 and 307.
Probate: (PCC Wills-Microfilm) PROB/11/108; PROB/11/109; PROB/145
    Hele F.2826.
State Papers Domestic: James I – SP/14/1, 6, 12, 15, 18, 20, 24, 34, 38, 63, 74,
    77, 130 and 192; Charles I – SP/16/255.
State Papers Ireland: SP/63/112, 129, 131, 132, 135, 144, 147, 164, 167, 183,
    186, 201, 205–13, 215–40.
State Papers, Philadelphia Papers: PRO/31/8/199–201.
State Papers, Supplementary: SP/46/130.

Oxford
Bodleian Library
Autog. MS: d.21.
Carte MSS: 1, 3, 30, 60, 61, 62.
D'Orville MSS: 52.
Fortescue MSS: 2.
Laudian MSS: 612, 614.
Rawlinson MSS: D.922; A.494.
Tanner MSS: 458.
University College MSS: 103.
Wood MSS: F.39.

Theses

Bradshaw, B., 'The Irish Constitutional Revolution, 1515–1557', University of Cambridge, unpublished Ph.D. thesis, 1975.

Brink, Jeanie R., 'Sir John Davies: His Life and Major Works', University of Wisconsin, unpublished Ph.D. thesis, 1972.

Canny, N. P., 'The Career of Hugh O'Neill, Earl of Tyrone, 1603–7', University College Galway, unpublished MA thesis, 1967.

Carpinelli, F. P., 'A Study of Renaissance Literary Conventions in Sir John Davies' *Orchestra*', University of Notre Dame, unpublished Ph. D. thesis, 1973.

Childs, T. J., 'An Edition of "Nosce Teipsum" by Sir John Davies with an Introductory Account of His Work', University of Oxford, unpublished M. Litt. thesis, 1939.

Cunningham, B., 'Political and Social Change in the Lordships of Clanricard and Thomond, 1569–1641', University College Galway, unpublished MA thesis, 1979.

Donaldson, A. G., 'The Application in Ireland of English and British Legislation before 1801', Queen's University, Belfast, unpublished Ph.D. thesis, 1952.

Ellis, S. G., 'The Administration of the Lordship of Ireland under the Early Tudors', Queen's University, Belfast, unpublished Ph.D. thesis, 1978.

Finklepearl, F. J., 'The Works of John Marston: A Critical Study', Harvard University, unpublished Ph.D. thesis, 1954.

Hunter, R. J., 'The Ulster Plantation in the Counties of Armagh and Cavan, 1608–41', 2 vols., TCD, unpublished M. Litt. thesis, 1968.

Kennedy, D. J., 'The Presidency of Munster under Elizabeth and James I', University College Cork, unpublished MA thesis, 1973.

Krueger, Robert, 'A Critical Edition of the Poems of Sir John Davies', University of Oxford, unpublished D.Phil. thesis, 1964.

Ranger, T. O., 'The Career of Richard Boyle, First Earl of Cork in Ireland, 1588–1643', University of Oxford, unpublished D.Phil. thesis, 1958.

Sanderson, J. L., 'An Edition of an Early Seventeenth-Century Manuscript Collection of Poems', University of Pennsylvania, unpublished Ph.D. thesis, 1960.

Treadwell, V. R., 'Irish Financial Administrative Reform under James I: The Customs and State Regulation of Trade', Queen's University, Belfast, unpublished Ph.D. thesis, 1961.

White, D. G., 'The Tudor Plantations in Ireland before 1571', TCD, unpublished Ph.D. thesis, 1967.

Published Sources and Calendars: State Papers

Calendar of Carew Manuscripts, ed. J. S. Brewer, 6 vols. (London, 1867–73).

Calendar of Letters and Papers, Foreign and Domestic, Henry VIII, ed. J. S. Brewer, 21 vols. (London, 1862–1932).

Calendar of State Papers Domestic Series, 1547–1625, ed. M. A. Green, 12 vols. (London, 1869).

Calendar of State Papers Domestic Series, 1625–1641, ed. John Bruce, 16 vols. (London, 1858).

Calendar of State Papers Relating to Ireland, 1509–1603, ed. H. C. Hamilton, 11 vols. (London, 1869).

Calendar of State Papers Relating to Ireland, of the Reign of James I, ed. J. P. Prendergast, 5 vols. (London 1872–80).

Calendar of State Papers Relating to Ireland, 1625–1660, ed. R. P. Mahaffy, 5 vols. (London, 1901).

State Papers, Henry VIII, 11 vols. (London, 1830–52).

State Papers: Foreign

'Brief Calendar of the Borghese Papers', ed. John Hagan, *Arch.Hib.*, 4 (1915), pp. 311–18.

Calendar of Letters and State Papers Relating to English Affairs Existing in the Archives and Collections of Venice and Other Libraries of Northern Italy, ed. R. Brown (London, 1890).

Calendar of Letters and State Papers Relating to English Affairs, Preserved Principally in the Archives of Simancas, 1558–1603, ed. Martin Hume, 4 vols. (London, 1894).

Calendar of State Papers Relating to English Affairs, Preserved Principally at

Rome, in the Vatican Archives and Library, ed. J. M. Rigg, 2 vols. (London, 1916).

'Miscellanea Vaticano-Hibernica', *Arch. Hib.*, 3 (1914), pp. 227–366; 4 (1915), pp. 215–321; 5 (1916), pp. 74–167; 6 (1917), pp. 94–155; 7 (1918–21), pp. 67–337.

Miscellaneous Records: Patent Rolls and Fiants

Calendar of Fiants, Henry to Elizabeth, *Reports of the Deputy Keeper of the Public Records in Ireland*, nos. 7–22 (Dublin, 1875–90).

Calendar of the Patent and Close Rolls of Chancery in Ireland of the Reign of Henry VIII, Edward VI, Mary and Elizabeth, ed. James Morrin (Dublin, 1861).

Calendar of the Patent and Close Rolls of Chancery in Ireland from the 18th to the 45th Year of Queen Elizabeth, ed. James Morrin, 2 vols. (Dublin, 1862).

Irish Patent Rolls of James I: Facsimile of the Irish Record Commissioners' Calendar Prepared Prior to 1930, ed. M.C. Griffith (Dublin, 1966).

A Repertory of the Inrolments on the Patent Rolls of Chancery in Ireland Commencing with the Reign of James I, ed. J. C. Erck (Dublin, 1846).

Rotulorum Patentium et Clausorum Cancellariae Hiberniae Calendarium, ed. E. Trasham (Dublin, 1828).

Miscellaneous Records: Privy Council

'Acts of the Privy Council in Ireland, 1556–71', ed. J. T. Gilbert in HMC, *Report 15*, appendix III (1897), pp. 1–256.

Acts of the Privy Council of England, 1542–1631, 46 vols. (London, 1890–1964).

'Calendar of the Irish Council Book, 1581–86', *An. Hib.*, 24 (1967), pp. 91–180.

Proclamations

A Bibliography of Royal Proclamations of the Tudor and Stuart Sovereigns and of Others Published under their Royal Authority, 1485–1714, ed. R. Steele, 2 vols. (Oxford, 1910).

Tudor Royal Proclamations, ed. P. L. Hughes and J.F. Larkin (New Haven, 1964).

Parliamentary Records: Statute Collections

'The Bills and Statutes of the Irish Parliaments of Henry VII and Henry VIII', ed. D. B. Quinn, *An. Hib.*, 10 (1941), pp. 71–169.

The Statutes at Large Passed in the Parliaments Held in Ireland, 21 vols. (Dublin, 1786).

The Statutes of Ireland Newly Perused and Examined, ed. Richard Bolton (Dublin, 1621).

Statutes of the Realm, Magna Carta to 13th Anne, 9 vols. (London, 1810–28).

Parliamentary Journals

Commons Debates 1621, ed. W. Notestein, 7 vols. (New Haven, 1935).

D'Ewes, Simon, *The Journal of All the Parliaments during the Reign of Queen Elizabeth* (London, 1682).

'John Hooker's Journal of the Irish Parliament, 17 January–23 February 1569', ed. C. L. Falkiner, *RIA Proc.*, Section C, 25 (1904–5), pp. 563–6.

The Journal of the House of Commons of England (London, 1742), vols. 1–5.

The Journal of the House of Commons of the Kingdom of Ireland, 23 vols. (Dublin, 1763–86).

The Journal of the House of Lords, England (London, 1834), vols. 1–9.

The Journal of the House of Lords of Ireland, 8 vols. (Dublin, 1779).

'Journal of the Irish House of Lords in Sir John Perrot's Parliament, 1585–86', ed. F. J. Routledge, *EHR*, 29 (1914), pp. 104–17.

Townshend, H., *Historical Collections, or an Exact Account of the Proceedings of the Four Last Parliaments of Queen Elizabeth* (London, 1680).

Municipal Records

Archives of the Municipal Corporation of Waterford, ed. J. T. Gilbert, HMC, *Report 10* (London, 1885), appendix v, pp. 265–339.

Archives of the Town of Galway, ed. J. T. Gilbert, HMC, *Report 10* (London 1885), appendix v, pp. 380–520.

Calendar of the Ancient Records of Dublin, in the Possession of the Corporation, ed. J. T. Gilbert, 17 vols. (Dublin, 1889–95).

The Council Book of Cork, ed. R. Caulfield (Guildford, 1876).

Council Book of the Corporation of Waterford, 1662–1700, ed. S. Pender (IMC, Dublin, 1964).

The Council Book of Kinsale, ed. R. Caulfield (Guildford, 1879).

The Council Book of Youghal, ed. R. Caulfield (Guildford, 1878).

'The Minute Book of the Corporation of Dublin, 1567–1611', ed. H. F. Berry, *RIA Proc.*, Section C, 30 (1912), pp. 477–514.

Report by J. T. Gilbert on Corporation Records of Waterford, HMC, *Report 1* (London, 1874), pp. 13–32.

Report on the Manuscripts of the Late Reginald Rawdon Hastings, 9 vols. (HMC, London, 1930–4).

The Town Book of the Corporation of Belfast, 1613–1816, ed. R. M. Young (Belfast, 1892).

Edited Collections of Documents

The Black Books of Lincoln's Inn, ed. W. P. Baildon, 4 vols. (London, 1899–1902).

The Books of Survey and Distribution, ed. R. C. Simington, 4 vols. (Dublin, 1949–67).

Calendar of the Manuscripts of the Marquess of Ormond Preserved at Kilkenny Castle, 11 vols. (HMC, London, 1895).

Calendar of the Manuscripts of the Marquess of Salisbury, 23 vols. (HMC, London, 1883–1973).

Calendar of Ormond Deeds, ed. E. Curtis, 6 vols. (IMC, Dublin, 1935–43).
The Civil Survey, ed. R. C. Simington, 10 vols. (Dublin, 1931–62).
Collectanea de Rebus Hibernicis, ed. C. Vallancey, 4 vols. (Dublin, 1781–4).
A Collection of Curious Discourses, ed. Thomas Hearne, 2 vols. (Oxford, 1771).
The Complete Peerage of England, Scotland, Ireland, Great Britain and the United Kingdom, ed. Vicary Gibbs, 13 vols. (London, 1910).
The Composition Book of Connaught, ed. M. A. Freeman (IMC, Dublin, 1936).
Court of Castle Chamber Records, Egmont MSS, HMC, *Report 17* (London, 1905), appendix 1, pp. 1–60.
Desiderata Curiosa Hibernica, ed. John Lodge, 2 vols. (Dublin, 1772).
Giraldi Cambrensis, Opera, ed. J. F. Dimock, 8 vols. (London, 1867).
Hibernia: Or Some Antient Pieces Relating to Ireland, Never Hitherto Made Publick, ed. W. Harris (Dublin, 1747).
Historic and Municipal Documents of Ireland, AD 1172–1320, ed. J. Gilbert (London, 1870).
The Historical Works of Giraldus Cambrensis, ed. T. Wright (London, 1863).
Ireland: A Documentary Record, ed. James Carty, 4 vols. (Dublin, 1949).
Ireland through Tudor Eyes, ed. E. M. Hinton (Philadelphia, 1935).
Ireland under Elizabeth and James I, Described by Edmund Spenser, by Sir John Davies and by Fynes Moryson, ed. Henry Morley (London, 1890).
Irish Historical Documents, ed. E. Curtis and R. B. McDowell (London, 1943).
Irish History from Contemporary Sources, 1509–1610, ed. C. Maxwell (London, 1923).
John of Salisbury's Metalogicon, ed. C. C. J. Webb (Oxford, 1924).
Letters and Memorials of State, ed. Arthur Collins, 2 vols. (London, 1746).
The Letters of John Chamberlain, ed. N. E. McClure, 2 vols. (Philadelphia, 1939).
Liber Munerum Publicorum Hiberniae, ed. R. Lascelles, 2 vols. (Dublin, 1810).
Manuscripts of the Marquess of Drogheda, HMC, *Report 9* (London, 1884), pp. 294–330.
The Montgomery Manuscripts, ed. G. Hill (Belfast, 1869).
National Manuscripts of Ireland, ed. James Henry, 4 vols. (Dublin, 1874).
Parliamentary Debates in 1610, ed. S. R. Gardiner (London, 1867).
The Poems of Sir John Davies, ed. Robert Krueger (Oxford, 1975).
Pontifica Hibernica: Medieval Papal Chancery Documents Concerning Ireland, 640–1261, ed. M. P. Sheehy, 2 vols. (Dublin, 1962).
Select Statutes and Other Constitutional Documents Illustrative of the Reigns of Elizabeth and James I, ed. G. W. Prothero (Oxford, 1898).
'Ulster Plantation Papers 1608–1613', ed. T. W. Moody, *An. Hib.*, 8 (1938), pp. 179–297.
Usher's Works, ed. C. A. Elrington, 17 vols. (Dublin, 1847).
The Works of Francis Bacon, ed. James Spedding, 7 vols. (London, 1905).

Personal Tracts, Treatises and Memoirs

Anonymous, *The Goverment of Ireland under Sir John Perrot, 1584–88* (London, 1626).
Attwood, W., *The History and Reasons of the Dependency of Ireland upon the Imperial Crown of the Kingdom of England* (London, 1698).

Beacon, R., *Solon His Follie or a Politique Discourse Touching the Reformation of Commonwealths Conquered* (Oxford, 1594).

Boate, G., *Ireland's Natural History* (London, 1652).

Bolton, R., *A Justice of the Peace for Ireland* (Dublin, 1638).

Borlase, E., *The Reduction of Ireland to the Crown of England* (London, 1675).

Campion, E., and Hamner, M., *Two Histories of Ireland* (Dublin, 1633).

Cary, J., *A Vindication of the Parliament of England in Answer to a Book Written by William Molyneux of Dublin* (London, 1698).

Chichester, Arthur, 'Letter Book of Sir Arthur Chichester 1612–14', ed. R. D. Edwards, *An. Hib.*, 8 (1938), pp. 3–178.

Darcy, P., *A Declaration Setting Forth How and by What Means the Laws and Statutes Came to be of Force in Ireland* (Dublin, 1747).

Davies, J., *A Discovery of the True Causes Why Ireland Was Never Subdued Nor Brought under Obedience of the Crown of England* (London, 1612).

Dialogue of the Exchequer, 1170, ed. E. Johnson (London, 1950).

Docwra, H., 'A Narration of the Services Done by the Army Employed to Lough Foyle', *Miscellany of the Celtic Society* (Dublin, 1849).

Finglas, P., *A Breviate of the Getting of Ireland and the Decaie of the Same* (Dublin, 1747).

Gainsford, T., *The True Exemplary and Remarkable History of the Earl of Tyrone* (London, 1619).

Grotius, H., *De Iure Belli et Pacis*, ed. S. P. Scott (Indianapolis, 1926).

Holinshed, R., *Chronicles*, 3 vols. (London, 1587).

Littleton, Thomas, *Tenures* (London, 1600).

Lombard, P., *De Regno Sanctorum Insula Hiberniae Commentarius* (Dublin, 1868).

Lynch, J., *Cambrensis Eversus*, 3 vols. (Dublin, 1795).

Mayart, S., *The Answer of Samuel Mayart to a Book Entitled a Declaration Setting Forth How and by What Means the Laws and Statutes Came to Be of Force in Ireland* (Dublin, 1747).

Molyneux, W., *The Case of Ireland's Being Bound by Acts of Parliament in England Stated* (Dublin, 1698).

Moryson, F., *An Itinerary of Ten Yeeres Travell* (London, 1617).

Rich, Barnaby, *A Catholic Conference* (London, 1612).

   The Irish Hubbub (London, 1617).

   My Ladies' Looking Glass (London, 1616).

   A New Description of Ireland (London, 1616).

   A Short Survey of Ireland (London, 1609).

   A True and Kind Excuse (London, 1612).

Santry, James, *The Case of Tenures* (Dublin, 1637).

Speed, John, *The Theatre of the Empire of Great Britain* (London, 1610).

Spenser, E., *A View of the State of Ireland, Written Dialogue-Wise between Eudoxus and Irenaeus* (Dublin, 1633).

Stafford, Thomas, *Pacata Hibernia* (London, 1633).

Strafford's Letters, ed. W. Knowler, 2 vols. (Dublin, 1740).

Ware, James, *The History and Antiquities of Ireland*, trans. by Richard Harris, 2 vols. (Dublin, 1764).

Wilbraham, Roger, 'The Diary of Sir Roger Wilbraham', *Camden Miscellany*, 10 (1902), pp. 1–139.

Gaelic Sources

Ancient Laws of Ireland, 6 vols. (Dublin, 1865).
Annals of Ulster, Otherwise Known as the Annals of Senat, Chronicles from AD 431 to 1540 (Dublin, 1887).
Binchy, D. A. (ed.), *Corpus Iuris Hibernici ad Fidem Codicum Manuscriptorum Recognivit* (Dublin, 1978).
Hennessy, W. (ed.), *The Annals of Loch Ce, a Chronicle from AD 1014 to AD 1590* (London, 1871).
MacAirt, S. (ed.), *Annals of Inisfallen* (Dublin, 1951).
Martin, A. (ed.), *Annals of Connacht* (Dublin, 1944).
O'Donovan, J. (ed.), *Annals of the Four Masters, from the Earliest Period to the Year 1616* (Dublin, 1851).
O'h Innse, S. (ed.), *Miscellaneous Irish Annals, AD 1114–1437* (Dublin, 1947).

Legal Records: Canon Law

Chassaneux, Barthélemy de, *Catalogus Gloriae Mundi* (Lyons, 1546).
Corpus Iuris Canonici, editio Lipsiensis secunda post Ludouci Richteri curas ad librorum manu scriptorum et editionis Romanae fidem recognovit et adnotatione critica instruxit Aemilius Friedberg, 2 vols. (Leipzig, 1879).
Decretum Gratiani emendatum et notationibus illustratum, una cum glossis, 2 vols. (Venice, 1600).
Gibson, Edmund, *Codex Juris Ecclesiastici Anglicani or the Statutes, Constitutions, Canons and Rubricke Articles of the Church of England*, 2 vols. (London, 1713).
Godolphin, John, *Repertorium Canonicum or an Abridgement of the Ecclesiastical Laws* (London, 1678).
Innocent IV, *Commentaria Super Libros Quinque Decretalium Gregory IX* (Frankfurt, 1570).
Lancelloti, Joannes Paulus, *Institutiones Iuris Canonici, Quibus Ius Pontificum Singulari Methodo Libris Quatuor Comprehenditur* (Louvain, 1578).
Lyndwood, William, *Provinciale, Sue Constitutiones Angliae* (Oxford, 1679).
Segusio, Henricus de, *In Quinque Decretalium Libri Commentaria et in Sextem Decretalium Librum*, 4 vols. (Venice, 1581).
Tudeschi, Nicholas de (Panormitanus), *Omnia Quae Extant Commentaria Primae Partis in Primum et Decretalium Librum*, 7 vols. (Venice, 1588).

Legal Records: Civil Law

Ancient Roman Statutes, ed. F. C. Bourne, P. R. Coleman-Norton and A. C. Johnson (Austin, 1961).
Baldus de Ubaldis, *Opera Omnia*, 7 vols. (Venice, 1577).
Bartolus of Sassoferrato, *Opera*, 11 vols. (Basle, 1588).
Bodin, J., *The Six Books of a Commonweale* (London, 1606).
Chassaneux, Barthélemy de, *Catalogus Gloriae Mundi* (Lyons, 1546).
Clerk, William, *An Epitome of Certaine Late Aspersions Cast at Civilians, the*

Civil and Ecclesiastical Laws, the Courts Christian, and at Bishops and their Chancellors (Dublin, 1631).

Corpus Iuris Civilis, Editio 16, Institutiones ed. by Paul Krueger, Digest ed. by Theodore Momsen, rev. by Paul Krueger, Codex ed. by Paul Krueger, Novellae ed. by Rudolf Schoell and Wilhelm Kroll, 3 vols. (Berlin, 1954).

Craig, Thomas, *De Unione Regnorum Britanniae Tractatus* (Scottish History Society, 60, 1909), pp. 1–498.

The Jus Feudale, ed. J. S. Clyde, 2 vols. (Edinburgh, 1934).

Cujas, Jacques, *Corporis Iuris Civilis*, 2 vols. (Amsterdam, 1681).

Digestum Vetus Seu Pandectorum Iuris Civilis Commentariis Accursii & Multorum Insuper Aliorum Tam Veterum (Lyons, 1569).

Gentili, Alberico, *De Iure Belli Libri Tres*, 2 vols. (Oxford, 1933).

Regales Disputationes Tres: id est de Potestate Regis Absoluta (London, 1605).

Gomesius, Loudovico, *Summaria Super Rubricum de Actionibus* (Lyons, 1568).

Grotius, H., *De Iure Belli et Pacis*, ed. S. P. Scott (Indianapolis, 1926).

The Freedom of the Seas (New York, 1916).

'Some Lesser Known Works of Hugo Grotius', *Bibliotheca Visseriana Dissertationum Ius Internationale Illustrantium*, 7 (1928), pp. 154–205.

Welwood, William, *An Abridgement of All Sea-Lawes* (London, 1613).

Wiseman, R., *The Law of Laws* (London, 1656).

Zouche, Richard, *Iuris et Iudicii Fecialis, Sive Iuris Inter Gentes et Quaestionam de Eodem Explicatio* (Washington, DC, 1921).

Legal Records: Common Law

Bacon, Francis, *The Elements of the Common Law*, 2 vols. (London, 1630).

Blackstone, William, *Commentaries on the Laws of England*, 4 vols. (Oxford, 1773).

Bracton, Henry de, *On the Laws and Customs of England*, 5 vols. (Cambridge, Mass., 1968).

Brooke, Robert, *Le Graunde Abridgement* (London, 1586).

Calendar of the Justiciary Rolls, in Proceedings in the Court of the Justiciar, ed. J. M. Mills, 3 vols. (Dublin, 1905–17).

Coke, Edward, *The Institutes of the Laws of England*, 4 vols. (London, 1671).

The Reports of Sir Edward Coke, 7 vols. (London, 1826).

Cowell, J., *The Interpreter* (Cambridge, 1607).

Davies, Sir John, *Le Primer Report des Cases in les Courts del Roy* (Dublin, 1615). Translated as *A Report of Cases and Matters in Law Resolved and Abridged in the King's Courts in Ireland* (Dublin, 1762).

A Perfect Abridgement of the Eleven Books of Reports by Sir Edward Coke (London, 1651).

Dyer, James, *Report of Cases in the Reigns of Henry VIII, Edward VI, Queen Mary and Queen Elizabeth*, 3 vols. (London, 1794).

The English Reports, Chancery (London, 1903–4), vols. 24 and 35.

The English Reports, King's Bench Division (London, 1909), vol. 91.

Fitzherbert, Anthony, *The New Natura Brevium* (London, 1677).

Fulbecke, W., *Directive or Preparative to the Study of the Law* (London, 1602).

Jacob, G., *A New Law Dictionary* (London, 1772).

Howell, T. B. (ed.), *A Complete Collection of State Trials*, 21 vols. (London, 1816–98).

The Law Reports, Appeal Cases before the House of Lords and the Judicial Committee of the Privy Council (London, 1889), vol. 14.

Les Reports des Cases in Les Ans des Roys Edward V, Richard III, Henrie VII and Henrie VIII (London, 1679).

Littleton, Thomas, *Tenures* (London, 1525).

Perkins, John, *A Profitable Book Treating of the Laws of England* (London, 1827).

Plowden, Edmund, *The Reports* (London, 1761).

Rastell, G., *Les Termes de la Ley* (London, 1629).

 (ed.) *Registrum Omnium Brevium* (London, 1634).

Ruggle, G., *Ignoramus* (London, 1622).

Selden, J., *Mare Clausam* (London, 1674).

Select Cases in the Exchequer Chamber before All the Justices of England, ed. M. Hemmant, 2 vols. (London, 1948).

Smith, Thomas, *De Republica Anglorum* (Cambridge, 1906).

Spelman, J., *The Reports*, ed. J. H. Baker, 2 vols. (London, 1977).

Taylor, Silas, *The History of Gavelkind* (London, 1663).

Vaughan, John, *The Reports and Arguements of Sir John Vaughan* (London, 1677).

Yearbooks of the Reign of Edward III, ed. C. O. Pike, Rolls Series (London, 1906).

Yelverton, Henry, *Les Reports* (London, 1674).

General Secondary Works

Bagwell, R., *Ireland under the Stuarts*, 3 vols. (London, 1963).

 Ireland under the Tudors, 3 vols. (London, 1963).

Curtis, E., *History of Medieval Ireland from 1086 to 1513* (London, 1938).

Gardiner, S. R., *The History of England from the Accession of James I to the Outbreak of the Civil War, 1603–42*, 10 vols. (London, 1899).

Lecky, W. E. H., *A History of Ireland in the Eighteenth Century*, 5 vols. (London, 1913).

Lydon, J. F., *The Lordship of Ireland in the Middle Ages* (Toronto, 1972).

Moody, T. W., Martin, F. X., and Byrne, F. J. *A New History of Ireland* (Oxford, 1976).

Orpen, G. H., *Ireland under the Normans*, 4 vols. (Oxford, 1968).

Secondary Works Concerning Sir John Davies

Ballard, G., *Memoirs of Several Ladies of Great Britain* (Oxford, 1752).

Brink, J. R., 'The Composition Date of Sir John Davies' *Nosce Teipsum*', *HLQ*, 37 (1973), pp. 19–32.

 'The Rhetorical Structure of John Davies' *Nosce Teipsum*', *Yearbook of English Studies*, 4 (1974), pp. 52–61.

Falkiner, C. L., 'Sir John Davies', in *Essays Relating to Ireland* (London, 1909), pp. 32–55.

Finklepearl, P. J., 'Sir John Davies and the Prince d'Amour', *Notes and Queries*, 208 (1963), pp. 300–2.

Grosart, A. B. (ed.), *The Works in Verse and Prose Including Hitherto Unpublished Manuscripts of Sir John Davies*, 3 vols. (Blackburn, 1869–76).

Hand, G. J., 'Sir John Davies, 1569–1626', *Gazette of the Incorporated Law Society of Ireland*, 64 (1971), pp. 174–7.

Hardacre, P., 'Gerrard Winstanley in 1650', *HLQ*, 22 (1958), pp. 345–9.

Hayes McCoy, G. A., 'Sir John Davies in Cavan in 1606 and 1610', *Breifne*, 3 (1960), pp. 177–92.

Krueger, R. (ed.), *The Poems of Sir John Davies* (Oxford, 1975).

Pawlisch, H. S., 'Sir John Davies, the Ancient Constitution and Civil Law', *HJ*, 23 (1980), pp. 689–702.

Roemer, Mary Von, 'Notes on the Descendants of Edward Combe of Bridsor in Tisbury', *Wiltshire Notes and Queries*, 8 (1914–16), pp. 63–73.

Sanderson, J. L., 'Recent Studies in Sir John Davies', *English Literary Renaissance*, 4 (1974), pp. 411–17.

Seeman, M., *Sir John Davies, Sein Leben und Seine Werke* (Vienna and Leipzig, 1913).

Spencer, Theodore, 'The History of an Unfortunate Lady', *Harvard Studies and Notes in Philology*, 20 (1938), pp. 43–59.

Stowell, Lord, 'Observations on, with a Copy of the Proceedings had in Parliament of the Middle Temple, respecting a Petition of Sir John Davies to be Restored to the Degree of Barrister, AD 1601', *Archaeologia*, 21 (1827), pp. 107–12.

Secondary Works: Civil and Canon Law

Buckland, W., *Roman Law and Common Law, a Comparison in Outline* (Cambridge, 1952).

A Textbook of Roman Law from Augustus to Justinian (Cambridge, 1932).

Cheney, C., 'William Lyndwood's *Provinciale*', *The Jurist*, 21 (1961), pp. 405–34.

Davies, H. W., 'The Canon Law in England', *Zeitschrift der Savigny-Stiftung für Rechtsgeschichte, Kanonistische Abteilung*, 3 (1913), pp. 344–63.

Donahue, Charles, 'The Civil Law in England', *Yale Law Journal*, 84 (1974), pp. 167–81.

'Roman Canon Law in the Medieval English Church: Stubbs vs. Maitland Re-examined after 75 Years in the Light of Some Records from the Church Courts', *Michigan Law Review*, 72 (1974), pp. 647–715.

Gilmore, M. P., *Argument from Roman Law in Political Thought, 1200–1500* (Cambridge, Mass., 1941).

Humanists and Jurists (Cambridge, Mass., 1963).

Gray, J. W., 'Canon Law in England: Some Reflections on the Stubbs–Maitland Controversy', *Studies in Church History*, 3 (1966), pp. 48–68.

Kantorowicz, H., and Buckland, W., *Studies in the Glossators of the Roman Law* (Cambridge, 1938).

Kelley, D. R., *Foundations of Modern Historical Scholarship: Language, Law and History in the French Renaissance* (New York, 1970).

'History, English Law and Renaissance', *P & P*, 65 (1974), pp. 24–51.

Kemp, E. W., *An Introduction to Canon Law in the Church of England* (London, 1957).

Kuttner, S. G., 'The Father of the Science of Canon Law', *The Jurist*, 1 (1941), pp. 2–19.

Harmony from Dissonance: An Interpretation of Medieval Canon Law (Latrobe, Pa., 1966).

'The Scientific Investigator of Medieval Canon Law: The Need and the Opportunity', *Speculum*, 34 (1949), pp. 493–501.

Levack, B., *The Civil Lawyers in England 1603–41* (Oxford, 1973).

Lloyd-Jacob, D. H., *The Ecclesiastical Courts* (London, 1954).

Logan, D., *Excommunication and the Secular Arm in Medieval England* (Toronto, 1968).

'The Henrician Canons', *BIHR*, 47 (1974), pp. 99–103.

Mears, T. L., 'The History of the Admiralty Jurisdiction', in *Select Essays in Anglo-American Legal History*, 3 vols. (Cambridge, 1907).

Mortimer, R. C., *Western Canon Law* (Berkeley, 1953).

Muldoon, J., 'The Contribution of Medieval Canon Lawyers to the Formation of International Law', *Traditio*, 28 (1972), pp. 483–97.

'The Remonstrance of the Irish Princes and the Canon Law Tradition of Just War', *AJLH*, 22 (1978), pp. 309–25.

Pennington, K., 'Bartolomeo de Las Casas and the Tradition of Medieval Law', *Church History*, 39 (1970), pp. 144–61.

Phillimore R., *The Ecclesiastical Law of the Church of England* (London, 1895).

Savigny, F., *Geschichte des Römischen Rechts in Mittelalter*, 7 vols. (Heidelberg, 1834–51).

Schwarzenberger, G., 'Function and Foundations of the Laws of War', *Archiv für Rechts und Sozialphilosophie*, 44 (1941), pp. 351–69.

Scrutton, T. E., *The Influence of the Roman Law on the Law of England* (Cambridge, 1885).

'Roman Law Influence in Chancery, Church Courts, Admiralty and Law Merchant', in *Select Essays in Anglo-American Legal History*, 3 vols. (Cambridge, 1907), vol. 1, pp. 238–43.

Sheehy, M. P., 'The Bull Laudabiliter: A Problem in Medieval Diplomatique and History', *Journal of the Galway Archaeological and Historical Society*, 29 (1960), pp. 45–70.

Spalding, J., 'The Reformatio Legum Ecclesiasticarum of 1552 and the Furthering of Discipline in England', *Church History*, 39 (1970), pp. 162–71.

Squibb, G. D., *Doctors Commons, a History of the College of Advocates and Doctors of Law* (Oxford, 1977).

The High Court of Chivalry, a Study of the Civil Law in England (London, 1956).

Stein, Peter, 'The Influence of Roman Law in the Law of Scotland', *Juridical Review*, new series, 8 (1962–3), pp. 205–43.

Legal Values in Western Society (Edinburgh, 1974).

Regulae Iuris from Juristic Rules to Legal Maxims (Edinburgh, 1966).

Stubbs, William, 'The History of the Canon Law in England', in *Select Essays in Anglo-American Legal History*, 3 vols. (Cambridge, 1907).

Introduction, Report of the Commissioners, *The Constitution and Working of the Ecclesiastical Courts* (London, 1883).

Sutherland, D., 'Conquest and Law', *Studia Gratiana*, 15 (1972), pp. 35–51.

Tejada, F. E., 'El Concepto del Derecho Natural y Las Commentarias Hispanos de Graciano', *Studia Gratiana*, 2 (1954), pp. 85–93.

Thomas, J. A. C., *Textbook of Roman Law* (New York, 1976).

Thorne, S. E., 'English Law and the Renaissance', *La Storia del Diritto nel Quadro delle Scienza Storiche* (Florence, 1966), pp. 437–45.

Tierney, B., 'Canonistics in England', *Studia Gratiana*, 2 (1954), pp. 521–8.

'The Prince is Not Bound by the Laws: Accursius and the Origins of the Modern State', *Comparative Studies in Society and History*, 5 (1963), pp. 378–400.

Ullman, W., *Law and Politics in the Middle Ages* (London, 1975).

Medieval Papalism: The Political Theories of the Medieval Canonists (London, 1949).

Vinagradoff, P., *Roman Law in Medieval Europe* (Oxford, 1961).

Wagner, A., 'Über Positives Göttliches Recht und Naturliches Göttliches Recht bie Gratian', *Studia Gratiana*, 1 (1953), pp. 505–18.

Secondary Works: Common Law

Abbott, L. W., *Law Reporting in England, 1485–1585* (London, 1973).

Allen, C. K., *Law in the Making* (Oxford, 1961).

Baker, J. H., 'Coke's Notebooks and the Sources of his Reports', *CLJ*, 30 (1972), pp. 59–86.

'The Dark Age of English Legal History, 1500–1700, in D. Jenkins (ed.), *Legal History Studies* (Cardiff, 1975).

An Introduction to English Legal History (London, 1971).

'New Light on Slade's Case', *CLJ*, 29 (1971), pp. 51–61, 213–36.

The Reports of Sir John Spelman (Selden Society, 93, London, 1976).

Barton, J. L., 'The Medieval Use', *LQR*, 81 (1965), pp. 562–77.

Bell, H. E., *Maitland: A Critical Examination and Assessment* (London, 1965).

Bingham, P., *Reports of Cases Argued and Determined in the Court of Common Pleas, 1822–1834*, 10 vols. (London, 1834).

Bland, D. S., 'Rhetoric and the Law Student in Sixteenth-Century England', *Studies in Philology*, 54 (1957), pp. 498–508.

Dawson, J. P., 'Coke and Ellesmere Disinterred: The Attack on the Chancery in 1616', *Illinois Law Review*, 36 (1941), pp. 127–52.

A History of Lay Judges (Cambridge, Mass., 1960).

Oracles of the Law (Ann Arbor, 1968).

Fisher, R. M., 'Reform, Repression and Unrest at the Inns of Court, 1518–1588', *HJ*, 20 (1977), pp. 783–801.

Gray, C. M., 'Bonham's Case Reviewed', *Proceedings of the American Philosophical Society*, 116 (1972), pp. 35–58.

Hall, G. D. G., 'Bates' Case and Lanes' Reports: The Authenticity of a Seventeenth-Century Legal Text', *Bulletin of the John Ryland's Library*, 35 (1952–3), pp. 405–27.

'Impositions of the Courts, 1554–1606', *LQR*, 69 (1953), pp. 200–18.

Hemmant, M., *Select Cases in the Exchequer Chamber, 1461–1509* (Selden Society, 51, London, 1933).

Holdsworth, W. S., 'Case Law', *LQR*, 50 (1934), pp. 180–95.
A History of English Law, 16 vols. (London, 1922–66).
Some Makers of English Law (Cambridge, 1966).

Ives, E. W., 'Common Lawyers in Pre-Reformation England', *TRHS*, 18 (1968), pp. 145–73.
'The Genesis of the Statute of Uses', *EHR*, 82 (1967), pp. 673–97.
'Promotion in the Legal Profession in Yorkist and Early Tudor England', *LQR*, 75 (1959), pp. 343–63.

Jones, W. J., *Politics and the Bench* (New York, 1971).

Kempin, F. G., 'Precedent and Stare Decisis', *AJLH*, 3 (1959), pp. 28–54.

Kiralfy, A. K. R., 'Law Reform by Legal Fiction, Equity and Legislation in English Legal History', *AJLH*, 10 (1966), pp. 3–14.

Knafla, L., *Law and Politics in Jacobean England* (Cambridge, 1977).

Lewis, T. E., 'History of Judicial Precedent', *LQR*, 46, 47, 48 (1930–2), pp. 207–24, 341–60, 411–27, 230–47.

McIlwain, C. H. 'The English Common Law as a Barrier against Absolutism', *AHR*, 49 (1943), pp. 23–41.
The Political Works of James I (Cambridge, Mass., 1918).

Maine, H., *Early History of Institutions* (London, 1880).

Maitland, F. W., *The Collected Papers of Frederick William Maitland*, 3 vols. (Cambridge, 1911).
The Constitutional History of England (Cambridge, 1908).
English Law and the Renaissance (Cambridge, 1901).
Select Passages from the Works of Bracton and Azo (Selden Society, 8, London, 1894).

Maitland, F. W., and Pollock, F., *The History of English Law before the Time of Edward I*, 2 vols. (Cambridge, 1973).

Malamont, T., 'The Economic Liberalism of Sir Edward Coke', *Yale Law Journal*, 76 (1967), pp. 343–5, 1321–8.

Montrose, J., *Precedent in English Law and Other Essays* (Shannon, 1968).

Ogilvie, C., *The King's Government and the Common Law, 1471–1641* (Oxford, 1958).

Plucknett, T. F. T., *Concise History of the Common Law* (London, 1956).
Early English Legal Literature (Cambridge, 1958).
'The Genesis of Coke's Reports', *Cornell Law Quarterly*, 27 (1942), pp. 190–213.

Pocock, J. G. A., *The Ancient Constitution and the Feudal Law* (Bath, 1974).

Pollock, Sir Frederick, *The Expansion of the Common Law* (London, 1924).

Prall, S., 'The Development of Equity in Tudor England', *AJLH*, 8 (1964), pp. 1–18.

Prest, W., *The Inns of Court under Elizabeth I and the Early Stuarts* (London, 1972).

Schoeck, R. J., 'The English Society of Antiquaries and Men of Law', *Notes and Queries*, 199 (1954), pp. 417–21.
'Rhetoric and Law in Sixteenth-Century England', *Studies in Philology*, 50 (1953), pp. 119–27.

Simpson, A. W. B., 'The Place of Slade's Case in the History of Contract', *LQR*, 74 (1958), pp. 381–96.

Stephen, J., *A History of the Criminal Law of England*, 3 vols. (London, 1883).

Thorne, S. E., *A Catalogue of the Library of Sir Edward Coke* (New Haven, 1950).

    'Courts of Record and Sir Edward Coke', *University of Toronto Law Journal*, 2 (1937), pp. 24–49.

    A Discourse upon the Exposicion and Understanding of Statutes with Sir Thomas Egerton's Additions (Los Angeles, 1942).

    'Dr Bonham's Case', *LQR*, 54 (1938), pp. 543–52.

    'The Early History of the Inns of Court', *Graya*, 50 (1959), pp. 79–96.

    'Praemunire and Sir Edward Coke', *HLQ*, 2 (1938), pp. 85–98.

    Readings and Moots at the Inns of Court in the Fifteenth Century (Selden Society, 71, London, 1954).

    'Tudor Social Transformation and Legal Change', *New York University Law Review*, 26 (1951), pp. 10–23.

Tucker, E.J., '*The Mirror of Justices*: Its Authorship and Pre-occupations', *Irish Jurist*, 9 (1974), pp. 98–109.

Usher, R., 'James I and Sir Edward Coke', *EHR*, 18 (1903), pp. 666–75.

Veall, D., *The Popular Movement for Law Reform, 1640–1660* (Oxford, 1970).

Wagner, D. O., 'Coke and the Rise of Economic Liberalism', *Economic History Review*, 6 (1935), pp. 31–51.

Wallace, J. W., *The Reporters Arranged and Characterized with Incidental Remarks* (Edinburgh, 1882).

Whittaker, J., *The Mirror of Justices* (Selden Society, 7, London, 1893).

Wilson, J., *The Common Law of Kent, or the Custom of Gavelkind* (London, 1822).

Wolff, H. J., 'Debt and Assumpsit in the Light of Comparative Legal History', *Irish Jurist*, 1 (1966), pp. 316–27.

Law, Lawyers and Ireland

Adewoye, O., *The Judicial System in Southern Nigeria 1854–1954* (London, 1977).

Archer, C. P., *Analytical Digest of All the Reported Cases in the Several Courts of Common Law in Ireland* (Dublin, 1842).

Ball, F. E. *The Judges in Ireland, 1221–1921* (New York, 1927).

Barry, J., 'The Coarb and the Twelfth-Century Reform', *IER*, 88 (1957), pp. 17–25.

    'The Erenagh in the Monastic Irish Church', *IER*, 89 (1958), pp. 424–32.

    'The Lay Coarb in Medieval Times', *IER*, 91 (1959), pp. 27–39.

Bartholomew, P. C., *The Irish Judiciary* (Dublin, 1971).

Bedwell, C. E., 'Irishmen at the Inns of Court', *Law Magazine*, 37 (1911–12), pp. 268–71.

Binchy, D. A., 'Irish History and Irish Law', *Studia Hiberniae*, 15 (1975), pp. 7–36.

    'Irish Law Tracts Re-Edited', *Eriu*, 17 (1955), pp. 52–85.

    'The Linguistic and Historical Value of the Irish Law Tracts', *Proceedings of the British Academy*, 29 (1943), pp. 195–227.

'Some Celtic Legal Terms', *Celtica*, 3 (1956), pp. 221–31.

Brooks, G. P., 'Abnormal Behaviour and the Law in Ancient Ireland: The Brehon Laws', *Papers in Psychology*, 5 (1960), pp. 13–15.

Brunker, T., *Digest of Cases in the Supreme and Other Courts of Common Law, Ireland, and Courts of Admiralty from Sir John Davies' Reports to the Present Time* (Dublin, 1865).

Bryant, S., *Liberty Order and Law under Native Rule* (London, 1923).

Burke, O. J., *Anecdotes of the Connaught Circuit* (Dublin, 1885).

Caiv, B. O., 'A Seventeenth-Century Legal Document', *Celtica*, 5 (1960), pp. 177–85.

Castles, A.C., *An Introduction to Australian Legal History* (Melbourne, 1971).

Cosgrove, L., 'The King's Inns', *Dublin Historical Record*, 21 (1967), pp. 45–52.

Crawford, J. G., 'The Origins of the Court of Castle Chamber: A Starchamber Jurisdiction in Ireland', *AJLH*, 24 (1980), pp. 22–55.

Cregan, D. F., 'Irish Catholic Admissions to the English Inns of Court, 1558–1625', *Irish Jurist*, 5 (1970), pp. 95–114.

'Irish Recusant Lawyers in Politics in the Reign of James I', *Irish Jurist*, 5 (1970), pp. 306–20.

Creighton, S., 'Innocent XII and Early Irish Penal Legislation', *IER*, 98 (1962), pp. 213–22.

Delaney, V. T. H., 'The History of Legal Education in Ireland', *Journal of Legal Education*, 12 (1956–60), pp. 396–406.

'A Note on the History of Legal Education in Ireland', *NILQ*, 21 (1955), pp. 216–18.

Diamond, A. S., *Primitive Law, Past and Present* (London, 1971).

Donaldson, A. G., *Some Comparative Aspects of Irish Law* (Durham, NC, 1957).

Duhigg, B. T., *A History of the King's Inns* (Dublin, 1806).

King's Inns Remembrances (Dublin, 1805).

Edwards, R. D., 'Conflict of Papal and Royal Jurisdiction in Fifteenth-Century Ireland', *Proceedings of the Irish Catholic Historical Committee*, 48 (1960), pp. 3–9.

Hamilton, G. E., *An Account of the Honorable Society of King's Inns, Dublin* (Dublin, 1915).

Hand, G. J., 'The Church and English Law in Medieval Ireland', *Proceedings of the Irish Catholic Historical Committee*, 47 (1959), pp. 10–18.

'The Common Law in Ireland in the Thirteenth Century: Two Cases Involving Christ Church, Dublin', *RSAI*, 97 (1967), pp. 97–111.

English Law in Ireland, 1290–1324 (Cambridge, 1967).

'The Forgotten Statutes of Kilkenny', *Irish Jurist*, 1 (1966), pp. 299–312.

'Proceedings without Writ in the Court of the Justiciar of Ireland', *RIA Proc.*, Section C, 62 (1961–3), pp. 9–20.

'Rules and Orders to be Observed in the Proceedings of Cases in the High Court of Chancery in Ireland, 1659', *Irish Jurist*, 9 (1974), pp. 110–65.

'Sir John Davies, 1569–1626', *Gazette of the Incorporated Law Society of Ireland*, 64 (1971), pp. 174–7.

'The Status of the Native Irish in the Lordship of Ireland', *Irish Jurist*, 1 (1966), pp. 93–115.

Hand, G. J., and Treadwell, V. W., 'His Majesty's Direction for Ordering and Settling the Courts within the Kingdom of Ireland, 1622', *An Hib.*, 26 (1970), pp. 177–233.

Hedges, I. C., 'The Blood Covenant among the Celts', *Revue Celtique*, 44 (1927), pp. 109–53.

Johnston, W. J., 'The English Legislature and the Irish Courts', *LQR*, 40 (1924), pp. 91–106.

'The First Adventure of the Common Law', *LQR*, 36 (1920), pp. 9–30.

'Ireland and the Medieval Law Courts', *Studies*, 12 (1928), pp. 553–7.

'The Parliament of the Pale', *LQR*, 34 (1918), pp. 291–303.

Joyce, P. W., *A Social History of Ancient Ireland*, 2 vols. (London, 1903).

Littledale, W. F., *The Society of King's Inns: Its Origins and Progress* (Dublin, 1859).

Lynch, W. A., *A View of the Legal Institutions, etc. Established in Ireland during the Reign of Henry II* (London, 1830).

MacNeill, E., 'Ancient Irish Law: The Law of the Status of Franchise', *RIA Proc.* Section C, 36 (1923), pp. 265–316.

'Communal Ownership in Ancient Ireland', *Irish Monthly*, 47 (1919), pp. 407–15.

'The Irish Law of Dynastic Succession', *Studies*, 8 (1919), pp. 367–82, 640–53.

MacNiocaill, G., 'Admissible and Inadmissible Evidence in Early Irish Law', *Irish Jurist*, 5 (1969), pp. 332–7.

'The Contact of Irish and Common Law', *NILQ*, 23 (1972), pp. 16–23.

'Irish Law and the Armagh Constitution of 1297', *Irish Jurist*, 6 (1971), pp. 339–44.

'Jetsam, Treasure Trove and the Lord's Share in Medieval Ireland', *Irish Jurist*, 6 (1971), pp. 103–10.

'Notes on Litigation in Late Irish Law', *Irish Jurist*, 2 (1967), pp. 299–307.

Maitland, F. W., 'The Introduction of English Law into Ireland', *EHR*, 4 (1889), pp. 516–17.

Mathews, Mary, 'Aspects of the Irish Law of Contract', *Irish Jurist*, 7 (1972), pp. 292–305.

Muldoon, J., 'The Contribution of Medieval Canon Lawyers to the Formation of International Law', *Traditio*, 28 (1972), pp. 483–97.

'The Remonstrance of the Irish Princess and the Canon Law Tradition of the Just War', *AJLH*, 22 (1978), pp. 309–25.

Murphy, B., 'The Status of the Native Irish after 1331', *Irish Jurist*, 2 (1967), pp. 116–28.

Newark, F. H., 'The Bringing of English Law to Ireland', *NILQ*, 23 (1972), pp. 3–15.

'The Case of Tanistry', *NILQ*, 9 (1950–2), pp. 215–21.

'The Medieval Irish Keepers of the Peace', *Irish Jurist*, 2 (1967), pp. 308–26.

Notes on Irish Legal History (Belfast, 1964).

'Notes on Irish Legal History', *NILQ*, 7 (1947–8), pp. 121–39.

Nicholls, K. W., 'Celtic Suretyship, a Fossilized Indo-European Institution', *Irish Jurist*, 6 (1971), pp. 360–72.

Gaelic and Gaelicized Ireland in the Middle Ages (Dublin, 1972).

Land, Law and Society in Sixteenth-Century Ireland (O'Donnell Lecture, University College Cork, 1976).

'Some Documents on Irish Law and Custom in the Sixteenth Century', *An. Hib.*, 26 (1970), pp. 103–30.

O'Brien, G. T., 'The Old Irish Inns of Court', *Studies*, 3 (1914), pp. 592–601.

Ó'Buachalla, L., 'Some Researches in Ancient Irish Law', *Journal of the Cork Historical Society*, 52 (1947), pp. 41–54, 135–48; 53 (1948), pp. 1–12, 75–8.

Ó'Corráin, D., 'Irish Regnal Succession: A Reappraisal', *Studia Hibernica*, 10 (1970), pp. 7–39.

O'Higgins, P., 'English Law and the Irish Question', *Irish Jurist*, 1 (1966), pp. 59–61.

O'Sullivan, Anne and William, 'A Legal Fragment From TCD MS H.4.22', *Celtica*, 8 (1970), pp. 140–3.

Otway-Ruthven, A. J., 'The Native Irish and English Law in Medieval Ireland', *IHS*, 7 (1951), pp. 1–16.

'The Request of the Irish for English Law, 1277–1280', *IHS*, 1 (1939), pp. 261–71.

Pennington, K., 'Bartolome de las Casas and the Medieval Legal Tradition', *Church History*, 39 (1970), pp. 149–61.

Quinn, D. B., 'Analysis of Survey Rolls and the Statutes with Some Unpublished Additions for the Period, 1485–1547', *An. Hib.*, 10 (1942), pp. 70–169.

'Government Printing and the Publication of the Irish Statutes', *RIA Proc.*, Section C, 49 (1943), pp. 45–129.

Sheehy, M. P., 'The Bull Laudabiliter: A Problem in Medieval Diplomatique and History', *Journal of the Galway Archaeological and Historical Society*, 29 (1960), pp. 45–70.

Simms, J. G., 'The Making of a Penal Law', *IHS*, 12 (1960), pp. 105–18.

Simms, K., 'The Legal Position of Irish Women in the Later Middle Ages', *Irish Jurist*, 10 (1975), pp. 96–111.

Sutherland, D., 'Conquest and Law', *Studia Gratiana*, 15 (1972), pp. 35–51.

Thurneysen, R., Power, N., Dillon, M., Mulchrone, K., Binchy, D. A., Knoch, A., and Ryan, J., *Studies in Early Irish Law* (Dublin, 1936).

Treadwell, V., 'The Irish Court of Wards under James I', *IHS*, 12 (1960), pp. 1–27.

Watt, J. A., 'English Law and the Irish Church', *Medieval Studies Presented to Aubrey Gwynn* (Dublin, 1961), pp. 133–67.

Weckman, L., *Las Bulas Alejandrinas de 1493 y la Teoría Politica del Papado Medieval: Estudio de la Supremacía Papal Sobre Islas, 1091–1493* (Mexico City, 1949).

'The Middle Ages in the Conquest of America', *Speculum*, 26 (1951), pp. 130–41.

Yale, D. E. C., 'Notes on the Jurisdiction of the Admiralty in Ireland', *Irish Jurist*, 3 (1968), pp. 146–62.

General Medieval and Early Modern Historiography of Irish Interest

Andrews, J. H., 'Geography and Government in Elizabethan Ireland', *Irish Geographical Studies*, 73 (1970), pp. 178–91.

Ashton, R., 'Revenue Farming under the Early Stuarts', *Economic History Review*, 2nd series, 8 (1956), pp. 310–22.

Ball, F. E., *Historical Review of the Legislative Systems Operative In Ireland from the Invasion of Henry II to the Union* (London, 1889).

Barnard, T. C., *Cromwellian Ireland* (Oxford, 1975).

'Planters and Policies in Cromwellian Ireland', *P & P*, 61 (1973), pp. 30–69.

Benn, G., *A History of the Town of Belfast*, 2 vols. (London, 1880).

Berry, H. F., 'The Records of the Dublin Guild of Merchants, 1438–1671', *RSAI*, 30 (1900), pp. 44–68.

Bevan, W. L., *Sir William Petty, A Study in English Economic Literature* (Baltimore, 1894).

Bigger, F. J., 'Sir Arthur Chichester, Lord Deputy of Ireland – With Some Notes on the Plantation of Ulster', *UJA*, 10 (1904), pp. 1–12, 56–66, 104–12.

Bradshaw, B., 'The Beginnings of Modern Ireland', in B. Farrell (ed.), *The Irish Parliamentary Tradition* (Dublin, 1973), pp. 68–87.

'Cromwellian Reform and the Origins of the Kildare Rebellion, 1533–34', *Transactions of the Royal Historical Society*, 27 (1977), pp. 475–502.

The Dissolution of the Religious Orders in Ireland (Cambridge, 1974).

'The Edwardian Reformation in Ireland, 1547–53', *Arch. Hib.*, 24 (1976–7), pp. 83–99.

'Fr Wolfe's Description of Limerick, 1574', *North Munster Antiquarian Journal*, 17 (1975), pp. 47–53.

'George Brown, First Reformation Archbishop of Dublin', *Journal of Ecclesiastical History*, 21 (1970), pp. 301–26.

The Irish Constitutional Revolution of the Sixteenth Century (Cambridge, 1979).

'The Opposition to the Ecclesiastical Legislation in the Irish Reformation Parliament', *IHS*, 16 (1969), pp. 285–303.

Burke, O., *The History of the Lord Chancellors of Ireland, from AD 1186 to AD 1874* (Dublin, 1879).

Butler, W. F. T., *Confiscation in Irish History* (Dublin, 1917).

Canny, N. P., 'Dominant Minorities: English Settlers in Ireland and Virginia, 1550–1650', *Historical Studies*, 12 (1977), pp. 51–69.

The Elizabethan Conquest of Ireland: A Pattern Established 1565–1576 (Hassocks, 1976).

'The Flight of the Earls, 1607', *IHS*, 17 (1971), pp. 380–99.

The Formation of the Old English Elite in Ireland (O'Donnell Lecture, University College Dublin, 1975).

'Hugh O'Neill, Earl of Tyrone and the Changing Face of Gaelic Ulster', *Studia Hibernica*, 10 (1970), pp. 7–35.

'The Treaty of Mellifont and the Reorganization of Ulster, 1603', *Irish Sword*, 9 (1969–70), pp. 249–62.

'Why the Reformation Failed in Ireland: Une Question Mal Posée', *Journal of Ecclesiastical History*, 30 (1979), pp. 423–50

Challis, C. E., *Tudor Coinage* (Manchester, 1978).

'The Tudor Coinage in Ireland', *BNJ*, 40 (1971), pp. 97–119.

Chart, D. A., 'The Break-up of the Estate of Con O'Neill', *RIA Proc.*, Section C, 10 (1942), pp. 119–51.

Clarke, A., 'Colonial Identity in Early Seventeenth-Century Ireland', *Historical Studies*, 11 (1976), pp. 57–71.

The Graces 1625–41 (Historical Association Pamphlet, Dublin, 1968).

'The History of Poynings' Law, 1615–41', *IHS*, 18 (1973), pp. 207–27.

'Ireland and the General Crisis', *P & P*, 48 (1970), pp. 79–99.

The Old English in Ireland, 1625–42 (Ithaca, 1966).

Cooper, J. P., 'The Fortune of Thomas Wentworth, Earl of Strafford', *EHR*, 11 (1958), pp. 227–48.

'Wentworth and the Byrnes Country', *IHS*, 15 (1967), pp. 1–20.

Cullen, L., 'Population Trends in Seventeenth-Century Ireland', *Economic and Social Review* (1975), pp. 149–65.

Dietz, F., *English Public Finance* (New York, 1932).

Dolley, M., 'Anglo-Irish Monetary Policies, 1172–1637', *Historical Studies*, 7 (1969), pp. 45–64.

'The Irish Coinage, 1534–1691', in Moody *et al.*, *A New History of Ireland*, pp. 408–18.

Edwards, R. D., *Church and State in Tudor Ireland* (London, 1935).

'Ireland, Elizabeth I and the Counter-Reformation', in S. T. Bindoff, J. Hurstfield and C. H. Williams (eds.), *Elizabethan Government and Society* (London, 1961), pp. 315–39.

'The Irish Reformation Parliament of Henry VIII, 1536–7', *Historical Studies*, 6 (1968), pp. 59–84.

Edwards, R. D., and Moody, T. W., 'The History of Poynings' Law: Part I, 1495–1615', *IHS*, 2 (1941), pp. 415–25.

Elton, G. R., *England under the Tudors* (London, 1974).

Reform and Reformation (London, 1977).

Reform and Renewal (Cambridge, 1973).

The Tudor Constitution (Cambridge, 1968).

The Tudor Revolution in Government (Cambridge, 1969).

Falkiner, C. L., (ed.), *Illustrations of Irish History* (London, 1904).

'The Parliament of Ireland under the Tudor Sovereigns', *RIA Proc.*, Section C, 25 (1904–5), pp. 508–41.

Fenlon, D. B., 'Wentworth and the Parliament of 1634: An Essay in Chronology', *RSAI*, 13 (1964), pp. 159–78.

Fitzmaurice, E., *The Life of Sir William Petty, 1623–1687* (London, 1895).

Gale, P., *An Enquiry into the Ancient Corporate System of Ireland* (London, 1834).

Green, Alice, 'The Irish Parliament in the Seventeenth Century', *Scottish Historical Review*, 7 (1910), pp. 232–43.

Hazlett, H., 'British Armies in Ireland, the Financing of 1640–49', *IHS*, 1 (1939), pp. 21–42.

Healy, T. M. *The Great Fraud of Ulster* (Dublin, 1917).

The Planter's Progress (Dublin, 1921).

Stolen Waters (London, 1913).

Hopkins, A. G., 'Property Rights and Empire Building: Britain's Annexation of Lagos, 1861', *Journal of Economic History*, 40 (1980), pp. 777–97.

Hughes, J. L., 'The Chief Secretaries in Ireland, 1566–1921', *IHS*, 8 (1953), pp. 59–82.

    Patentee Officers in Ireland, 1173–1826, Including High Sheriffs, 1161–1684, and 1761–1816 (Dublin, 1960).

Kearney, H. F., 'The Court of Wards and Liveries in Ireland, 1622–41', *RIA Proc.*, Section C, 57 (1956), pp. 29–69.

    'The Irish Wine Trade, 1614–1615', *IHS*, 9 (1955), pp. 400–42.

    'Mercantilism and Ireland, 1620–1640', *Historical Studies*, 1 (1958), pp. 59–68.

    'Richard Boyle Ironmaster', *RSAI*, 33 (1953), pp. 156–67.

    Strafford in Ireland (Manchester, 1959).

Longfield, A., *Anglo-Irish Trade in the Sixteenth Century* (London, 1929).

Loomie, A. J., 'Sir Robert Cecil and the Spanish Embassy', *BIHR*, 49 (1969), pp. 30–57.

    'Toleration and Diplomacy: The Religious Issue in Anglo-Spanish Relations, 1603–05', *Transactions of the American Philosophical Society*, 53 (1966), pp. 1–60.

Lough, S. M., 'Trade and Industry in Ireland in the Sixteenth Century', *Journal of Political Economy*, 24 (1916), pp. 713–30.

Lydon, J. F., 'The Irish Church and Taxation in the Fourteenth Century', *IER*, 103 (1965), pp. 158–68.

    The Lordship of Ireland in the Middle Ages (Toronto, 1972).

    'A Survey of the Memorandum Rolls of the Irish Exchequer, 1294–1509', *An. Hib.*, 23 (1966), pp. 1–27.

    'Three Exchequer Documents from the Reign of Henry III', *RIA Proc.*, Section C, 65 (1966–7), pp. 1–27.

MacFarlane, A., *The Origins of English Individualism* (Cambridge, 1978).

Maguire, W. A., 'The 1822 Settlement of the Donegall Estates', *Irish Economic and Social History*, 3 (1976), pp. 17–32.

    'Lord Donegall and the Sale of Belfast: A Case History from the Encumbered Estates Court', *Economic History Review*, 2nd series, 29 (1976), pp. 570–84.

Moody, T. W., 'The Irish Parliament under Elizabeth and James I: A General Survey', *RIA Proc.*, Section C, 45 (1939), pp. 41–82.

    Londonderry Plantation, 1609–41: The City of London and the Plantation in Ulster (Belfast, 1939).

    'Sir Thomas Phillips of Limavady, Servitor', *IHS*, 1 (1939) pp. 251–72.

    'The Treatment of the Native Population under the Scheme for the Plantation in Ulster', *IHS*, 1 (1939), pp. 59–63.

Moody, T. W., and Simms, J.G., *The Bishoprics of Derry and the Irish Society of London, 1602–1705* (Dublin, 1968).

Müller, W., *Sir William Petty als Politischer Arithmetiker, eine Soziologisch-Statistische Studie* (Baden, 1932).

Newton, A. P., 'The Establishment of the Great Farm of the English Customs', *Transactions of the Royal Historical Society*, 4th series, 1 (1918), pp. 129–55.

O'Brien, G., *The Economic History of Ireland in the Seventeenth Century* (Dublin, 1919).

O'Domnhaill, S., 'The Maps of the Down Survey', *IHS*, 3 (1943), pp. 381–92.

O'Mahoney, C., *The Viceroys of Ireland* (London, 1912).

Otway-Ruthven, A. J., 'The Chief Governors of Medieval Ireland', *RSAI*, 95 (1965), pp. 227–36.

  A History of Medieval Ireland (London, 1968).

  'The Medieval Irish Chancery', *Album Helen Maude Cam*, 2 (1961), pp. 119–38.

  'Royal Service in Ireland', *RSAI*, 98 (1968), pp. 37–46.

Pasquier, M., *Sir William Petty* (Paris, 1903).

Pender, S., *Waterford Merchants Abroad* (National University of Ireland, O'Donnell Lecture, Tralee, 1964).

Perceval-Maxwell, M., *The Scottish Migration to Ulster in the Reign of James I* (London, 1973).

Prestwich, M., *Cranfield, Politics and Profits under the Early Stuarts* (Oxford, 1966).

Quinn, D. B., 'Analysis of the Parliamentary Subsidy', *RIA Proc.*, Section C, 42 (1935), pp. 219–46.

  'The Early Interpretation of Poynings' Law: Part I, 1494–1534', *IHS*, 2 (1941), pp. 415–24.

  The Elizabethans and the Irish (Ithaca, 1966).

  'Parliaments and Great Councils in Ireland, 1461–1585', *IHS*, 3 (1943), pp. 60–77.

Ranger, T. O., 'Richard Boyle and the Making of an Irish Fortune', *IHS*, 10 (1957), pp. 257–97.

  'Strafford in Ireland, a Revaluation', *P & P*, 19 (1961), pp. 26–45.

Richardson, H. G., and Sayles, G. O., *The Administration of Ireland, 1172–1377* (Dublin, 1963).

  The Irish Parliament in the Middle Ages (Philadelphia, 1964).

Roebuck, P., 'The Making of an Ulster Great Estate: The Chichesters, Barons of Belfast and Viscounts of Carrickfergus, 1597–1648', *RIA Proc.*, Section C, 79 (1979), pp. 1–25.

Ronan, M. V., *The Reformation in Ireland under Elizabeth, 1558–1580* (London, 1930).

Schuyler, R. L., *Parliament and the British Empire* (New York, 1929).

Silke, J. J., *Ireland and Europe, 1559–1607* (Dundalk, 1966).

  Kinsale – The Spanish Intervention in Ireland at the End of the Elizabethan Wars (New York, 1970).

  'Spain and the Invasion of Ireland, 1601–2', *IHS*, 14 (1965), pp. 295–312.

Simington, R. C., 'A Census of Ireland, 1659', *An Hib.*, 13 (1943), pp. 177–8.

  The Transplantation to Connaught (Dublin, 1970).

Simms, J. G., 'Irish Catholics and the Parliamentary Franchise', *IHS*, 12 (1961), pp. 28–37.

  The Jacobite Parliament of 1689 (Dundalk, 1966).

  'Land Owned by Catholics in Ireland in 1688', *IHS*, 7 (1951), pp. 189–99.

  'The Making of a Penal Law', *IHS*, 12 (1961), pp. 105–18.

The Treaty of Limerick (Dundalk, 1965).

The Williamite Confiscation in Ireland (London, 1956).

Smith, C., *The Antient and Present State of the County and City of Cork* (Dublin, 1750).

The Antient and Present State of the County and City of Waterford (Dublin, 1746).

The Antient and Present State of the County of Down (Dublin, 1746).

The Antient and Present State of the County of Kerry (Dublin, 1744).

Tawney, R. H., *Business and Politics in the Reign of James I* (Cambridge, 1958).

Treadwell, V., 'The Establishment of the Farm of the Irish Customs', *EHR*, 93 (1978), pp. 580–602.

'The House of Lords in the Irish Parliament of 1613–15', *EHR*, 70 (1965), pp. 92–107.

'The Irish Court of Wards under James I', *IHS*, 12 (1961), pp. 1–27.

'The Irish Customs Administration in the Sixteenth Century', *IHS*, 21 (1977), pp. 385–417.

'The Irish Parliament of 1569–71', *RIA Proc.*, Section C, 65 (1966–7), pp. 55–89.

Webb, J. J., *Municipal Government in Ireland, Medieval and Modern* (Dublin, 1918).

White, D. G., 'The Reign of Edward VI in Ireland: Some Political Social and Economic Aspects', *IHS*, 14 (1965), pp. 197–211.

Woodward, D. M., 'Anglo-Irish Livestock Trade in the Seventeenth Century', *IHS*, 18 (1973), pp. 489–515.

Zweigert, K. (ed.), *Legal Aspects of Economic Development, Surveys Made at the Request of UNESCO* (Paris, 1966).

Materials for Irish Colonization

Andrews, J. H., 'The Maps of the Escheated Counties of Ulster, 1609–1610', *RIA Proc.*, Section C, 74 (1974), pp. 133–70.

Andrews, K. R., Canny, N. P., and Hair, P. E., (eds.), *The Westward Enterprise: English Activities in Ireland, the Atlantic and America, 1480–1650* (Liverpool, 1978).

Bonn, M. J., *Die Englische Kolonisation in Irland* (Stuttgart and Berlin, 1906).

Bottigheimer, K. S., *English Money and Irish Land, the Adventurers in the Cromwellian Land Settlement of Ireland* (Oxford, 1971).

Canny, N. P., 'The Ideology of English Colonization: From Ireland to America', *William and Mary Quarterly*, 30 (1973), pp. 575–99.

Clark, A., 'A Discourse between Two Councillors of State, the One of England and the Other of Ireland, 1642', *An. Hib.*, 26 (1970), pp. 177–233.

Davies, R. R., 'Colonial Wales', *P & P*, 65 (1974), pp. 3–23.

Dunlop, R., 'The Plantation of Leix and Offaly', *EHR*, 6 (1891), pp. 61–73.

'The Plantation of Munster, 1586–9', *EHR*, 3 (1888), pp. 250–69.

'The Sixteenth-Century Schemes for the Plantation of Ulster', *Scottish Historical Review*, 21 (1924), pp. 52–60, 200–12.

Hanke, L., *The Spanish Struggle for Justice in the Conquest of America* (Philadelphia, 1949).

Hechter, M., *Internal Colonialism* (London, 1975).

Hill, G., *An Historical Account of the Plantation of Ulster* (Belfast, 1877).

Hunter, R. J., 'Carew's Survey of Ulster, 1611: The Voluntary Works', *UJA*, 38 (1975), pp. 81–3.

James, F. G., *Ireland in the Empire, 1688–1770* (Cambridge, Mass., 1973).

Jensen, M., and Reynolds, R., 'European Colonial Experience: A Plea for Comparative Studies', *Studi in Onore di Gino Luzzatto*, 4 (1950), pp. 75–90.

Jones, H. M., *Ideas in America* (Cambridge, Mass., 1944).

Knorr, K. E., *British Colonial Theories, 1570–1850* (Toronto, 1968).

McIlwain, C. H., *The American Revolution – A Constitutional Interpretation* (New York, 1923).

Moody, T. W., *The Londonderry Plantation, 1609–41: The City of London and the Plantation in Ulster* (Belfast, 1939).

'The Treatment of the Native Population under the Scheme for the Plantation of Ulster', *IHS*, 1 (1939), pp. 59–63.

'Ulster Plantation Papers, 1608–1613', *An. Hib.*, 8 (1938), pp. 179–297.

Parry, J. H., *Age of the Reconnaissance* (London, 1963).

The Spanish Theory of Empire in the Sixteenth Century (Cambridge, 1940).

Quinn, D. B., 'Discourse of Ireland, *c.* 1599', *RIA Proc.*, Section C, 47 (1942), pp. 151–66.

'Edward Walsh's Conjectures Concerning the State of Ireland (1552)', *IHS*, 5 (1947), pp. 303–22.

'Ireland and Sixteenth-Century European Expansion', *Historical Studies*, 1 (1958), pp. 20–32.

'The Munster Plantation: Problems and Opportunities', *Journal of the Cork Historical and Archaeological Society*, 71 (1966), pp. 19–40.

'Renaissance Influences in English Colonization', *Transactions of the Royal Historical Society*, 26 (1976), pp. 73–95.

'Sir Thomas Smith and the Beginnings of English Colonial Theory', *Proceedings of the American Philosophical Society*, 89 (1945), pp. 543–60.

Rabb, T. K., *Enterprise and Empire: Merchant and Gentry Investment in the Expansion of England, 1575–1630* (Cambridge, Mass., 1967).

Ranger, T. O., 'Richard Boyle and the Making of an Irish Fortune', *IHS*, 10 (1957), pp. 257–97.

Reynolds, R., *Europe Emerges* (Madison, 1961).

Robinson, P., 'British Settlement in County Tyrone, 1610–66', *Irish Economic and Social History*, 5 (1978), pp. 5–26.

'Irish Settlement in Tyrone before the Ulster Plantation', *Ulster Folklife*, 22 (1976), pp. 59–69.

Verlinden, C., *The Beginnings of Modern Colonization* (Ithaca, 1970).

Index

Act of Supremacy: application to
  Ireland, 106–7
Act of Uniformity: application to
  Ireland, 106–7
Adrian IV, Pope: issues bull *Laudabiliter*,
  63
Africa: administration of English law in,
  13–14
aliens: law concerning, 59–60; applied to
  Ireland, 67
Alton Woods: case of, 44
Antrim, county of: the Rout and Glens,
  84
Ardglass: customs duties in, 126
Aristotle: influence on Irish reform, 7
Arklow: customs duties in, 126
Armagh, county of: title to, 75
army: size of in 1603, 5
Ashley, Serjeant: cites *ius gentium* in
  parliamentary debate, 163
Aubrey, John: describes Richard Martin,
  18

Bacon, Francis, Baron Verulam and
  Viscount St Albans: comments on
  Davies' Irish appointment, 30; on
  authority of judicial resolutions, 44;
  discussion of Irish sovereignty, 56;
  supports recusant policies, 110;
  reaction to Coke's *Reports*, 166
Baldus: medieval Italian jurist, 173
Baltimore: customs duties in, 126
Bann, fishery of: judicial resolution
  over, 46; granted to Sir Randall
  MacDonnell, 85; description of, 85–6;
  annual cash value of, 96; granted to
  city of London, 96; civil law in dispute
  over, 173; title before Tudor
  conquest, 194–5 n. 6; *see also*
  MacDonnell, Sir Randall

Barnewall, Sir Patrick: role in mandates
  controversy, 110–13
bills of exchange: for base money, 148
Bingley, John: notes Cecil's
  involvement in customs reform, 125;
  see also Cecil, Sir Robert
Blackstone, Sir William: discussion of
  overseas plantations, 13; on conquest
  right, 210 n. 47
Blount, Charles, Lord Mountjoy, Earl
  of Devonshire: defeats rebel forces, 3;
  presents Davies at court, 17; role in
  formulating Irish policy, 66; marches
  from Dublin to pacify towns, 103;
  threatens Waterford, 104; leniency
  towards towns, 105; suggests revival
  of High Commission, 106; plans to
  eliminate corporate privilege, 124;
  complains of base coin, 142; notes
  inflation, 152; Davies' patron, 179 n.
  16
Bodin, Jean: theory of sovereignty
  applied to Ireland, 55; cited by Davies,
  167
Bolton, Richard, Recorder of Dublin:
  attorney in case of tanistry, 77; in case
  of customs, 134–5; opposes bill to
  terminate customs exemptions, 140
Boyle, Richard, Earl of Cork: origins of
  estate, 89
brehon law: concepts of property, 11;
  structure of, 55–9 *passim; see also*
  Gaelic Irish
brehons: arbitrators in legal disputes, 57
Brouncker, Sir Henry: proclaims
  expulsion of recusant clergy, 108;
  deposes mayors in Munster, 109;
  recusants allege remorse, 110
Budelius, René: civil lawyer cited in base
  money case, 154, 155, 156, 173

Cambridge Studies in the History and Theory of Politics

Editors: Maurice Cowling, G. R. Elton and J. R. Pole

A series in two parts, studies and original texts. The studies are original works on political history and political philosophy while the texts are modern, critical editions of major texts in political thought. The titles include:

1867: Disraeli, Gladstone and Revolution: The Passing of the Second Reform Bill, by Maurice Cowling

The Social and Political Thought of Karl Marx, by Shlomo Avineri

Idealism, Politics and History: Sources of Hegelian Thought, by George Armstrong Kelly

Alienation: Marx's Conception of Man in Capitalist Society, by Bertell Ollman

Hegel's Theory of the Modern State, by Shlomo Avineri

The Impact of Hitler: British Politics and British Policy 1933–1940, by Maurice Cowling

The Liberal Mind 1914–1929, by Michael Bentley

Revolution Principles: The Politics of Party 1689–1720, by J. P. Kenyon

John Locke and the Theory of Sovereignty: Mixed Monarchy and the Right of Resistance in the Political Thought of the English Revolution, by Julian H. Franklin

Adam Smith's Politics: An Essay in Historiographic Revision, by Donald Winch

Lloyd George's Secretariat, by John Turner

The Tragedy of Enlightenment: An Essay on the Frankfurt School, by Paul Connerton

Religion and Public Doctrine in Modern England, by Maurice Cowling

Bentham and Bureaucracy, by L. J. Hume

A Critique of Freedom and Equality, by John Charvet

The Dynamics of Change: The Crisis of the 1750s and English Party Systems, by J. C. D. Clark

Resistance and Compromise: The Political Thought of the Elizabethan Catholics, by P. J. Holmes

Nationalism, Positivism and Catholicism: The Politics of Charles Maurras and French Catholics, 1890–1914, by Michael Sutton

The Christian Polity of John Calvin, by Harro Höpfl